SUSTAINABLE TOURISM PLANNING AND DEVELOPMENT

All India Tourism Teachers' Association
National Seminar Proceedings
March 1-2, 2004

Editor

Prof. S.C. Bagri

Bishen Singh Mahendra Pal Singh
23-A, New Connaught Place
Dehra Dun - 248 001 (INDIA)

Centre for Mountain Tourism and Hospitality Studies
HNB Garhwal University, Srinagar Garhwal, Uttaranchal

2006

Sustainable Tourism Planning and Development
© 2006, Bishen Singh Mahendra Pal Singh

ISBN: 81-211-0505-6

Printed by Gajendra Singh Gahlot at Shiva Offset Press, and composed by Doon Phototype Printers, 14 Old Connaught Place, Dehra Dun, India for Bishen Singh Mahendra Pal Singh, Dehra Dun, India.

FOREWORD

I am happy to know that All India Tourism Teachers Association, *a recently constituted academic body*, is publishing the proceedings of its first National Seminar on Sustainable Tourism Planning and Development held at Rishikesh. The Centre for Mountain Tourism of our University, had taken up the responsibility to organize this event. It is good to know that a number of academicians from all over the country participated in the event to discuss trends and issues related to Sustainable Tourism Planning and Development.

Everyone knows about the economic significance of Tourism. In the global context, travel and tourism sector is one of the largest service sectors accounting for 3.6% of world's GDP and 2.8% of world's employment. In terms of the larger travel and tourism economy concept (which will include secondary and tertiary sectors benefiting from tourism), travel and tourism accounts for 10% of world's GDP and 7.8% of the world's employment.

In the Indian context, although travel and tourism sector accounts for 2.15% of India's GDP and 2.6% of the country's employment, its relative share in relation to both South East Asia and the world is considerably low. Therefore, India needs to adopt suitable policy measures to increase the travel and tourism sector to its full potential. The tourism growth rate projected in the sub-continental region by various agencies are higher as compared to other regions and the world average as a whole.

Indian economy growing at around 7% per annum and rise in the disposable incomes of Indians, an increasing number of people are going on holiday trips within the country and abroad resulting in the tourism industry growing wings. Tourism is no more being seen as the rich man's pass time. An increasing number of ordinary people are now going on holiday tours, giving a fillip to the industry's growth. Foreign tourists' inflow has risen 20% during the last two years. It is fast turning into a volume game where an ever-burgeoning number of participants are pushing up revenues to industry players. Thus, the tourism sector is expected to perform very well in future and stocks of some leading players in the industry offer an interesting investment opportunity for long-term investors.

Some major international events like 9/11, U.S. led war against terrorism and SARS hit the tourism industry over the past few years. The adverse travel advisories by many countries to their citizens too contributed significant slowdown in tourism in India. There were other negatives too. Expenses per night of stay for a tourist in India during SE Asian currency crisis was $ 100 whereas it was around $ 35-40 in SE Asian Countries. This hurt Indian tourism. Though this discrepancy has come down, still there is some gap. Some of the reasons for this are high luxury and entertainment taxes and high landing charges applicable in Indian Airports. Costs are also high because tourism is a state subject. Each state separately spends on tourism and tourism related activities, whereas if these funds were spent in cohesive manner by a nodal agency to showcase the entire country as one destination, the results would probably have been far more spectacular. Currently, the centre is only allocating finances for tourism projects. With some exemptions implementation is left to the states. This leads to time and cost overruns of tourism projects. But the government is trying to convince states on the benefits of bringing tourism under the aegis of the central government and get the subject on to the concurrent list.

India is now chalking up one of the strongest growth charts in a long time. As the Indian economy opens up in an effort to integrate with the world economy, benefits of doing business with and in India are increasing. With the result, hundreds of thousands of jobs are moving to the Indian shores from the west. This brings in its wake transit travellers, business travellers, business meets and holiday seekers. This is resulting in greater room occupancies and average room revenues (ARRs) in the country. ARRs have moved up from Rs. 3200-3400 in 2003 to Rs. 4000-4200 in 2004. Room occupancy rates have shot up from 75-80% in 2002 to over 90% now. In fact, in Bangalore it is now estimated at 100%.

During 2002, 2.2 million foreigners visited India. This number is up by 20% in 2003. India should be aiming at getting the kind of tourist inflows that countries like Singapore are attracting. Despite its low profile, tourism industry was the second –largest foreign exchange earner for the country during the year ended March 2003. In the Union Budget for 2004-05, government extended infrastructure status to tourism, thus opening the doors to cheap, long term funds to help finance tourism infrastructure.

With these few words I am sure that the research papers included in the proceedings would be useful for planning and development of Tourism in our country.

30th August, 2005

(Prof. S.P. Singh)
Vice Chancellor
HNB Garhwal University
Srinagar Garhwal

EDITOR'S NOTE

Travel and Tourism, perhaps more than any other industry, creates a wealth of opportunities and challenges particularly to the environmental and ecological aspects of a given community. Studies conducted by International Air Transport Association (IATA), Pacific Asia Travel Association (PATA) and World Leisure and Recreation Association (WLRA) indicate that travel demands within and to the Pacific Asia region grew from 1985 to 1990 at an average annual rate of 12.1 per cent. Therefore, this region's share of worldwide scheduled passenger traffic in 2010 is expected to become 51.1 per cent. According to the research findings, the growing economies of countries like Japan, South Korea and Taiwan will boost their outbound travel to a great extent. Other newly industrialised countries like Singapore, Thailand, Malaysia and even India will follow this. With the expected doubling of passenger traffic by the year 2010, there would have to be a better utilisation of airspace and navigation systems etc. The airports and other infrastructure, including roads, surface transport, hotels, will have to be modernized and updated to be able to service and absorb new demands. There would be a creation of mega resorts. There would be an improved life style and therefore there would be greater demands for improvement of quality of tourism. Business travel and special interest tourism would flow by leaps and bounds. There would be greater demands for proper technology and human resources to meet both the qualitative and quantitative needs. In India, in the earlier years, people used to head for the hill stations and in Europe, there used to be a traditional seaside holiday and one has seen how all this has changed.

In view of increased visitors, both interregional and intraregional, a number of trends and issues have been noticed all over the world. A large number of tourists are agreed that budget hotels are more economical because customer prefers to pay on the basis of per room and not per person. The budget hotel proposition, providing basic commodity-type accommodation at a standard price, consistent throughout the chain, reassures many people who may otherwise not have been happy to book room in an independent hotel. To some extent, the success of budget hotels has led the industry into a new period of development.

Natural health care has been tapped by known hoteliers to promote health tourism. Hotel properties will develop or convert their hotels into

Spa resorts on the ayurvedic concepts and other rejuvenating formula. Kerala Tourism has already introduced this concept, followed by Himachal and Uttaranchal Tourism. In the private sector, Hilton Hotel Chain recently tied up with the Singapore-based Banyan Tree Hotel and Resorts to announce its intention to tap this market. The Hyatt Regency is already in it, with its Goa resort and spa scheduled to open soon. The Indian Hotels and Health Resorts is also hoping to repeat the success it had with Ananda in Rishikesh. Add to this, Medical Tourism has been growing at the rate of 15% over the last five years. By 2012, if medical tourism were to touch 25% of revenues of private up market players, then upto Rs.10,000 crore will be added. However, for this promise to be fulfilled, certain measures are to be adopted. The broad areas of action are insurance, tax concessions, infrastructural facilities and establishment of standards. India has a natural advantage of lower cost. Our government needs to negotiate at WTO and at the bilateral level so that health insurance cover in the original country should also cover medical care provided in India.

A few years back, Indians were not receptive to the idea of franchising. But with tourism increasing in India, all big names in mid market segment started enhancing their visibility by lending their brand names through franchise agreements. Choice Hotels group is promoting both Quality Inns and Comfort Inns brands in a big way through franchise agreements. The group has 18 operational properties in India and few others are in the pipeline. ITC Hotels also have started a Fortune Park brand and the Oberoi Group has launched the Trident brand for catering to this segment. An amazing 110-hotel property is expected to come up throughout India in the next four years. The new hotels will add nearly 10,000 rooms, one third of India's existing room capacity in the branded hotel category. The country has caught the fancy of leading international groups, such as Marriott International, Accor, Carlson Hospitality, Hyatt, Hilton and Le Meridian, all of which are expanding their presence in India. The early years of the present century will be marked by major social and economic shifts that will change the way consumers behave. By 2006, more than two-thirds of the country's 1.1 billion people will be literate. Close to half the population will be very young, under the age of 20. Higher education will also be expanded due to the increasing international linkages that the Internet and other interactive media will provide. One of the biggest changes that will occur in the tourism market in the 21st century will be the increasing size of the mature travellers segment. The preferred guided tour of the future may not be conducted via motor coach but instead via the oldest form of transportation, i.e. on foot. Recently there has been a boom in the number of tourists taking walking tours. Rising numbers of the aged (above 60 years) in our population signifies a vast new opportunity for our marketers. They are likely to have savings and as they grow older, will not be averse to spending on themselves not just the income but their capital as well. They constitute a niche market for a variety of goods and services.

Aging populations in the developed countries, and most immediately Japan, provide India with another opportunity. It has been projected that between 1991 and 2016 the number of the aged person will grow by from 54.5 million to 113.0 million. Television will cover practically all of urban India and over 60 per cent of rural India. The number of households earning over $ 10,000 a year, in terms of purchasing power parity, will double from 16 million to 31 million. A further 165 million homes will provide a vast pool of consumers for the mass market. Promoting IT use is a key element of the Government's agenda now. Steps will be taken to increase personal computer penetration from 1 in every 500 persons to 1 in every 50 by 2008. These developments will give rise to two major opportunities: new demand at the lower end of the market spectrum, and a dramatic shift in the nature of demand at the upper end. The key to capturing these opportunities will be technology. Numerous customer enquiries (related to airline schedules, travel bookings, hotel reservations, rent-a-car service, tour guides, check-in facilities) have to be logged on to a centrally connected database. With the introduction of voice mail and integrated chips, everything will be instantaneous. User requirements have been validated in a very interactive manner. The availability of a PC on each desk will ensure quick processing of specific requirements of customers across a zonal, regional or national level. With the growing popularity and use of the internet as a distribution channel, absolute control over distribution and pricing has become increasingly difficult. Experts anticipate that online reservations for hotels will grow from an estimated $6 billion in 2002 (up from $4.1 billion in 2001) to nearly $10 billion in 2004. The challenge is to manage this growth through an effective channel distribution strategy that addresses the impact on the customer experience, the transparent nature of pricing over multiple channels and the increasing cost of reservations delivery. Another demographic shift, which will have an impact on international travel, has been the shift in the ethnic mix of North America. During the 19th and first half of the 20th century, most immigrants to the United States and Canada were Europeans by birth. These individuals, as they become more affluent, will also want to visit the lands of their heritage, generating a substantial increase in travel to their homelands.

Single holiday concept shall be the newest market spin from leading hotel chains in the country. However, most single people in India do not take a holiday alone as they feel awkward and lonely. The singles package, and the special events that go along with it, is aimed at promoting companionship. The target clientele is mostly 35 to 40 year old upmarket executives, senior managers and entrepreneurs coming form MNCs and banks.

Business travel or corporate travel constitutes about 12 per cent of the share of the global travel industry sweepstakes. And that share is bound to rise. According to most industry estimates, the Indian business travel industry should touch the $ 1 billion mark (including both domestic and international). Busy corporate executives and other professionals can leave all the intricate and complex details of their regular travel 'agendas' to these travel management specialists. Indeed, these companies through innovative and effective use of technology are already managing the huge travel budgets of some major Indian companies and in the process effecting many savings. In order to attract repeat visitors, hotel industry shall extend special emphasis on personal attention to their customers. To record guest preferences hoteliers shall store records into the hotel database so that likes and dislikes of an individual customer could be kept in mind during return visits.

Adventure tourism, such as, water sports, snow skiing, cycling and Jungle Safaris are likely to grow in popularity. For example, the U.S. Parachute Association reports that its membership has increased by 10% in each of the past 2 years. Although young men are most likely to seek out extreme thrills, non-traditional groups, such as women and those over 40 years old, have been noticed the fastest-growing sub-segments.

Where the size of the ecotourist segment expected to increase dramatically in the 21st century it would be necessary to dispersing a large number of lodging properties throughout a natural region, would necessitate widespread development of both infrastructure and superstructure, and would mean that little of the area could remain entirely undeveloped. Unless the emerging rank of ecotourists are willing to go without the most basic standards of comfort and convenience, most ecotourism destinations will need to cater to Western tastes to be able to attract a substantial number of visitors. Therefore, ecotourism may be the double-edged sword of the 21st century.

In the Explore India Millennium year, golf has been chosen as a thrust area and the Department of Tourism is working with major courses to attract potential golf tourists. What makes golf particularly attractive is the fact that it is an all-season passion. So, states like Himachal Pradesh and Uttaranchal, which are trying to address the problem of seasonality, are looking at the golf niche. There are an estimated 62 million keen golfers around the world, who are believed to venture out at least twice or thrice a year to test their skills on unknown terrain.

With the increasing number of visitors to a common destination, managing visitors requirements shall become difficult for service organisations in the near future. There would be increased number of mergers, acquisitions, alliances and cooperative agreements. Airlines have pioneered the development of cooperative alliances to gain greater brand recognition and operating synergies. The Indian tourism industry is looking at alliances with other countries, especially those in the neighborhood. The ideas that are being mooted now include joint promotion of the Himalayas in alliance with Nepal and China, marketing of beaches in collaboration with Maldives and Sri Lanka, and launching cricket tourism packages in association with Australia and New Zealand. Buddhist pilgrimage centers like Bodh Gaya and Lumbini can be developed into major tourist attractions in collaboration with Nepal to tap markets like Japan and Sri Lanka. However, there is no question of these destinations competing of with each other. Both Bodh Gaya (located in India) and Lumbini (the birthplace of Buddha in Nepal) will benefit if joint promotions are undertaken. Though there are various views on the nature of alliances, selection of partners and impact on business, representative of a number of leading Indian travel companies feel that basic concept of joint promotions would do well in the long term. During one of the international conference organised by the Confederation of Indian Industries (CII) in 2004, a large number of industry veterans expressed the desire to go in for long-term promotions as the current size of the cake is too small. The Indian market has the potential to grow to a much larger size.

After the recent wars and terrorist strikes, tourists seem to prefer short-haul destinations with an established reputation for safety. Therefore, there is no question of their choice being influenced by financial considerations alone. The cricket world cup in South Africa was a clear example of how cricket can be a large attraction. India, Pakistan, Sri Lanka, Australia and New Zealand can promote cricket tourism together. There are no geographical boundaries for these concepts and it is a question of a common theme. Beaches should be promoted as 'India beaches' rather than Goa or Kerala separately.

Liberalisation to local airlines should be treated as the prescription for revving up civil aviation. The government should allow for 49% FDI in domestic airlines and lift the ban on foreign airlines from investing in domestic airlines. The government is required to permit private airlines, like Jet Airways and Air Sahara, to operate on all major international routes. The other sweeping changes suggested is to include scrapping of the route disbursal guidelines which stipulate mandatory operations by domestic carriers to service remote areas like the north-east. Instead, such uneconomic services, which are essential for connectivity, should be subsidized. Inception of low cost Airlines like Deccan and Kingfisher have changed the shape of tourism industry. The low-cost model is now in its third wave of development. It has carriers like Deccan Air in India, Southwest in the US and Ryanair in Europe that have introduced cost effective fares. The industry is now in the middle of the third phase, with new low-costs being launched every week in some part of the world. On the runway are Snowflake, Jump Song, Ted, Baboo, Duo, Jet Magic, Sterling, Wind Jet, Tango, Flying Finn, Air Asia and the Thai Airways. Worldwide, the low-cost phenomenon has revolutionized the point-to-point airline market and, in turn, the way all airlines think about costs. Low-cost airlines like Air Asia, promoted by Tony Fernandes, which was launched in Malaysia, have shaken up established players in the region.

The hardest work for the industry lies in convincing its constituents that it is not an industry by the rich for the rich. In many parts of Asia, luxury hotels are still an incongruous embarrassment in the midst of surrounding poverty. Either orientation will have to be replaced by modesty or the industry will have to work harder at explaining why it is paying housekeepers as much as it charges guests for 20 cups of coffee. Non-governmental organisations still blame travel and tourism for abetting the problem of child prostitution even though the industry is working very hard to combat it.

Climate models used by the US's Inter-governmental Panel on Climate Change and thousands of scientists worldwide who advise government on climate change, project that the Earth will warm up by two to six degrees Fahrenheit by the year 2100 if emissions that trap the sun's heat are not reduced. Evidence suggests that shorter winters, longer of drier summers, and increased frequency of flooding, and summer droughts will be associated with global warming. The countries that would suffer the most from global warming are island nations. These countries have long coastlines, sensitive tourism industries and small undeveloped economies. Tiny low lying Caribbean islands, with economies based primarily on agriculture and tourism, are extremely vulnerable to the impacts of potential global warming. Winter tourism may also be affected, as the Alps and other skiing destinations like Auli, Kufri, and Narkanda in Indian shall experience less snowfall and shorter skiing seasons. Global warming is expected to cause a substantial reduction in the duration of winter snow cover in Australia. Therefore there would be possible effects on the tourism industry in alpine regions and its environs.

Hospitality business leaders have long recognized the difficulty of attracting and retaining quality employees as a continuous threat to the health of the industry. The current bad situation is worsening. Labour costs are increasing as hotels compete with retailing and fast food outlets for the unskilled and semi-skilled workers. All workers are demanding greater benefits. Labour unions appear to be regaining strength, and the tightening of immigration standards in the wake of 9/11 will place an increased burden on the industry. Highly skilled and trained workers have better carrying capacity in other industries. Productivity is declining, as employees demand more favorable hours and the hotel business modernizes its wage and hour policies. The spirit of hospitality is deteriorating and guest service is being compromised by turnover, lack of training, corporate earning requirements and staff reductions. Comparing profit potential with a brand or without a brand is becoming a serious exercise for hotel owners. At the same time, the proliferation of brands means fewer independents that struggle for fair share using price as the preferred strategy. While independent hotel operators use the Internet to level the playing field, continued downward pressure on rates results in destabilized markets and further erodes profitability.

In view of the foregoing issues and trends the All India Tourism Teachers Association decided to hold its maiden seminar on sustainable tourism planning and development at Rishikesh. The conference was attended by a large number of professionals and academicians who shared their ideas and thoughts on sustainable tourism planning and development. The present report is an outcome of the discussions held during the two days conference. Around 35 research papers were presented during the conference which were discussed in the proceedings. Out of the total 35 papers, we included in this publication papers presented by some eminent academicians and researchers. These include S.P. Bansal and Prashant Gautam, Himachal University, Shimla; M.R. Dileep, KITTS, Thiruvananthapuram; Mohit Kukreti, University of Gondar, Ethiopia, Africa; Ravi Bhusan and Surendra Pal Singh, Kurukshetra University, Kurukshetra; Anjana Sharma, IndraPrastha University, New Delhi; S.M. Ambli, Goa University, Goa; Prachi Rastogi, the Centre for Tourism Research, Lucknow; Adarsh Batra, Assumption University, Thailand; Tarun Roy, New Delhi; Saurabh Dixit, Devesh Nigam and Nidhi Bhatia, Bundelkhand University, Jhansi; S.K. Gupta, Rakesh Dhodi, Ashok Kumar, Rashmi Dhodi, Sanjay Dhyani, Jitendra Mohan Misra and S.C. Bagri, HNB Garhwal University, Srinagar, Garhwal.

(Prof. S.C. Bagri)
Dean & Director
Centre for Mountain Tourism & Hospitality Studies
HNB Garhwal University, Srinagar Garhwal, Uttaranchal

CONTENTS

Sustainable Tourism Planning and Development, 1-10, 2006
Edited by Bagri, S.C.
Published by Bishen Singh Mahendra Pal Singh, Dehra Dun, India

A Brief History of AITTA and Seminar Proceedings

All India Tourism Teachers Association was formed towards the end of the year 2002 by a group of leading tourism and travel academicians who felt that the time had come to create an association to regulate tourism and travel manpower training and research programmes in India along organised lines. The primary purpose is to enhance the standard of teaching and research of those engaged in the academic institutions and to promote its orderly growth and development. The association membership is currently around 100 consisting of life and yearly membership.

What is AITTA?

❑ AITTA is a professional coordinating body of different segments of the tourism and travel institutions.

❑ It is the National Association of India.

❑ It is Non political, Non commercial and Non profit making organisation

Aims and Objectives

AITTA aims at the development of tourism education in India by constantly improving the standard of teaching, research and professionalism in the industry so as to cater to the needs of tourist traffic from within India and overseas. AITTA is also engaged in promoting mutual cooperation among the different segments of the tourism teaching and research institutions, academicians by contributing to the sound progress and growth of the industry as a whole.

ACTIVITIES

❑ AITTA functions as powerful platform for interaction of thoughts and experiences.

- AITTA helps to promote, maintain and stimulate the growth of travel and tourism research in the industry.

- AITTA educates and equips the members to meet the challenges of tomorrow through conventions and seminars.

- AITTA draws the attention of travel trade operators in the country and discusses with them the problems of manpower development.

- AITTA maintains close contact with world bodies and represents matters affecting the travel and tourism training and research in the country.

- AITTA gathers useful information on travel and tourism and disseminates the same to its members for their guidance.

- AITTA helps better understanding among the different segments of the travel industry and bring them into its fold by offering membership under different categories.

- AITTA fosters fraternity among its members.

Seminar Proceedings

Centre for Mountain Tourism and Hospitality Studies, HNB Garhwal University, Srinagar Garhwal organized the maiden All India Tourism Teachers' Association's conclave on "Sustainable Tourism Planning & Development" on March Ist and IInd 2004 at Rishikesh, Uttaranchal. This is an annual event wherein a large number of eminent personalities both from the trade and academia were invited to debate a particular theme with an audience of delegates and invitees from far and wide.

At the start of the conclave, there was a slight apprehension to comment on the theme as it was too grandiose. After listening to the rich content which emerged from the speakers and the discussions of the delegates, everyone was reassured. The conclave format was carefully planned in keeping with the theme. AITTA conclave 2004 though will surely be remembered for the grandstanding of our keynote speaker Mr. M. Ramachandran, Additional Chief Secretary and Secretary Education, Govt. of Uttaranchal, Dehradun, who spoke at length, regarding the efforts of the government in developing infrastructure to keep up with the pace of the tourism scenario in the world. Mr. M. Ramchandran in his welcome address mentioned the economic growth of Uttaranchal as the outcome of tourism and hydroelectric potential of the state. He emphasized on planning and development of state with equitable resource utilization without affecting the local areas and host community. He identified the areas that should be taken care of for tourism promotion in the state like infrastructural growth, uplifting transport facilities, provision of airport and expansion of information technology. He portrayed the picture of tourism in a way that should not effect local beliefs and will lead to employment generation.

Prof. D.S. Bhardwaj, Department of Tourism, Kurukshetra University, Kurukshetra and President AITTA, was the next speaker on the occasion and described tourism industry as fastest growing and emerging industry which have economic potential for earning foreign exchange, generating revenue, employment opportunities, talked about impacts of tourism, social and physical but more importantly economic impacts. He gave data of 700 million international tourists crossing borders spending 430 billion US $. He spoke about the unemployment problem and said one out of every nine is indulged in tourism. By 2010 volume of international tourism would be one billion and by end of 2020 it would reach to 1.8 billion. At present 20 million persons are indulged in the industry directly and at the end of 2020 this figure will reach to 40 million in India alone. He said "if one million is invested in tourism, then approx. 49 jobs will be generated. Therefore no country can afford to ignore to tourism development. In 1984 we were at 34th number at global level and China was at 44th number. Today China is among top 5 nations in tourist arrivals whereas India is still struggling to achieve its position. However we have more then 250 million domestic tourists so we should emphasise more on domestic tourism". Prof. Bhardwaj further explained that international tourism generated seasonal employment whereas domestic tourism is helpful in providing permanent employment. He laid emphasis/stressed more on domestic tourist satisfaction that will lead to more international tourists. Prof. S.C. Bagri, Director, Centre for Mountain Tourism, HNB Garhwal University, Srinagar Garhwal who was also the Chief Organiser of the conclave emphasized on the use and relevance of sustainable tourism in context of Indian tourism. He cited the examples of India's tourism resources and expressed his deep concern over the present condition especially the excess number of visitors and depleted nature of tourism resources and attractions. He cautioned and warned the delegates about the serious consequences if not updated and timely preventive measures are not taken. Dr. S.P. Bansal, Secretary AITTA, and Chairman of MTA Programme, HP University Shimla, proposed vote of thanks and acknowledged the contribution of all concerned.

After the opening ceremony post luncheon session declared the opening of the first plenary session and it emphasized on sustainable tourism development, its relevance & challenges. The session was chaired by Prof. Manjulla Chaudhary, Chairperson, Department of Tourism, Kurukshetra University, Kurukshetra. In her key note address she spoke at length about the concept of overlooking the sustainability as we are getting obsessed with the theory of sustainability of resources. She even spoke about the services being offered to the tourists that must satisfy their expectations so as to improve the quality of incoming tourists. She further spoke on multiplier effect and myopic approach created by tourism industry and stressed that if marketers would increase customers' expectation and work for customer satisfaction, automatically sustainability would be maintained. The session was further enlightened by various scholars and professors like Dr. S.P. Bansal, Chairman, Institute of Vocational studies, HP University Shimla, who gave his views on "Synergistic Relationship Between Tourism, Biodiversity, Local People : A Tool for Achievement of Sustainable Tourism Development". The paper was discussed by Mr. Prashant Gautam, Lecturer, HP University, Shimla. He explained the framework for conservation of Maharana Pratap Sagar wetland in district Kangra of Himachal Pradesh. He put forward various findings by using questionnaires method and identified different problems in development of tourism in the area. He concluded that tourism is a tool for economic growth and recommended involvement of community, local NGO's, NSS camps in the local area. H.K. Mandal, from Tamilnadu, asked about the treatment of cassamodia about which Prashant Gautam said that he has already talked about those details which can only be found by wetland expert committee. Kaushik Mandal, Lecturer Deptt. Of Tourism, Burdwan University, Burdwan presented his paper on "Accounting and Comparing Resources of West Bengal with other states. He mentioned different dimension of Sustainable Tourism Development and spoke about report of World Commission on Environment and Development in 1987. He also talked about sectional, environmental & sustainable tourism development approaches. He rated West Bengal to be greater than Goa, Orissa, Assam & Bihar. A very spontaneous question was raised by Amit K. Singh, Lecturer, Uday Pratap College, BHU, Varanasi, about why they have considered Goa for comparison with West Bengal and similar question came from Jitendra Mishra, Research Scholar, CMTHS, HNB Garhwal University, Srinagar, about Kerala being better option to compare in-spite of Orissa & Assam. Mandal told about his source of information and different publication & statistical abstract he had with him. The next speaker was Surinder Pal Singh, Research

Scholar, Kurukshetra University Kurukshetra, discussed about "Sustainable Tourism in Developing Countries – relevance and challenges" where he spoke about accountability, affordability, long run Vs short run focus, high value and low value proposition of tourism operators, ensure education and awareness of tourism in communities where he quoted the help of US to Kenya. First question came from Jitendra Mishra, CMTHS, Srinagar, about the need for more educational programme to which Pal answered, "tourism is people's industry and all the points of tourism should be known to students of young generation". Then D.K. Vaid, Head, Pd. Sunderlal Sharma Central Institute of Vocational Education, Bhopal, talked about the scope for improvement where he said wage employment are shrinking and Pal said training should be given to encourage self employment opportunities. On this Ashok Kumar, CMTHS, Srinagar, strongly opposed the opinion of Pal regarding wage structure being offered by the organizations to trained and untrained manpower.

The next presentation was delivered by Dheerendra Laxman Rao Ekbote MASC College, Karnataka, who spoke on "India's Tourism - Beyond an Artist's Brush", where he described various features of tourism as a service of intangibility, perishability, inseparability, heterogeneity and changing demand and talked about incidents of Bin Laden and Kargil and described tourism as *'more Gham than Khushi'* and tourists wanting to *"Pay Aadha and enjoy Jyada"*. He suggested ensuring safety, discounted fares, proper planning and professional marketing etc. for better tourism prospects. Tarun K. Roy from Delhi, discussed the environmental codes of conduct and positive attitude of tourist, sustainable tourism development in India and presented national forest policy and opportunity for promoting domestic tourism in context of Garhwal Himalaya and suggested for bringing a change in behavior of locals and creating awareness.

The second day's plenary session was headed by D.K. Vaid, Professor P.D. Sunderlal Sharma, Central Institute of Vocational Education, Bhopal. The first speaker was R.A. Sharma, Coordinator, Centre for Tourism studies, Jiwaji University, Gwalior, who presented on the topic, Tourism Education in India and its problem, in which he discussed the present scenario of tourism education and suggested the uniformity in the nomenclature and course content. Vaid questioned if Sharma had any suggestion for teachers' education? To this, Sharma answered that there should be indepth exposure to trainees and teachers in all major interactive disciplines. Answering to the question by Sarla Shahi, Tehri Campus,

HNB Garhwal University, Srinagar Garhwal, asked about the jobs prospects. Sandeep Kulsheshtra, Prof. IITTM Govindpuri, Gwalior, in between informed the participants regarding IITTM refresher courses in tourism and allied disciplines and said such courses are being organised frequently. Saurabh Dixit, CMTHS, Srinagar, presented a case study on sustainability and ecofriendliness for the hospitality industry and discussed about concern for environment in hotels and other accommodation units and suggested the ecofriendly measures, carrying capacity management plans, integrated planning, appropriate standards for the hotel industry.

The next speaker of the session was Arvind Dubey, Delhi Institute of Heritage Research, New Delhi. He spoke on the Backbone of Sustainable Tourism Development and described carrying capacity as base for sustainable tourism development. He found out development should be based upon the education of young generation. He emphasized on conservation about sustainability. S.C. Bagri CMTHS, HNB Garhwal University, asked if he had any formula for carrying capacity measurement and then suggested the author to present a case study. Kulshestra cited the example of Lakshadeep and explained the measures they have undertaken for carrying capacity fixation. There was presentation by S.M. Ambli, S.P. Chowgule College, Goa on Temporal Distribution of Tourism in Goa. He presented facts and figures on foreign tourist arrivals to Goa. He made scientific analysis of tourist arrivals and pointed out that due to socio cultural reasons potential market of Maharashtra and Karnataka doesn't come to Goa. Praveen Rana, BHU Varanasi raised doubts on the reliability of Govt. supplied data. Ambli explained the doubt and clarified that all available data have been obtained from reliable sources and have been interpreted extensively. H.K. Mann asked about variation of climate in Goa and Europe and viability of making advertisement of 365 days holidays making in Goa. Ms. Sarla Shahi enquired if cultural impacts were prevailing which he answered it is not because of tourism but pseudo propaganda by the media. Jitendra Mishra asked how to use data in making some strategies and policy making for betterment of tourism, which was answered that society supports any promotion of culture and accordingly strategies should be implemented. The next presentation was given by Majumdar, Department of Economics, S.P. Chowgule College, Goa, on the Prospect of Ecotourism in Goa: a case study of Cabo de Roma. In which he laid emphasis on Beach Tourism and its prospects for development through coral reefs, marine rafting, fishing, natural environment involvement of host community. He answered that Goa has numerous forts which can be promoted as ecotourism destination. He said tourism promotion will automatically develop nearby villagers. After this Ms. Usha Aggarwal, Govt. PG College Mandsaur, Madhya Pradesh discussed on prospects and problems of tourism in Western Madhya Pradesh. She explained many potential destinations which can come up as a hot destinations for future. Her objectives were to explore tourism potentials, create awareness, eradicate economic impacts, and rejuvenate poor information. She disseminated useful information based on various field surveys, questionnaires, interviews, research analysis. To fulfill her objectives she suggested solution to shortcomings like lack of publicity and accommodation shortage, poor advertisement, poor transport and infrastructure in and around tourist places.

Ms. Prachi Rastogi, Centre for Tourism Recreation Research, Lucknow, spoke next on Yoga which was described as oldest discipline to keep mind and soul healthy. She emphasized Yoga as the remedy to overcome isolation, depression, stress, restore physical and mental strain focused on self awareness through continuous practice of *pranayams* and *aasnas*. Next presentation was given by Lav Kush Mishra, Co-ordinator, Department of Tourism, B.R. Ambedkar University Agra. He spoke on Tourism Problems in Agra where night stay is not prevalent because of high tariff structure of accommodation units being offered to inbound visitors. Tourists even carry drinking water which leads to poor participation of local entrepreneur in tourism promotion. So there should be training programmes to *coolies, rikshawala, dhabawala* to motivate and influences the tourist behavior.

Sandeep Verma, Devshree University, Shantikunj Haridwar, was the next speaker who analysed the input of state as well as central govt. regarding *Kumbh Mela*. He expressed surprise at the nature of work been done on ground and question reliability of the data for *Kumbh Mela* and also data about hotels, *dharamshalas* obtained from Dept. of Tourism. Then Ashok Kumar, CMT&HS, HNB Garhwal University, Srinagar Garhwal, discussed on the innovative idea of promoting entrepreneurship at various locations by Tourist Guests Houses (TGH) project in Uttaranchal. He presented relevant data regarding the financial statement and achievement of objectives of the group. He projected opening of religious packages, trekking routes, adventure wings at TGH units that can reduce unemployment problems by providing chance to youth to make run different ventures. Next presentation was by Harshiet Kumar Mandal on Promoting Sustainable Tourism in Himalayan region. He described various impacts of tourism on Himalayan ecology and environment. He suggested in making links, breaking negative links and clarifying and managing certainty links. Mr. Jitendra Mohan Mishra presented his viewpoint on Sustainable Tourism Planning: A Case study of Kausani – Almora – Jageshwar – Binsar and Ranikhet circuit. He suggested various means of developing tourist traffic to this region by focusing on development standards and style that intermingles with the local milieu like rural tourism, health tourism, agriculture tourism etc. He further presented the idea of developing ecotourism model in the region thereby protecting the nature for the future generation.

The second day's valedictory function started with welcome note by S.C. Bagri, organizer of the conclave. On this occasion N.N. Prasad, the then Secretary Tourism, Govt. of Uttaranchal was the special invitee and Air Vice Marshall (Retd.) Dr. N. Natrajan, the then Vice Chancellor HNB Garhwal University was the chief Guest. Prasad addressed guests, delegates and academicians regarding his 3 years experience as Secretary Tourism after formation of new state. He spoke at length about the expectations of people at the initial stages. He said bureaucrats are not magician they can not do miracles with such limited resources and regulatory aspect and emphasized on the need of understanding ground realities that hinders the actual development. In his speech he mentioned Uttaranchal as gold mine with ample hill stations, lakes, glaciers, pilgrimage centres, wild life, flora and fauna, with sand beaches, rafting etc. He said we don't even miss sea because we have *Ganga* undone by man not by God. He presented relevant data of tourist arrivals in Uttaranchal in the previous years and its growth. According to his data 1,30,00,000 tourists visited the region with 85 lakhs population of local people (2003) and predicted an increase in 2004 because of *Ardh Kumbh*. Focus was on developing tourism in such a way that it will lead to minimum destruction, like in-spite of constructing five star hotels emphasis should be given in constructing resorts made of local material that will suite the local milieu and further help local people in getting direct benefits. He pointed out certain locations and circuits to be developed in the near future viz., *Mana village*, Valley of Flowers, *Binsar, Kausani* in an ecofriendly way.

His speech was accompanied by very enthusiastic and realistic speech by Air Vice Marshal (Retd.) Dr. N. Natrajan, the then Vice Chancellor, HNB Garhwal University. He expressed his pleasure on issues concerning tourism industry. He appreciated N.N. Prasad's promising speech and described the problems as site and region specific and quoted example of his own native state Tamilnadu. He mentioned strengths of Uttaranchal state in the field of tourism, hydro-electricity, natural resources, wild flora and fauna etc. He said university must be considered to make centres for training manpower professionals. He assured university support by including foreign languages and emphasized on maintaining economic support. The vote of thanks was proposed by Sandeep Kulsherestha, Prof. at IITTM Gwalior. The conclave witnessed its closing with a gala dinner at Chotiwala near Swargashram.

The final outcome of the conclave that were put forward by various renowned personalities were as follows:-

- Uttaranchal being an upcoming destination needs intensive planning and management with keeping Sustainability as the central idea.

- Environmental conservation and tourist safety must be given priority while developing new tourism products and travel circuits.

- Tourism should be promoted to benefit a wider community by increasing tourism-community involvement.

- Services provided to tourists should have consistency right from the time of tourist arrival to departure and must be of a high standard.

- All stakeholders along with host community must be involved in the planning process.

- Design and building of new accommodation units should have sound visual impact, technological efficiency, attractive and locally relevant landscaping.

- Efforts must be made to reduce the amount of garbage produced by hoteliers and eateries runners.

- Recycling in yet another way to reduce garbage, whereby the original product is transformed into some other useful purpose. All non-biodegradable products can be recycled.

- There is a need to support private institutes developing manpower skills in different areas of tourism like - adventure tourism activities, hospitality training etc. from the government.

- It is imperative to device effective tourism legislation for protection of tourist rights at the places of tourist visit and stay.

- Intensive financial and other ancillary encouragement should be given to host community to promote winter tourism at specific locations and routes in order to reduce congestion during the summer season.

- Encourage watershed management to reduce soil erosion and lake sedimentation.

- Proper signage should be used at road sides as well as on trek routes.

- Comprehensive and updated information of tourist attractions should be displayed on boards in order to keep tourist informed of the visiting destinations.

- In order to increase tourist arrivals in Uttaranchal efforts should be made to make the prefabricated accommodation at all tourist places.

- Effective measurement methods and techniques should be devised for measuring the arrivals and to know the expenditure pattern of tourists visiting Uttaranchal.

- Efforts should be made to reduce negative impact of over grazing by cattle's at mountain meadows and highlands by a continuous monitoring agency.

- Entry into parks and sanctuaries should be charged and moreover cattle should be strictly prohibited into it.

- Run-of the- river technology for power generation should be adopted and applied at different locations.

Sustainable Tourism Planning and Development, 11-27, 2006
Edited by Bagri, S.C.
Published by Bishen Singh Mahendra Pal Singh, Dehra Dun, India

Sustainable Synergistic Relationship between Tourism, Bio-diversity, Local People and Management: Maharana Pratap Sagar (Pong Dam Wetland) in Himachal Pradesh

S.P. Bansal

Chairman, Institute of Vocational Studies,
Master of Tourism Administration,
Himachal Pradesh University, Shimla 171005.
E-mail: spbansal_mtahpu@rediffmail.com

Prashant Kumar Gautam

Lecturer, Institute of Vocational Studies,
Master of Tourism Administration,
Himachal Pradesh University, Shimla 171005.
E-mail: prashantgautam76@rediffmail.com

Abstract : Sustainable Tourism can contribute to both conservation and development and involves positive synergistic relationship among tourism, bio-diversity and local people, facilitated by appropriate management. Present paper is taking an example of Maharana Pratap Sagar Wetland in district Kangra of Himachal Pradesh – a wetland of International importance- and applies a framework/action plan for the development of tourism and conservation of the wetland. The study of tourism phenomenon near this wetland is important because it attracts a lot of migratory birds during the winters, and is home for a lot of species of fishes. Due to its bio-diversity, the area has the potential for providing quality nature experiences and also there is a need for conservation of the wetland and how a sample of residents of nearby areas of Maharana Pratap Sagar Wetland perceived the effect of tourism on the development of the community. This paper also examines how tourism is responsible for the development of the area. By using questionnaire, local opinions and the perceptions regarding tourism contribution towards the community development were also identified. It is revealed that the natural beauty as well as the diversity of animal and plant life in many wetlands make them ideal locations for tourists. By taking example of the Maharana Pratap Sagar Wetland the authors have tried to develop an action plan for the development of sustainable tourism.

Key Words : Himachal, sustainable, development, tourism, management.

Concept of Sustainable Tourism Development

The World Commission on Environment and Development (The Brundtland Commission) brought the term 'sustainable tourism development' into common use in its seminar report (1987) called "Our common future". "Sustainable Development is the development that meets the needs of the present without compromising the ability of future generations to meet their own needs." The definition incorporates two concepts:

- The concept of 'needs', especially the needs of the poor.
- Ability to meet the present and the future needs (Srivastva; 1996).

"Basically, when discussions take place on sustainable development, the easiest definition is what we, the present generation, have inherited as certain amount of ecology and environment surrounding in terms of land, water and air; when we leave it to the next generation, we should leave it at least in the same condition, if not in a better condition than what we inherited. This is the sum and substance of sustainable development, putting it in elementary terms (Geethakrishnan; 1990)."

Concept of Ecotourism

Ecotourism is often considered to be a potential strategy to support conservation of natural ecosystems while at the same time promoting sustainable development (Ross and Wall; 1999). Ecotourism is usually considered to be more than just tourism to natural areas. However, the absence of a widely accepted definition of ecotourism is associated with a lack of consensus concerning the distinctiveness of ecotourism and the extent to which it differs from other forms of tourism. Since the formal introduction of the term by Ceballos-Lascurain almost two decades ago, controversies over appropriate uses for the term and inconsistency in its application have hindered the development of the concept and its practical realization at specific sites (Bottrill and Pearce; 1999). Those at the forefront of ecotourism research and development now provide definition, which address the fundamental goals of conservation of natural areas and local development. The Ecotourism Society defines ecotourism as "Purposeful travel to natural areas to understand the culture and the natural history of the environment; taking care not to alter the integrity of the ecosystem; producing economic opportunities that make the conservation of the natural resources beneficial to the local people" (Wood, Getz and Lindberg; 1995). The World Conservation Union's (IUCN) Commission on Natural Parks and Protected Areas (CNPPA) defines ecotourism as "Environmentally responsible travel and visitation to relatively undisturbed natural areas, in order to enjoy and appreciate nature (and any accompanying cultural features – both past and present) that promotes conservation, has low visitor impact, and provides for beneficially active socio-economic involvement of local populations (Ceballos-Lascurain; 1996).

Ecotourism is neither a simple concept to define nor a straightforward phenomenon to implement and evaluate. Ecotourism should be regarded as being more than tourism to natural areas and should be viewed as a means of combining the goals of resource conservation and local development through tourism in a synergistic fashion. This means that care should be taken to ensure that the goals of tourism development do not interfere with the goals of protecting natural areas and bio-diversity (Ross and Wall; 1999). While providing an enjoyable experience in nature, the fundamental functions of ecotourism are protection of natural areas, production of revenue, education and local participation and capacity building. While difficult to measure, ecotourism is believed to be the fastest growing tourism segments. In 1988 there were between 157 and 236 million international ecotourists, generating economic impacts of $93 billion (Filion *et al.*; 1994). There is a considerable debate over what ecotourism really means. However, the estimates of value generated are based upon a definition of the form, which allows tourists to enjoy and appreciate nature.

Ecotourism and Community Participation

Ecotourism development is not possible, if it remains the responsibility of the Govt. alone. It is an admitted fact that many environmental problems cannot be solved without the active participation of the local people and people-centered environmentally active grass-root organizations. Their involvement in the environmental protection programmmes is essential for discharging a variety of vital functions; because they know better as to which kind of environmental protection programs are in their best interest. Any program of environmental protection, which is thrust upon people will not succeed unless it embodies their explicit acceptance in terms of their perceived needs.

Figure 1 illustrates how the economic benefits of tourism flow through the local economy. As shown in this diagram, there is some loss of economic benefits to purchasing goods from outside the area while use of locally produced goods and services leads to increased benefits within the local economy. The diagram also shows that some attractions, facilities and services – parks, sport centres, theatres, stores and art and craft galleries developed for tourism are ones that community residents can also use.

Tourism and the Community

When tourist spends money, it creates a chain reaction that produces additional economic benefits. They trade with businesses that purchases supplies and services locally or elsewhere. The business, in turn, purchases supplies and services they need to operate and, through successive rounds of purchases, the initial direct expenditures of visitors spread and multiply throughout the local and regional economy. The following chart demonstrates how tourism spending flows through the economy.

Tourism, the Environment and the Community

Tourism and the environment are closely interrelated. The natural and built environment provides many of the attractions for tourists and tourism development can have both positive and negative impacts on the environment. Sustainable tourism development depends on protecting the environmental resources for tourism. The partners for sustainable tourism development are the tourism industry - owners and managers of tourism commercial enterprises, the environment supporters - advocates for environmental conservation, and the community-residents, community groups and leaders and the local authorities. Typically some members of the community will also be involved in the tourism industry or be environment supporters.

Figure 2 illustrates the interaction needed among these partners that is necessary to achieve improved quality of life for the community.

A Case of Tourism Wetlands

The natural beauty as well as the diversity of animals and plant lives in many wetlands make them ideal locations for tourists. Many of the finest sites are protected as National Parks or World Heritage Sites and

Tourism and the Community

When tourist spends money, it creat a chain reaction that produces additional economic benefits. They trade with businesses that purchases supplies and services locally or elsewhere. The business, in turn, purchases supplies and services they need to operate and, through successive rounds of purchases, the initial direct expenditures of visitors spread and multiply throughout the local and regional economy. The following chart demonstrates how tourism spending flows through the economy.

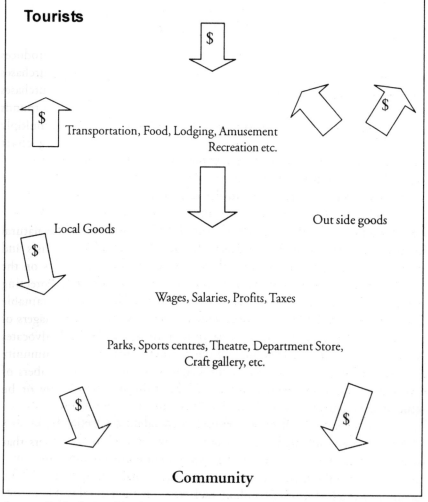

Tourists

Transportation, Food, Lodging, Amusement Recreation etc.

Local Goods

Out side goods

Wages, Salaries, Profits, Taxes

Parks, Sports centres, Theatre, Department Store, Craft gallery, etc.

Community

Source : Guide for Local Authorities on Developing Sustainable Tourism, A Tourism and Environment Publication, WTO, Spain.

Fig. 1.

16

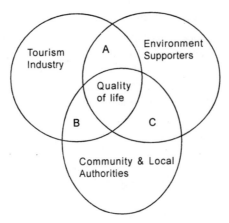

Source : Guide for Local Authorities on Developing Sustainable Tourism, A Tourism and Environment Publication, WTO, Spain.

Fig. 2: The Tourism Industry, Environment and the Community

are able to generate considerable income from tourists and recreational uses. In some countries the revenue is a significant component of the national economy. Caribbean countries rely on their beaches and reefs to attract millions of visitors each year; their tourist industry was valued at US$ 8.9 billion in 1990, one half of their GNP (Gross National Product). In Australia, the Great Barrier Reef Marine Park recorded 1.6 million visitors with an approximate annual value in excess of US$ 540 million in 1997, while Kakadu National Park collects over US$ 800,000 in visitor fees annually. At the Bonaire National Park in the Netherlands Antilles, divers pay a US$ 10 fee each year, which covers the operational costs of the park, and they are estimated to contribute about US$ 30 million per year to the island's economy through other expenditures. Similarly, a small marine protected area in the Cayman Islands attracts 168,000 divers per year, who spend around US$ 53 million. The Florida Keys wetland area generates at least US$ 800 million annually from tourism. Freshwater recreational fishing is entirely dependent on wetlands. In the USA it has been estimated that half of the seawater catch is also associated with wetlands. Recreational fishing can generate considerable income; more than 45 million people take part in recreational fishing in the USA, spending a total of US$ 24 billion each year on their hobby. There are of course a wide range of recreational activities associated with wetlands that generate income locally and nationally, from boating and other water sports to hunting, watching wildlife and even art and literature. For example, Monet has inspired millions of people with his paintings of water lilies. More than 60 million people watch migratory birds and 3.2 million people hunt ducks and geese in North America (Canada, USA and Mexico); collectively they generate US$ 20 billion annually in economic activity.

Table I: Wetlands of International Importance in India

Name	Date	State	Area	Position
Ashtamudi Wetland	19/08/02	Kerala	61,400 ha	08°57'N 076°35'E
Bhitarkanika Mangroves	19/08/02	Orissa	65,000 ha	20°39'N 086°54'E
Bhoj Wetland	19/08/02	M.P.	3,201 ha	23°14'N 077°20'E
Chilika Lake	01/10/81	Orissa	116,500 ha	19°42'N 085°21'E
Deepor Beel	19/08/02	Assam	4,000 ha	26°08'N 091°39'E
East Calcutta Wetlands	19/08/02	W.B.	12,500 ha	22°27'N 088°27'E
Harike Lake	23/03/90	Punjab	4,100 ha	31°13'N 075°12'E
Kanjli	22/01/02	Punjab	183 ha	31°25'N 075°22'E
Keoladeo National Park	01/10/81	Rajasthan	2,873 ha	27°13'N 077°32'E
Kolleru Lake	19/08/02	A.P.	90,100 ha	16°37'N 081°12'E
Loktak Lake	23/03/90	Manipur	26,600 ha	24°26'N 093°49'E
Point Calimere Wildlife and Bird Sanctuary	19/08/02	T.N.	38,500 ha	10°19'N 079°38'E
Pong Dam Lake	19/08/02	H.P.	15,662 ha	32°01'N 076°05'E
Ropar	22/01/02	Punjab	1,365 ha	31°01'N 076°30'E
Sambhar Lake	23/03/90	Rajasthan	24,000 ha	27°00'N 075°00'E
Sasthamkotta Lake	19/08/02	Kerala	373 ha	09°02'N 076°37'E
Tsomoriri	19/08/02	J & K	12,000 ha	32°54'N 078°18'E
Vembanad-Kol Wetland	19/08/02	Kerala	151,250 ha	09°50'N 076°45'E
Wular Lake	23/03/90	J & K	18,900 ha	34°16'N 074°33'E

Source: http://www.ramsar.org/ramsarlist.html
ha = hactare

There are many wetlands with great recreational value for which a dollar figure cannot easily be given because visitors use the area without direct payment. Employing economic valuation techniques to investigate how members of the public "value" the Norfolk Broads wetland area in the United Kingdom, researchers estimated that the recreational value of the area to users amounted to US$ 32.5 million per year for people living relatively close to the Broads and US$ 12.9 million per year for those living further away.

Although not strictly speaking a "recreation" function, the educational value of wetlands is closely related; there are many wetland education centres and programmes around the world that involve the general public and school children in practical activities in their local wetland environments; these activities span the border between education and recreation. Water-watch Australia is a community-based programme with 50,000 volunteers in 1,800 groups from all over the country who monitor water quality in local rivers. Using simple but effective water monitoring kits, the general public and school children are better able to understand environmental concepts through hands-on activities and at the same time contribute significantly to the conservation of their local watershed. The importance of tourism on the wetlands has been identified for the overall development of area. Country towns in Victoria (Australia) will benefit financially by introducing Nature-based Wetlands Tourism to their regions.

Objectives

The main objectives for the completion of study are:

- To study the residents perceptions towards tourism development and its impacts.

- To study the problems in the development of tourism in the area.

- To identify that how tourism in the wetland area can be developed on sustainable basis through positive synergistic relationship between tourism, bio-diversity, locals and management.

- To suggest a framework/action plan for the development of sustainable tourism through conservation of wetlands.

Methodology

The above objectives were achieved with the help of a questionnaire based on Likert Scale[1]. It was prepared for the perception of the local community regarding the tourism development and its impacts.

---

[1] A Likert scale provides a measure of the degree to which a respondent agree or disagrees with the each series of statements. The degree of agreement in a Likert scale is often measured with a five-point scale: (Likert R., 1932, *A Technique for the Measure of Attitudes*, Achieves of Psychology, No. 140, Columbia University Press, New York.)

Furthermore mail survey[2] was undertaken with the help of questionnaire containing open-ended questions based on Delphi technique.[3] Panel of experts' include; local community representatives, people belonging to the district administration, tourism department, forest department, fisheries, environment and zoological survey. Main focus was upon identifying problems in the development, how tourism in the wetland area can be developed on sustainable basis through positive synergistic relationship between tourism, bio-diversity, locals and management, and to develop a framework /action plan for the development and conservation of wetlands. The sample of local people selected for the present study was 50 from the 5 places near to the wetland on quota basis.

DESIGNING QUESTIONNAIRE

A questionnaire was prepared to identify the perception of the local community regarding tourism development and its impacts. The questionnaire was based on Likert scale and was having 16 items. Five items were focussed on the study of role of tourism in the development of area, seven items were focussed on identifying the role of tourism for the community and five items were focussed on identifying the impacts of tourism development.

Case of Maharana Pratap Sagar Wetland (Pong Dam)

Pong Dam wetland is one of the largest man-made wetlands of northern India. Situated at the base of the Dhauladhar ranges in Kangra district of Himachal Pradesh, the wetland came into existence in 1975-76. This is the first major wetland which potentially offers a transitory resting reserve for the migratory water birds coming from the Trans-Himalayan zone. Pong dam wetland was declared a wild life sanctuary in 1983, and in 1994, the Ministry of Environment and Forests, Government of India declared it a National wetland and now it has been

---

[2] The use of mail format has a major advantage that it avoids the potential biasing effects of peer or committee pressure and other psychological influences on the respondents' answers (Smith, Stephen L.J., 1995, Forecasting Tourism Demand and Market Trends, *Tourism Analysis: A handbook*, Harlow, Longman, p. 143).

[3] The Delphi technique is one of the best known forecasting method developed by RAND Corporation in the early 1950s as a method for forecasting events when historical data are unavailable or when the forecast requires significant levels of subjective judgement (Dalkey N. and Helmer, O., 1963, An experimental application of the Delphi method of the use of experts, *Management Science* 9(3): 459-67).

given the status of Wetland of International Importance or Ramsar Site No. 1211 on 19/08/02.

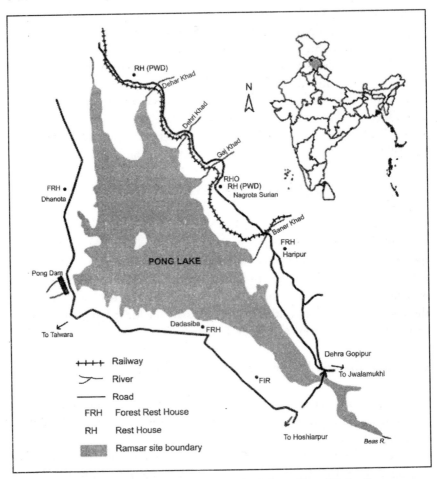

Fig. 3: Maharana Pratap Sagar Wetland (Pong Dam Wetland)

Being fed by 5 major streams emerging from the Dhauladhar ranges, the reservoir has an area of about 45,000 hectares at maximum possible flooding – the level varies with every season and averages around 30,000 hectares. Over 200 villages with a population over 85,000 lies along the wetland. The Beas River on which the Pong Dam is created itself originates from the Pir-Panjal ranges in the Kullu valley. The Beas river is joined by the other tributaries such as Baner Khad, Yaj Khad, Dehra Khad, and Buhal Khad, which also feed the Pong Dam Wetland.

The towns located in the wetland periphery are Dehra Gopipur, Jawali, Talwara, Dadasiba and Nagrota Surian. The towns of Nagrota Surian and Jawali are also connected with the narrow gauge Kangra Valley railway line. The nearest airport is at Gaggal (40 km). The nearest railway stations are Mukerian-30 km, and Pathankot-32 km. Important road distances are Chandigarh-170 km, Amritsar-110 km, Dharmshala-55 km. The climate of the wetland is sub-tropical. The summer season extends from mid-March to mid-July and the maximum temperature goes up to 44.3C in summers. Monsoon starts from mid-July and lasts till end of the September followed by autumn. The winter lasts from mid-December to mid-March and the minimum temperature recorded is 5-6C. The mean annual rainfall for the wetland is 1780 mm. The surface water temperature of the wetland varies from 20-40 C.

Pong Dam wetland has immense potential for bird watching, water sports, angling and many other activities. Other attractions near by are places of cultural and religious importance in the vicinity of Pong Dam wetland. Famous heritage village of Paragpur is located just 15 km from the lake. The hilltops and ridges are also the setting for numerous forts and temples. Kangra fort (25 km), Haripur fort, and the ruins of the fort stand majestically on the Shore of Ransar Island. Many temples are also found near the lake and it includes monolithic rock cut temple at Masroor, Jwala ji Temple, Dadasiba temple with its mid- 19th century wall paintings, and Chintpurni Temple. A number of Rest Houses, Hotels and other type of accommodation are available near the wetland. Forest Inspection huts at Amela, Barikalan, Dadoa, Gwaldhar, Habrol, Maghin, Nandpur, Sadwan; Forest rest houses at Dehra, Dadasiba, Haripur, Nagrota Surian; PWD Rest houses at Bharoli, Paragpur, Indora, Kandrori, Jwali, Kotla, Sansarpur Terrace; BBMB rest hoses at Talwara and Sansarpur terrace are some of accommodation units. A number of private hotels and guest houses are also located at various places.

The right bank of the Beas has meagre forests in small pockets whereas on the left bank from Dehra to Terrace, there are linear strips of scrub forests. There are several tree species, which produce edible fruit for the birds. There is also some submerged aquatic vegetation in the wetland but pronounced seasonal changes in the water level and shoreline does not support extensive areas of emergent vegetation. Main tree species of the trek offer attraction for the birds. Besides this a variety of shrubs, grasses and climbers are also found in these forests. The important fauna includes Barking Deer, Leopard, Samber, Nilgai, Wild boar and clawless otter. Indian Cobra, Indian Pythen and common Ratsnake, are some of the reptiles (Balokhra; 1997).

Figure 4 is the map of the Pong reservoir showing fish assembly centres. A large variety of fish such as Mahasheer, Katla, Mirror carps, Rohoo, Singhara, etc. are found in the Pong dam lake and its tributaries. Low-yield subsistence fishing existed prior to impoundment, but since a lucrative fishery has grown up with 27 fish species and a yield increasing markedly each year – some 1800 fishermen now have direct employment and 1000 families benefit directly, and fish worth 197 lakhs was harvested from the reservoir (Dept. of Fisheries, 2003). A total of 400 avian species have been recorded from the Maharana Pratap Sagar wetland and the surrounding farmlands and hills. The wetland attracts more than 220 species of migratory and resident birds and is an important wintering area for a large number of Black headed Gulls, Brahminy ducks, Bar headed gees, Shovlers, Plovers, Grebes, Cormorants, Darters, Herons, Moorhens, Egrets and Storks etc. The first sighting of Red Necked Grebe in India was reported from the Pong Dam Wetland.

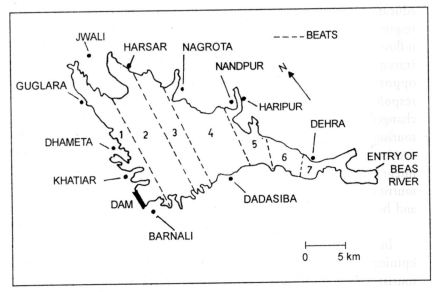

Fig. 4: Map of Pong Reservoir showing fish assembly centres

Results and Analysis

In the first part of the questionnaire respondents have reflected their opinion regarding the role of tourism in the development of the area. The first question attempted to know the tourism's contribution for the overall regional growth; 80% of the respondents were 'strongly agreed' with the statement. In response to the second statement that tourist inflows provide foreign exchange to the state; 68% of the respondents were agreeing with the statement. When asked if tourism inflow increases occupational opportunities; 72% of the respondents agreed with the statement; 58% of the respondents felt that tourist inflow creates awareness among local youth, which leads them towards urbanization; 60% of the respondents agreed with the statement that tourist inflow provides guidelines for modernization in infrastructural facilities. Hence it is assumed that most of the respondents were agreed that tourism can act as an ideal tool for the overall regional growth. It generates foreign exchange to the state, increases occupational opportunities and improves infrastructural facilities.

In the second part of the questionnaire, respondents have reflected their opinion regarding the role of tourism in the development of the community. In response to the first statement that tourism increases educational opportunities to the children of the area, only 44% of the respondents were agreed with the statement. When asked whether tourist inflow improved the self-image of the community; 50% agreed with the statement; 50% of the respondents felt that tourism provides the opportunities to local people to learn something new; 62% of the respondents agreed with the statement that increased tourist inflow changed the life style of local people; 46% of the respondents felt that tourism increases the standard of living; 52% of the respondents felt that tourism increases social interaction, which further boost the cultural integration among the tourists and hosts. Hence it was concluded that tourist interaction increases the social inter-integration, among the tourists and hosts, and changes the life style of the local people.

In the last part of the questionnaire, respondents have reflected their opinion regarding the impacts of tourism. In the first statement that tourist inflow affects the local culture; 60% of the respondents agreed with the statement; 52% of the locals' felt that tourism leads towards

24

overcrowding, congestion and environmental problems; 80% of the respondents replied as 'strongly agree' or 'agree' with the statement that increased tourist inflow, created demand for capital and consumer goods resulting an increase of GDP 64% of the respondents agreed with the statement that tourism provides employment to the local youth; 80% of the respondents felt that, if planned carefully, the negative impacts of the tourism can be minimised. Hence integrated planning was found necessary for sustainable tourism development.

Conclusions and Recommendations

The natural beauty as well as the diversity of animals and plant lives in many wetlands make them ideal locations for tourists. There are of course a wide range of recreational activities associated with wetlands that generate income locally and nationally. These include boating and other water sports to hunting, watching wildlife and even art and literature. Necessary steps should be taken for the conservation of wetlands and development of the ecotourism in the nearby areas. But these steps will not be enough until the community is involved in conservation and development. For the development of tourism in a sustainable manner there must be a positive synergistic relationship among tourism, living and nonliving spheres. These all are linked with each other and interdependent, and are each of them requires proper attention for the development of tourism in a sustainable manner.

As regards to the local people opinion regarding tourism development in the area most of the respondents were of the view that tourism is a tool for the overall regional growth as it generates additional revenue that increases occupational opportunities and improves infrastructural facilities. The tourist–host encounter further increases the social interaction, which ultimately boosts natural integration among the tourists and hosts. The increased tourist inflow also changed the life style of the local people and therefore, a proper synergistic relationship can be obtained for sustainable tourism development. However, some problems like illegal extraction of resources, such as fishing, hunting, overlapping of fishing birds arrival season and agriculture expansion in the area are some of the problems that may hamper the conservation development plans.

The state Govt. had constituted a Wetland Expert Committee to identify various management objectives and problems in conservation of wetland. It identifies the major stake holders of its development including

Council for Science Technology, Environment and Forest Department, Pollution Control Board, Fisheries, Dept. of Tourism and Research and educational institutions. For the proper site conservation, the following action plan should be taken into consideration:

- Survey and mapping of the wetland and its catchment area.
- Proper treatment of catchment area and soil conservation.
- Environment awareness among the locals.
- Socio-Economic study of the area.
- Fisheries, conservation and development.
- Water quality monitoring.
- Hydro biological studies.
- Strengthening of infrastructural facility.
- Fencing of the important points of the wetland.
- Development of the nature parks on the pattern of nearby Rajiv Gandhi Nature Park at Jawali
- Complete ban on poly bags.
- Proper open space for bird watching.
- Development of the Ramsar Island and fort (in the middle of the lake) for tourism activities.

However, steps taken for the conservation will not be enough until the community is involved in conservation and development. Some points for the involvement of the community are as follows.

- Local NGOs should be involved in ecotourism awareness programme.
- NSS camps of school children should be organized from time to time. This will increase awareness among local.
- Local people should be made a part of the development.
- Financial Assistance with 20% subsidies should be given to the local people for the development of alternate tourism like ecotours, camping, adventure sports, etc.
- Local educated people should be trained as guides and instructors for water sports activities.
- Declare some of the area for the fishing by the locals.

26

Table II: Total Responses

S. No.	Statement	Strongly Agree	Agree	Uncertain	Disagree	Strongly Disagree
	Role of Tourism in the development of area					
1.	Tourism is responsible for overall regional growth	12 (24)	28 (56)	4 (8)	6 (12)	0 (0)
2.	Tourist inflow provides foreign exchange to the state	7 (14)	27 (54)	3 (6)	10 (20)	3 (6)
3.	Tourist inflow increases the occupational opportunities	11 (22)	25 (50)	8 (16)	3 (6)	3 (6)
4.	Tourist inflow creates awareness among local youth, which leads them towards urbanization	7 (14)	22 (44)	7 (14)	17 (34)	7 (14)
5.	Tourist inflow provides the guidelines for modernization in infrastructural facilities Tourism and the community	8 (16)	22 (44)	9 (18)	6 (12)	5 (10)
6.	It increases educational opportunities to the children of the area	4 (8)	18 (36)	12 (24)	10 (20)	6 (12)
7.	Tourist inflow improved the self image of the community	7 (14)	18 (36)	10 (20)	8 (16)	7 (14)
8.	It provides opportunities to local people to learn something new	6 (12)	19 (38)	12 (24)	8 (16)	5 (10)
9.	The increased tourist inflow changes the life style of local people	10 (20)	21 (42)	10 (20)	8 (16)	1 (02)
10.	It increases the standard of living	3 (06)	20 (40)	17 (34)	5 (10)	5 (10)
11.	It gives the concept of social interaction which further boost the natural integration among the tourists and hosts	7 (14)	19 (34)	15 (30)	7 (14)	2 (04)
	Impacts of Tourism					
12.	Tourists' inflow affects the local culture	10 (20)	20 (40)	7 (14)	7 (14)	6 (12)
13.	Tourism leads towards overcrowding, congestion and environmental problems	7 (14)	19 (38)	13 (26)	5 (10)	6 (12)
14.	Increased tourist inflow creates demand for capital and consumer goods resulting in increase of G.D.P.	12 (24)	28 (56)	1 (2)	5 (10)	4 (8)
15.	Tourism provide employment to local youth	10 (20)	27 (54)	9 (18)	4 (8)	0 (0)
16.	If planned carefully the negative impacts of tourism can be minimised	15 (30)	25 (50)	4 (8)	4 (8)	2 (4)

Source : Data collected through Questionnaire.

Note : Figures in Parenthesis are percentage

References

Balokhra, Jagmohan (1997). *Himachal Pradesh: The Wonderland*, New Delhi, H.G. Publication, p-548.

Bottrill, C. and Pearce D. (1995). Ecotourism: Towards a key Elements : Approach to Operationalizing the concept, *Journal of Sustainable Tourism*, 3(1), pp. 45-54.

Ceballos-Lascurain, H. (1996). *Tourism, Ecotourism and Protected areas*. Gland, Switzerland, IUCN, p. 20.

Chisnal, P.M. (1986). *Marketing Research*, London, McGraw-Hill.

Dept. of Fisheries (2003). *Fisheries Development in Himachal Pradesh, Shimla*.

Filion, F.L., J.P. Foley and A.J. Jacquemot (1994). The Economics of Global Tourism, in *Protected Area Economics and Policy: Linking Conservation and Sustainable Development*, M. Munasignhe and J. McNeely (Eds.), Washington D.C. World Bank, pp. 234-254.

Geethakrisnan K.P. (1996). Sustainable Development in Operation, in Malcom S. Adiseshiah (ed.) *Sustainable Development : Its content, scope and prices*. Lancer International.

Likert, R. (1932). A Technique for the Measure of Attitudes, Archives of Psychology, No. 140, New York: Columbia University Press.

Middleton, Victor T.C. and Rebecca Hawkins (1998). *Sustainable Tourism: A Marketing Perspective*, Butterworth and Heinemann, Oxford p.232.

Ross, Sheryl and Wall Geoffrey (1999). Ecotourism: Towards Congruence between Theory and Practice, *Tourism Management*, 20, pp. 123-133. Site List, http://www.ramsar.org/ramsarlist.html accessed on dated 02.02.2004

Srivastava, S.P. (1996). Sustainable Development: Issues and considerations in K. Gopal Iyer (ed.) *Sustainable Development: Ecological and Socio-cultural Dimensions*, Vikas Publishing House N.Delhi. Wetland Tourism, http://www.duck.org.au/wetland tourism.html accessed 16.02.2004. Wetland Values & Functions recreation and tourism: Recreation and Tourism, http://www.ramsar.org/\Wetland Values & Functions recreation and tourism.htm accessed on dated 02.02.2004.

Wood, E. Gatz, M.F. and Lindberg, K. (1991). The Ecotourism Society: An action Agenda, In J. Kusler (Ed.), *Ecotourism and Resource Conservation*, Madison, Omni press, pp. 75-79.

Sustainable Tourism Planning and Development, 29-43, 2006
Edited by Bagri, S.C.
Published by Bishen Singh Mahendra Pal Singh, Dehra Dun, India

Nature Rock Garden: The Valley of Flowers Destination Interpretation and Infrastructure Auditing

S.C. Bagri

Dean & Director
Centre for Mountain Tourism and Hospitality Studies
HNB Garhwal University, Srinagar Garhwal, bagri_sc@hotmail.com

&

Ashok Kumar

Faculty
Centre for Mountain Tourism and Hospitality Studies
HNB Garhwal University, Srinagar Garhwal

Abstract : The Valley of Flowers needs effective physical tourism planning not just to reap the rich crop of tourism benefits so to ensure that the industry presents minimum of its ills which are not only devastating but often irreversible as well. There are examples of habitat destruction due to construction of facilities like approachable paths, camping sites, mule stables, wooden huts and other residential buildings for essential services and transmission lines etc. The present flow of visitors are neither culture nor it consists of nature lovers. They leave behind litter and a legacy of disturbances that continuously affect the local inhabitants. The type and scale of tourism development often exceeds the carrying capacity because least efforts have been undertaken to assess physical carrying capacity of the area of trekking route. Those responsible for conservation and protection are not equipped to deal with the hordes of trekkers who descend on them.

Key Words : Valley of Flowers, Garhwal, sustainable, conservation, tourist.

Physical Set-up of the Valley

One amongst the most beautiful valleys of Garhwal Himalaya is the Valley of Flowers. Situated at an altitude of 3352 mt it is located in the North-Eastern part of Garhwal Himalaya above Ghangaria, in the upper catchment of the Bhyundayar Ganga, an Eastern tributary of river Alaknanda. Today the Valley has been incorporated under Nanda Devi Biosphere Reserve. Its inception dates back to 1931. The park covers an area of 87.5 sq.kms which is located between North latitude 30° 42' and

30° 48', and longitude 79° 33' and 79° 46' east. The entire park area falls under Badrinath Forest Division in Chamoli district. The area of valley starts from the timberline beyond Ghangaria at an altitude of 3200 mt and runs in East West direction along the banks of river Puspawati up to the snow clad peaks of Ratanban (6126 mt) and Gauri Parvat (6590 mt). The trek starts from Govindghat, 20 km away from Joshimath on the bank of river Alaknanda on way to Badrinath at an altitude of 1829 mt. From there a continuous ascend leads one to Pulna village (3 km) at an altitude of 1920 mt (Bagri 1993). A further ascend leads to Ghangria transit point (3049 m) crossing Bhyundayar village. The total trek till Ghangria is of 14 km and from there a trek goes to Hemkund Sahib (4400 mt), one among the various sacred places of Sikhs. Ghangria is located at the confluence of river Pushpawati, coming from Valley of Flowers and Lakshman Ganga descending from Hemkund. A further climb from Ghangria leads one to the Valley of Flowers. The terrain has been carved by glacial action. The boulder strewn Pushpawati River flows along the valley's bottom. A gigantic snow clad ridge hems this valley from almost all sides. The climatic conditions vary from temperate to sub-arctic. Very heavy snowfall occurs during winters when the entire valley is covered under thick blanket of snow. Summers are mild and the maximum temperature rarely rises to over 20°C. The end of the rainy season sees the blooming of thousands of beautiful flowers in this valley (Kumar 2003, Bagri 2003).

Objectives

The research study was undertaken with the aim of analyzing the basic problems associated with the Valley of Flowers and to find out the root cause of continuous degradation of the trek. The present research has been conducted and the findings analysed to reach a particular result.

Methodology

Extensive survey was undertaken in the Valley of Flowers and adjoining tourist transit locations i.e., Joshimath, Govindghat, Bhyundayar, Phulna and Ghangria from May to October 2001. A Number of organizations and government agencies have been consulted viz., municipal boards, town area committees, notified area committees and local people of each place en-route to the Valley of Flowers. The size of the universe at all places was 100 persons and it comprised of local people, village heads, business class persons, school teachers, students and tourism professionals. The topic of discussions was related to accommodation, transportation, economic base and garbage and sanitation problems etc.

Discussion and Interpretation

The findings reveal that, out of the total population of Joshimath, a major transit point and a major town on Badrinath pilgrimage route, has a total literacy of 82 per cent. As regards Govindghat and Ghangria, the literacy was 63 and 39 per cent respectively. So the first and foremost work was to concentrate on eradicating illiteracy and create general awareness for environment in this part of the Himalaya.

Apart from literacy the other aspects taken into consideration were the percentage of local persons employed in tourism and related business. Table I reveals that Ghangria and Govindghat, though very small transit points, are mostly dependent on tourism business whereas in the case of Joshimath the percentage of dependency on tourism was quite low. This means that the major economy of the previous locations were highly dependent on tourism related activities hence cumulative steps should be taken by the state government and the locals to increase the length of tourist season. Instead of inviting private entrepreneurs from outside, proper direction and support should be given to the local community to reap the benefits of tourism activities in the Valley. Proper marketing strategy should also be adopted by the government to promote and advertise the tourist attractions of the area. Incidentally, quite a large number of visitors visit the valley either by chance or having very meager amount of knowledge. Persons visiting without the proper motivation ends up creating a mess.

Table I: Social Demography of Places Enroute to the Valley of Flowers.

Place	Total Population	Literacy (%)	Average Literacy Level	Major Occupation	Employed in Tourism & Related Fields (%)	Tourism Awareness
Joshimath	12000	82	Intermediate	Agriculture & Horticulture	43	Low
Govindghat	200	63	High School	Agriculture	87	Nil
Ghangria	33	39	High School	Agriculture	82	Nil

The findings of the survey further reveal that despite of tremendous tourism potential, it seems difficult to utilize tourism resources in the right direction. Thus a great share of Valley of Flowers tourism market is lost but still the existing amenities and facilities in the Valley, as displayed in Tables-II and III, if properly managed and handled, can work towards promotion of tourism in this valley. The Tables below are a complete checklist for evaluating the existing resources in the transit and destination regions through audit matrix method. The tables show that the area is excellent in primary natural resources along with good secondary features but the tourism infrastructure is poor whether it be accommodation units, restaurants, eateries or other facilities. Hence the first and the foremost step to be taken develop proper infrastructure is involving the local community.

Agriculture being the major source of the economy in the area remains the source of unending supply to local eateries and restaurants. Incidentally the findings of the survey, as presented in Table-IV, reveal that the present level of agriculture is degrading as compared to the previous years. There is a continuous decline in the land utilization for agricultural purposes along with agricultural productivity by 20- 30%. Locales are still using the traditional methods of farming and growing the traditional crops. Climatic conditions and soil productivity are declining and crop rotation or introduction of new crops is not practiced by the society. It is not a good indication for appropriate tourism promotion. However, the place is very well suited for developing orchard and floriculture. A very limited number of the locals are opting for it and those limited farmers doing the job are partially or totally unaware of various practices of or floriculture. Looking into the picture of agriculture and farming in the region, efforts were made to initiate planning at the grassroot level to get positive results. For this the basic initiative should be taken by the local community and the nongovernmental agencies in perfect tuning with the government. Moreover, local community should understand their negatives and jump over from traditional system to new methodology of farming and agricultural practices.

As of dependency on trade the region has an agriculture-based economy and tourism business still offers only seasonal jobs in the society (Table-IV). But with the increasing trend of tourism promotion and pouring in of outsiders for tourism trade, there are indications of locals getting attracted towards trade and commerce. One of the major sources of economy in terms of trade is its accommodation units, which is coming up at a tremendous pace at Ghangria, with 16 units in 2004 as compared to 5 units some four to five years back. From table-V below it is noticed that Joshimath has a high value for trade and commerce in relation to other transit points, but proper steps should be taken to ensure involvement of the local people in the trade, apart from tourism related business.

Table II: Destination Development Audit Matrix of Joshimath

Element	Current			Potential for Improvement			Impact		
	P	G	E	P	G	E	P	G	E
Primary Features									
Attraction	=	●	=	=	●	=	=	●	=
Climate	=	=	●	=	●	=	=	=	=
Environment	=	●	=	=	●	=	=	●	=
Ecology	=	●	=	=	●	=	=	●	=
Secondary Feature									
Accessibility	=	●	=	=	●	=	●	=	=
Accommodation	=	●	=	=	●	=	●	=	=
Enjoyment Facilities	●	=	=	=	●	=	=	●	=
Safety/ Security	=	●	=	=	=	=	=	●	=
Tourism Infrastructure									
Roads	=	●	=	●	=	=	●	=	=
Power	●	=	=	=	=	●	●	=	=
Drinking Water	●	=	=	=	=	●	●	=	=
Sewerage	●	=	=	●	=	=	=	=	=
Means of Communication	●	=	=	=	●	=	=	●	=
Business Climate									
Tourism Investors	=	●	=	=	●	=	●	=	=
Local Residents' Attitude									
Cooperative	=	=	●	=	●	=	=	●	=
Participatory	=	●	=	=	=	●	=	=	●
Staff Skill									
Competent, Dedicated, Skilled	●	=	=	=	●	=	=	=	●
Competition									
Degree of Competition and Rivalry	=	●	=	=	●	=	●	=	=

Terms : P- Poor, G- Good, E- Excellent

Table III: Destination Development Audit Matrix of Govindghat

Element	Current			Potential for Improvement			Impact		
	P	G	E	P	G	E	P	G	E
Primary Feature									
Attraction	*	=	=	=	*	=	=	*	=
Climate	=	*	=	=	*	=	=	=	=
Environment	=	*	=	=	*	=	=	*	=
Ecology	=	*	=	=	*	=	=	*	=
Secondary Feature									
Accessibility	*	=	=	=	*	=	*	=	=
Accommodation	*	=	=	=	*	=	*	=	=
Enjoyment Facilities	*	=	=	*	=	=	=	*	=
Safety/ Security	=	*	=	=	*	=	=	*	=
Tourism Infrastructure									
Roads	*	=	=	*	=	=	*	=	=
Power	*	=	=	=	=	*	*	=	=
Drinking Water	*	=	=	=	=	*	=	=	=
Sewerage	*	=	=	*	=	=	=	=	=
Means of Communication	*	=	=	=	*	=	=	*	=
Business Climate									
Tourism Investors	*	=	=	=	*	=	*	=	=
Local Residents' Attitude									
Cooperative	=	*	=	=	*	=	=	*	=
Participatory	=	*	=	=	*	=	=	=	*
Staff Skill									
Competent, Dedicated, Skilled	*	=	=	=	*	=	=	=	*
Competition									
Degree of Competition & Rivalry	*	=	=	=	*	=	*	=	=

Terms : P- Poor, G- Good, E- Excellent

Table IV: Socio-Economic Indicators of Sustainability at Places to the Valley of Flowers

Study Area	Sub Area	Indicators			
		Cultivated Land	Agricultural Productivity	Irrigation Facility	Manure Availability
Valley of Flowers	Agriculture				
(a) Joshimath		Scarce	Medium	Low	Declining
(b) Govindghat		Nil	Low	Low	Declining
(c) Bhyundhar		Medium	Medium	Medium	Declining
(d) Phulna		Medium	Medium	Medium	Declining
(e) Ghangria		Scarce	Low	Low	Declining

Table V: Socio-Economic Indicators of Sustainability at Places Enroute to Valley of Flowers

Study Area	Sub Area	Indicators
Valley of Flowers	Dependency on Tourism Trade	Percentage of Households
(a) Joshimath		Medium
(b) Govindghat		Low
(c) Bhyundhar		High
(d) Phulna		High
(e) Ghangria		Medium

Modernization and developmental changes are ever dynamic processes and an integral part of nature, but the fragile and sensitive environment of Uttaranchal Himalaya could not withstand many processes of change. Perhaps, few of them came so abruptly or in such a haphazard manner that brought in a series of negative consequences like loss of floral or faunal wealth, loss of craftsmanship, weakening of socio-cultural tie-ups, dilution of moral values and lack of enthusiasm in celebrating fairs and festivals. The region in haste of achieving its target of tourism promotion failed to incorporate its native spirit in selling eco-cultural and nature tourism products to domestic or international tourists.

Table VI and VII below indicate the amount of litter deposited by domestic as well as international tourists en-route the Valley of Flowers trek. The figures indicated are alarmingly shocking for the fragile ecosystem of the study area. If the present scenario of litter deposition is taken into consideration at Ghangria, it would be abundantly clear that Ghangria is soon going to convert the place into a stack of garbage and litter. The Valley of Flowers is still safe from such practices of litter and garbage because of certain regulations implied by the state government to prevent the ecosystem of the valley. But with the increasing pace and pressure of tourists and negligence of the governing authorities it is soon going to get a severe knock down in terms of ecosystem destruction due to the following reasons:

- Increased level of grazing in the valley
- Poaching
- Plucking of wild species of flowers, roots, shoots and cutting
- Soil erosion due to deforestation and glacier recession

Table VI: A Comparative Analysis of Litter Deposits by Domestic Tourists, Trekkers Excursionists (in kg) 2000-2001

Area	No. of Tourists	Average Litter Deposited	Visitors used Area in (sq. km.)	Total Litter Deposited (kg)
Joshimath	106909	1.5	2.5	1,60,363.5
Govindghat	93900	2.5	0.6	2,34,750
Ghangria	110953	3	0.8	3,32,859
Valley of Flowers	752	0.2	-	150.4
Hemkund	109246	2	0.2	2,18,492

Table VII: A Comparative Analysis of Litter Deposits by Foreign Tourists, Trekkers and Excursionists (in kg) 2000-2001

Area	No. of Tourists	Average Litter Deposited	Visitors used Area in (sq. km.)	Total Litter Deposited (kg)
Joshimath	646	3	2.5	1,938
Govindghat	79	3	0.6	237
Ghangria	46	4	0.8	184
Valley of flowers	12	0.2	-	2.4
Hemkund	52	3	0.2	156

To stop these disastrous activities in the valley it is imperative to make an Environment Impact Assessment analysis of various places enroute to the valley. From Table II & III, denoting the present infrastructural status of conditions at Joshimath, one can easily make out that the condition of primary features are as good as that of Govindghat but status of secondary features seems comparatively poor. If comparative study of both the data is made, it would reveals that Govindghat though having better environment resources lags behind Joshimath. As far as negative impacts are concerned, it takes place due to improper and unplanned development at Joshimath and consequently, the place is suffering from severe danger of extinction as compared to Govindghat.

With the increased pressure of incoming tourists, the environment and ecology of Joshimath is continuously degrading and further expansion of tourism promotion is almost equal to nil. Further expansion is possible by keeping the environment and ecology at stake. One can presume this by looking into the state of continuous declining snowfall at Auli and Joshimath and therefore shifting of skiing slopes from Auli towards Gorson has already begun.

Apart from considering the above findings, an effort has been made to assess the present status of facilities and amenities en-route to the Valley of Flowers. The nature and scale of development needs effective and environment friendly methods of garbage and litter disposal. In view of an unprecedented number of domestic tourist arrivals especially to Hemkund heaps of plastic bottles, polythene bags, wrapping material, pieces of glasses etc. were noticed all around the area. Further, excessive construction at Govindghat and Ghangria and large number of visitors assemblage at Joshimath have gradually depleted the green cover. Intensified demographic pressure on its limited resources has badly mutilated this once beautiful Valley of Flowers. The following two Tables (VI & VII) reveal the existing condition of litter deposits during the year 2000-2001.

The number of accommodation units coming up is definitely promoting tourism but it also creates an adverse impact on the fragile and delicate ecosystem of the region due to lack of proper management of garbage disposal and unplanned drainage system, monitoring and regulatory aspects etc. As far as employment generation is concerned, despite a number of accommodation and eatery units the proportion of seasonal jobs are still very low. From Table VIII, one can easily make out the contribution of tourism in promoting economic status in the region, which is almost negligible. A number of new accommodation units have come up but they are not as per the requirement of the ecosystem of the mountain environment and contribute little to the economic upliftment of the region. Incidentally, the basic problem of know-how and technical skills are limited in the people.

The primary concern is to develop and provide technical know-how to the local community through establishing workshops and camps at different locations by grassroot agencies like NGO's, educational centres, village organizations, *Zila Panchayats, Gram Panchayats* etc. Such camps will provide opportunities to the locals to avail further opportunities for their physical wellbeing. Moreover, this way they can also provide better and satisfying services to the tourists visiting the region. The word of mouth publicity will help in increasing tourist traffic to the area.

Table VIII: Assessing Accommodation Structure at Ghangria

Name of the Units	Number of Rooms	Bed Capacity	Dormitory	Manpower Involved
Priya Lodge	10	30	—	8
Gangotri Lodge	7	24	—	10
Himalaya Lodge	28	80	—	12
Krishna Lodge	12	24	—	3
Himlok Travel Lodge	6	10	—	4
Gurukripa Lodge	18	50	—	10
Kuber Lodge	30	80	—	18
Murrey Lodge	14	40	—	4
Deepak Lodge	16	52	—	5
Gurdwara	—	5000		40
Forest Guest House	2	4	—	1
GMVN Tourist Bungalow	10	38	5	18
Chauhan Lodge	18	60	—	4

To have a comprehensive environment programme, the role of accommodation units specially constructed to facilitate visitors' arrival is notable. Although in view of 5 months tourist season the nature of business operations is proportionately low as the nature of operation initiated by accommodation units seems to enhance pollution. Further analysis have been made on various aspects of accommodation units including building architecture, raw material used and disposal methods adopted for disposal of garbage and solid wastes. On the basis of personal contact programmes and visual observations, it was noticed that the way these accommodation units have been constructed and are operated they could disfigure and degrade the very heritage of this Valley. The results of the findings have been projected in Tables IX and X and the findings reveal that out of 13 accommodation units surveyed at Ghangria, 11 lodges have been categorized moderately functioning. The surveys could not locate any property that can cross the optimum level. The same condition was noticed at Govindghat (Table X) where more percentage of hoteliers use open space for waste disposal, leaving the surrounding areas polluted.

Table IX: Accommodation Structure and their Approach for Sustainable Tourism Development at Govindghat

Name of the Unit	Person Involved	Nature of Building	Sources of Fuel	Agency of Garbage Disposal	Building Design	Acquired Valuation
Saptshram Hotel	4	Tinned Roof Concrete Structure	L.P.G Gas, Stove, Wood	*Gram Panchayat**	Double Storey	5
Himsarovar Hotel	2	Tinned Roof Concrete Structure	L.P.G Gas, Stove, Wood	*Gram Panchayat*	Double Storey	6
Bharat Guest House	3	TRCS	L.P.G Gas, Stove, Wood	*Gram Panchayat*	Double Storey	5
Hem Tourist Lodge	6	TRCS	L.P.G Gas, Stove, Wood	*Gram Panchayat*	Double Storey	6
Mehta Guest House	7	TRCS	L.P.G Gas, Stove, Wood	*Gram Panchayat*	Double Storey	4
Gurdwara	NA	TRCS	L.P.G Gas, Stove, Wood	*Gram Panchayat*	Double Storey	5

Note : Acquired Valuation has been determined on the basis of optimum level 7 points and above, moderate 5-7 points and marginal level below 5 points.

*Gram Panchayat is the development committee in each village founded by Centre State Government.

Conclusion and Recommendations

The Valley of Flowers, once known for its splendid view of natural flowers, needs implementation of sustainable tourism development approach in order to meet the need of the present without compromising the ability of future generations to meet their own needs. There are a number of problems, which are the root cause of destruction of the Valley. It seems that the surrounding villages, especially those located en-route the Valley of Flowers, need to have proper literacy, proper supply of electricity and water, sufficient number of good schools, well maintained roads, and well equipped hospitals. It seems strange when efforts are concentrated on greater terms like sustainability and the area lacks basic facilities. The first motto should be proper schooling of new generation, setting environment awareness camps and environment protection cells along with emphasis on fulfilling the basic needs of the locals (Negi 1982).

Fundamental concept of sustainable tourism is carrying capacity or to the measurement of the level of use, which is sustainable. Proper

Table X: Accommodation Structure and their Approach for Sustainable Tourism Development at Ghangria

Name of the Unit	Person Involved	Nature of Building	Sources of Fuel	Agency of Garbage Disposal	Building Design	Acquired Valuation
Priya Lodge	8	Tinned Roof Concrete Structure	L.P.G Gas, Stove, Wood	Gram Panchayat	Double Storey	5
Himalaya Lodge	12	Tinned Roof Concrete Structure	L.P.G Gas, Stove, Wood	Gram Panchayat	Double Storey	6
Gangotri Lodge	10	TRCS	L.P.G Gas, Stove, Wood	Gram Panchayat	Double Storey	5
Krishna Lodge	3	TRCS	L.P.G Gas, Stove, Wood	Gram Panchayat	Double Storey	6
Himlok Travel Lodge	4	TRCS	L.P.G Gas, Stove, Wood	Gram Panchayat	Double Storey	4
Guru Kripa Lodge	10	TRCS	L.P.G Gas, Stove, Wood	Gram Panchayat	Double Storey	5
Kuber Lodge	14	TRCS	L.P.G Gas, Stove, Wood	Gram Panchayat	Double Storey	5
Marry Cottage	4	TRCS	L.P.G Gas, Stove, Wood	Gram Panchayat	Double Storey	6
Deepak Lodge	5	TRCS	L.P.G Gas, Stove, Wood	Gram Panchayat	Double Storey	5
Gurudwara	40	TRCS	L.P.G Gas, Stove, Wood	Gram Panchayat	Five Storey	3
Forest Guest House	1	TRCS	L.P.G Gas, Stove, Wood	Gram Panchayat	Single Storey	7
G.M.V.N Tourist Bungalow	13	TRCS	L.P.G Gas, Stove, Wood	Gram Panchayat	Single Storey	7
Chauhan Lodge	4	TRCS	L.P.G Gas, Stove, Wood	Gram Panchayat	Double Storey	5

Note : Acquired Valuation has been determined on the basis of optimum level 7 points and above, moderate 5-7 points and marginal level below 5 points.

management and planning can help in achieving the much needed and talked about term sustainability. Proper management here means minimum destruction to environment and ecology of the place by reducing human intervention like conserving certain areas during off season, total ban on firewood collection, protecting some selected areas as green areas thereby prohibiting grazing in those areas (Bagri, 1998; Bagri and Bhatt, 1997). It is also advisable to have a monitoring unit that should be made responsible to look after the pattern and type of construction in that area. Use of remote sensing and satellite system in construction of roads, drinking water, sewage system, etc. is immensely required. Encouraging local entrepreneurs by providing them incentives and concessions is the need of the hour. What is exactly required is to propose some control measures towards sustainable approach in tourism development, which include-

- Collect historical information along with maps, charts, photographs, to determine the use pattern and extent of changes that have taken place on the mountain environment of the Valley of Flowers and nearby areas, and define the extent of ecological problems.

- Survey the existing physical environment with sufficient precision to enable future changes to be measured.

- Review available information on mountain processes (tectonic movement, shifts) and their effect on land movement in the slopes and erosion prone areas.

- Document the various structural schemes and other development works that have been undertaken enroute the Valley of Flowers trek and assess their existing and future effects on behavioral pattern of hosts and guests as well as on the regional geography.

- Predict changes likely to occur on the flora and implement Environment Impact Assessment option in terms of these predictions.

- Totally restrict grazing in and around the Valley.

- Set up camps for environment awareness in the region along with reforestation programmes in and around the Valley.

- Strict regulations should be laid down for tourists, locals and other stakeholders for garbage disposal and sanitation conditions.

- Provide LPG, Kerosene on subsidized rates. Forest Department should demarcate waste wood and provide this waste wood as firewood to the entrepreneurs and local community to reduce the pressure on forests at Ghangria.

- Forest Department should demarcate grazing land for the locals and grazing should be banned on rest of the areas (Deptt. of Tourism 1998).

- The local community as well as the entrepreneur of the areas should set up pressure group to enforce government authority for management and handling of tourists.

- Monitoring agency should involve local people, entrepreneurs to ensure better performance.

- Special permits should be issued to tourists visiting the Valley with a fee structure.

Regulatory practices like ban on firewood collection, grazing of animals may result in protests by the local community. Hence an alternative or a middle path has to be chosen to create an understanding between the regulatory authority and the community. More emphasis should be given to encourage local people for entrepreneurship along with promotion of local handicrafts, art and culture. These small but inevitable efforts will go a long way in achieving the urgently needed sustainability in a mountain region like Uttaranchal.

Acknowledgement

Authors would like to acknowledge the assistance of GB Pant Institute of Himalayan Environment and Development, Ministry of Environment and Forest Govt. of India, Kosi Katarmal, Almora by way of funding the research project on "Sustainable Development Approach for Trekking Tourism Promotion in Chamoli District of Garhwal Himalaya". The present paper is a part of the project undertaken by authors.

References

Bagri, S.C. (1993). *Mountain Tourism in the Himalayas: Some Observations on Trekking in Garhwal Himalaya.* Journal of Tourism, HNB Garhwal University, Srinagar Garhwal.

Bagri, S.C. (1998). *Domestic Tourism in India: Analysing Tourism Destinations and Policies for Sustainable Development.* In Kandari, O.P. et al (eds.), *Domestic Tourism in India,* Indus Publishing Company, New Delhi

Bagri, S.C. and A.K. Bhatt (1997). Sustainable Tourism Planning and Development. *Proceedings of the Conference on Sustainable Tourism Planning and Development,* Indian Institute of Tourism and Travel Management, Gwalior (M.P.).

Bagri, S.C. (2003). *Sustainable Development Approach for Trekking Tourism in Chamoli District of Garhwal Himalaya.* A project report submitted to the GB Pant Institute

of Himalayan Environment and Development, Govt. of India Kosi Katarmal, Almora.
Department of Tourism, Government of India. (1988). *HIMTAB*.

Kumar, Ashok (2003). *Tourism in Pindar Valley: An Approach for Sustainable Tourism Development,* Unpublished Ph. D. Thesis, Submitted to HNB Garhwal University, Srinagar Garhwal.

Negi, S.S. (1982). *Environmental Problems in Himalayas,* Bishen Singh and Mahendra Pal Singh, Dehradun.

Sustainable Tourism Planning and Development, 45-60, 2006
Edited by Bagri, S.C.
Published by Bishen Singh Mahendra Pal Singh, Dehra Dun, India

Ecotourism a Tool for Sustainability in Afar Region of Ethiopia

Mohit Kukreti

Assistant Professor
Department of Tourism Management, Gondar University,
Gondar, Ethiopia

Abstract : Tourism has been hailed as an engine for economic growth and prosperity for the 21st century. Yet, over the past few years, concern has been mounting at the negative impacts of this smokeless industry on domestic economies, social and cultural systems and natural resources. Since the late 1980's, there emerged more benign types of tourism, giving rise to a number of alternative approaches. These represent a paradigm shift rather than a simple repackage of conventional tourism products. The search for approaches to, and more socially responsible types of tourism is a global phenomenon. These new perspectives of tourism open up wide opportunities for the economic development of the underdeveloped countries with vast untapped tourism potential. Ecotourism as a tool for sustainability in Afar region of Ethopia is one of such case studies.

Key Words: Ecotourism, Afar Ethopia, Environment Tourism.

The Echoes of Ecotourism

The world has started listening to the call of ecotourism since 1980's. Ecologically responsible tourism or, simply stated, ecotourism has many definitions. Dianne Brouse defines ecotourism as "responsible travel in which the visitor is aware of and takes into account the effects of his or her actions on both the host culture and the environment." (Brouse 1992). Other definitions reported in the Travel Industry Association of America's Study, (Tourism and Environment, 1992) are as follows:

- Ecotourism is environmentally friendly travel that emphasizes seeing and saving natural habitats and archeological treasures.

- Ecotourism is a tool for conservation.

- The World Wild Life Fund, which issued a study on ecotourism in 1990, defines it in general terms: "tourism to protect natural areas, as a means of economic gain through natural resources preservation ...any kind of tourism that involves nature..."

- The ecotourism Society defines ecotourism as "purposeful travel to natural areas to understand the culture and natural history of the environment, taking care not to alter the integrity of the ecosystem, while producing economic opportunities that make the conservation of natural resources beneficial to the local people."

- Broadly defined, ecotourism involves more than conservation. It is a form of travel that responds to a region's ecological, social, and economic needs. It also provides an alternative to mass tourism. It encompasses all aspects of travel – from airlines to hotels to ground transportation to tour operators. That is, each component of the ecotourism product is environmentally sensitive.

- As a form of travel, ecotourism nurtures understanding of the environment's culture and natural history, fosters the ecosystem's integrity, and produces economic opportunities and conservation gains.

Principles of Ecotourism

Dingwall and Cessford (1996) and Eagles (1996) provide principles of ecotourism. The following Table summarizes these principles:

Ecotourism as a tool for sustainable development

Ecotourism is widely believed to be the perfect economic activity to promote both sustainability and development. Third world countries host many ecotourists. In Brazil, nature travel has become the country's largest new source of revenues. In south central Africa, Rwanda's ecotourism is the third largest source of foreign exchange earnings. Much of this is generated by visitors to the Mountain Gorilla Project begun in the 1970s. Ecuador's Galapagos Islands in the eastern Pacific had about 50,000 ecotourists in 1990, about twice the number that the government deemed optimal (Molner, 1992).

Several African countries are set to cash in on the development, particularly in ecotourism. Zimbabwe, for example, which targets ecotourists who spend more and stay longer, is expected to earn more than Z$6 billion this year, making tourism the third largest foreign currency earner after agriculture and mining.

Table I: Principles of Ecotourism

1.	Ecotourism should lead to nature conservation and economic benefit.
2.	Both public and private ecotour businesses should have an environmental strategy and an environmental officer. Well-educated staffs are essential.
3	Tour operators and tourists should demand high environmental standards from their associates, hotels, transportation providers and destinations.
4.	Culturally and economically sensitive community development is necessary.
5.	Ecotourism should be designed to benefit local communities, socially, economically and ecologically.
6.	High Quality information and service delivery are essential. Well-educated guides are essential.
7.	Planning and management capabilities are essential for long-term success.
8.	Environmental protection is based upon fiscal viability of management, both public and private.
9.	Environmental protection requires the development of management structures to handle use of sensitive environments.

Source : (Dingwall and Cessford, 1996)

The business of ecotourism can be categorized under the small and medium sized tourism and travel enterprises. It is therefore important to promote the development of ecotourism in coordination with the rest of the activities, which fall under small and medium sized tourism and travel enterprises. To maximize the economic and social benefits of tourism, attention should be given not only to the earnings from tourism but also to the way in which those earnings are redistributed through the destination's economy and thereby ensure sustainable development through the encouragement of the local community in managing their own resources. The small and medium sized enterprises find their places in number of economic activities related to tourism. The following are some of the areas where local investors should be encouraged to participate:

- Establishment of small ecotourism centers.
- Lodging

- Catering

- Organizing travel guide services

- Manufacture and sales of souvenirs

- Transport (automobile, bicycles, boats, animal driven carts, animals)

- Organizing cultural events

- Sales of agricultural produces

- Sales of fish and poultry products

- Animal husbandry

Key management issues in ecotourism

Paul F.J. Eagles in his study revealed key management issues in ecotourism (Eagles, 1996). These issues are:

- Tourist travel motives and marketing

- Management of environmental quality

- Limits of acceptable change

- Management of tourist use

- Allocation of access

- Market specialization

- Management of recreation conflict

- Enforcement and monitoring

- Consumer assurance of quality

- Facility design

- Community development

- Financial viability

- Public and private sector co-operation

Benefits of ecotourism

The development of ecotourism can have wide range of social, cultural, environmental and economic benefits. If it is encouraged and well managed to flourish along side the small and medium sized tourism and travel enterprises, it can bring the following benefits:

Socio-Cultural benefits

- Creating employment opportunities for local communities.

- Organizational capacity building by involving local manpower.

- Ecotourism camps can be owned and managed by domestic investors.

- Artisanal crafts development or souvenirs production and sales are one of the areas in tourism where ecotourism can have significant contribution in preserving and reviving the vanishing art and craft of the region.

- Little known cultural and folk dances, songs, etc. could be revitalized.

- Local cuisines could be popularized.

- Cultural pride could also be instilled in the locals.

- Tourist cannot be the bystander; he could be a part and parcel of the total activity.

Environmental benefits

- If properly handled ecotourism can prove to be an effective tool for conservation and preservation of the environment.

- It can create many sources of revenues for the local community in the protected area by discouraging traditional activities such as deforestation, over-grazing, poaching, etc.

- Preservation of globally threatened flora and fauna.

- Determination of impact assessment on environment and its management.

- Resource depletion could be minimized.

- Better planning of land use and other natural resources endemic to the region.

Economic benefits

- The advantage of low investment cost and high return minimizes investment risks, and attracts investors and stimulates the economy in a sustainable manner.

- In case of small and medium sized travel and tourism enterprises the leakage of foreign currency could be minimized.

- High multiplier effect of the earnings.

- Better ecofriendly infrastructure facilities.

- Another advantage of ecotourism is that it is not seriously affected by economic recession while large sized enterprises are highly affected and take more time to recover.

- Resources, which cannot be exported through the channel of foreign trade such as anthological and natural resources can easily, become foreign currency generating products through ecotourism.

- Economic benefits, including entry fees, licenses and concessions, often generate substantial funds to support conservation and management of natural environments.

Ethiopia-the land of extremes, remote and wild places

Ethiopia, which covers an area as large as France and Spain combined, is situated in the northeastern Horn of Africa, equidistance between the equator and the tropic of Capricorn. Ethiopia, the land of queen of Sheba, the birthplace of the Blue Nile, is regarded as the cradle of mankind. That Ethiopia has a heritage from the beginning of mankind was underlined when the remains of 'Lucy' dated from 3.5 million years ago, and 4.4 million year old Homo Ramidus Afranus, man's oldest anthropoid ancestor, were uncovered. Traders from Greece, Rome, Persia, and Egypt knew of the riches of Abyssinia (ancient name of Ethiopia).

Ethiopia is a land of extremes and a land of remote and wild places. The physical features of the country are highly remarkable for they incorporate high plateaus, long mountain range, lofty peaks, deep gorges, the largest cave in Africa (Sof Omar), the lowest depression on earth (Dalol), the greatest rift valley, savannah land, tropical forest, desert, beautiful Lakes, including source of Blue Nile Lake 'Tana', mighty rivers, spectacular waterfalls and volcanic hot springs.

Ethiopia's wealth of varied attractions gives it a great potential for cultural and educational tourism, conference tourism, photo safaris, jungle safaris, desert safaris, bird watching, water sports, health spas, mountain trekking and camping, and other forms of ecotourism.

Ethiopia, including Afar Regional State (ARS), posses unique, attractive, and untapped tourism resources with great potential to attract inbound as well as domestic tourists. However, due to various natural and manmade reasons the level of development of tourism in Ethiopia is still in its infancy.

Ecotourism Potential of the Afar Regional State (ARS)

The Afar region is located within the rift valley system in the northeastern part of Ethiopia. It has unique geo-ecological formation with altitude ranging from below 100 meters above sea level within the Dalol depression to the higher altitudes around 2000 meters above sea level along the rift escarpment in the north western part of the region.

The whole region can be characterized as 20% hyper arid (i.e. below 500 meters above sea level) and 80% arid (i.e. above 500 meters above seal level). The average rainfall in the hyper arid is below 200 mm and for arid it is above 500 mm. The annual mean temperature in arid areas is below 20-degree centigrade and in hyper arid it is above 30 degree centigrade. Most part of the area is dominated by loose shallow sandy soils. The soils are low in organic contents and are prone to salinization and soil erosion.

The vegetation of the region includes deserts, shrub lands, grasslands, and open acacia woodlands. The diversity and species of trees in the region differ from the high altitude and /or low land moist forest tree species. The vegetation along Awash River and the acacia trees of the open savannah provide attractive scenery in the arid, semi-arid and desert areas of the region. The forest and parklands in the region can be ideal for the development of ecotourism and other outdoor activities.

Table II: Conservation areas in Afar region

	Conservation Area	Area in sq. km
1.	Awash National Park	756
2.	Yangudi-Rassa National Park	4731
3.	Alledege Wild Life Reserve	1832
4.	Awash West Wild Life Reserve	1781
5.	Gewane Wild Life Reserve	2439
6.	Mille-Serdo Wild Life Reserve	8766
7.	Gewane Controlled Hunting Area	5932 *
8.	Awash West Controlled Hunting Area	9136

* Includes Afdem – an area, which is not within Afar Region

Source : (Hillman, 1993)

The different geomorphologic and climatic conditions have contributed to the wide-ranging wild life habitats of the Afar Regional State (ARS). This includes gallery forest, savannah woodland, bush/shrub lands, grasslands, wetland Lake, rivers, ponds and marshlands. The habitat types support many wild life species that are globally threatened. This includes African wild ass and the globally threatened species like Gravy's zebra, Dorcas gazelle, Soemmering gazelle, cheetah, and Swayne's heart beast. Among birds the region is a strategic site for large number of globally threatened birds like pallid harrier, and various Warblers. Afar ecosystem serves as refueling and nesting grounds for a large number of arctic and intra Africa migratory birds. In view of initial measures required to conserve selected ecosystems and to ensure the survival of selected species in the region, conservation areas of various categories are established. Based on international criteria, the Afar Region has the following national parks, wild life reserves and controlled hunting areas.

Awash National Park

Establishment of this park was initiated and proposed by the UNESCO to conserve the rich flora and fauna of the region in 1964. A total of 81 species of mammals, over 453 species of birds and 340 different species of plants are recorded in the park. The weak level of management and social pressure are the major problems of the park.

Yangudi-Rassa National park

The Park is located in the central part of the region with an area of 4731 sq. Km and was proposed in 1977 to protect the Wild Ass, Dorcas gazelles, soemmering gazelles, and Oryx. The park has 36 species of mammals and 230 species of birds with various types of microhabitats. The park is not properly managed and protected and lacks basic tourist services. Habitat destruction for fuel wood and charcoal, overgrazing and a low level of management capacity are some of the main problems of the park.

The Wild Life Reserves

The Allidege Wild life Reserve, the Awash West, the Gewane and Mille Serdo Wild Life reserve are set aside primarily for the conservation and nature-oriented management objectives. These reserves could well function as multiple-use management areas for the sustained production of water, timber, wildlife, pasture and for the development of ecotourism.

Controlled Haunting Areas

The already established Afdem-Gewane and Awash West controlled hunting areas in the region are primarily set for consumptive use of wild life resources on sustained yield basis. These areas are quite extensive but with limited wildlife resources.

Other National and Cultural Attractions

Other than the above-mentioned natural attractions Lakh Hertale, which possess hippopotamus, crocodiles and some fish can be developed as a tourist site where camping, fishing. sailing, and other water sports can be practiced. The world famous Dalol depression, which ranges between 100 meters above sea level in addition, the area consists of a variety of wild life species, hot and cold springs, Lakes, forests, mountains, with fascinating features and rivers all of which have significant tourist attraction potentials if provided with proper infrastructure and facilities necessary for the development of ecotourism.

Mile – Serdo-Asayita-Afamb, and derbti areas have abundant wildlife, Lakes, forests and sites that can be considered for conservation or wild life reserve. The area consists of large Lakes like Gemeri, Adabed, Afamo and Abe located at the border with Djibouti. This route comprises date rest patches and a variety of waterfowls in a swamps and or marshy areas at less then half an hour drive from Aysaita.

Afar falls under the ancient land of the punts and used to be the crossroads of civilizations. It is believed that afar had a strong trade ties and cultural exchanges with pharonic Egypt and Saudi Arabia. The region also claims the burial places of the first Muslim migrants from Saudi Arabia. These graveyards could go back as far as the first half of the seventh century. Moreover, Afar played a major role for the formation and growth of the Arab Sultanate, after the tenth century. This sultanate had left behind important historical sites such as mosques and shrines.

Handicraft production and the technologies used in the region are quite rudimentary. Most of the handicraft products are meant for self-reliance of families. Except simple farming, tools and dagger (gile) are produced. Blacksmith technologies are not developed. Woodwork products like small headrests, milk containers, bowls, spoons, stick combs for men (fidhim), comb for women (sakara) and comb for young girls are made by men. Leather works, baskets and mat making, light sandals (kabob), leather containers to keep the water cool (soufar) are a well developed crafts and usually done by women.

Afar people are direct, honest ad hospitable. Thir songs, folklore and dances are quite attractive. However these cultural values are not displayed or performed for tourists or visitors. These are yet to be organized as a tourist product.

Anthropological and Archaeological Resources

Afar is a very important region to study the origin and evolution of human being. According to many scientists concerned with the issue of the origin of human being, Middle Awash is known as the birthplace of diverse families of hominids. Research studies conducted in the region have identified a number of pale anthropological sites, which include the Hadar, Gona, Middle awash, Melka Werer, Kesem – Kebena, Megchelle, Ledi, Waranso and Dara Lakh sites. If properly developed and managed, the above-mentioned sites in Afar Region State could become a famous attraction.

Infrastructure and tourist facilities

The overall situation of infrastructure and tourist facilities in the Afar Regional State is underdeveloped. In the whole region there are no accommodation facilities that could meet the minimum requirements of a non-sophisticated tourist. Further off the Assab-Addis Ababa high way, road connections are very poor and most of the tourist attractions sites are not easily accessible. Except Awash National Park none of the tourist attraction sites have electricity, water, and communication facility.

Constraints and challenges of Ecotourism development in Afar

The following are the major constraints and challenges for developing the Ecotourism in Afar region:

Resource depletion

The natural resources are not well preserved, conserved and developed. Hence the depletion rate is high. The majority of people in the area is pastoralist and practices a traditional way of life. Due to rapid human and animal population, pressure on the natural resources of the region is very high. As a result, overgrazing, fuel wood consumption, etc. have become an acute problem causing excessive resource depletion.

Legislative and policy framework

The investment proclamation issued in the region is a positive step forward in attracting foreign donation institutions and domestic investments. However, issuance of investment proclamation and attractive incentives alone is not enough to create enabling environment for investment. Land use policy is one of the problems, which still exists. Further, there is no policy frame work in place to change the traditional way of life of the people into a more cost-effective and modern way of living. People are not fully aware of the values and benefits of tourism. Resource ownership is not clear and fully understood.

Institutional elements

Tourism, being one of the most promising sector of the region, it is organized as a small division under the Culture, Tourism and Information Bureau (not even as a department), so tourism resource management is hardly getting due attention. Further, the office lacks qualified and required number of staff. Lack of skilled manpower is also a big problem faced by the tourism sector of the region.

Guest host relationship

The local communities are not helping for tourism in an organized manner. This has negative effect on the conservation of the environment and on the safety and security of the tourists. The locals sometimes prohibit tourists to enter the area. Therefore it is important to improve guest host relationship by creating awareness and devising benefit sharing mechanism.

Infrastructure and tourist facilities

Most of the tourist areas including Bilen, Hadar, and Yangudi Rassa National Park do not have the necessary infrastructure such as road, electricity, telephone, fax, internet and potable water and are hardly accessible. According to Ethiopian Tourism Commission (ETC) there are only three hotels in Aysaita with a total of 42 rooms. Generally speaking, tourist facilities such as accommodation and catering services are almost inexistent in tourist sites except the Kereya lodge in Awash National Park and The Village Ethiopia Lodge in Bilen. Medical facilities, and other tourist service such, as information, entertainment, cultural shows, shopping, and security are not up to the expectation of the international tourists. It should be remembered that ecotourists do not travel to areas at risk from war, civil strife, or where there are several health problems. The eruption of any of these factors quickly dries up the supply of would be ecotourists.

Measures for the development of ecotourism as a tool for sustainable development in Afar region

1. Visions and Policy

- The Regional Government of Afar must develop a clear vision and policy for the sustainable development of the entire region.

- Based on region's pale anthropological, cultural, and natural resources, the Afar Regional Government should give priority to the development of ecotourism to ensure a sustainable management and use of the resources. Ecotourism ensures not only sustainable development but it is also relatively cost effective type of tourism, which is appropriate for regions such as Afar where infrastructure is less developed.

2. Review of the current status

- It is necessary to accord special protection to those species, including globally important sites, that are highly threatened. A review of region's current status of the natural resources with the view to sustainably managing and utiliging them is of paramount importance.

3. Strategic Initiatives

- A long term development strategy, with due priority to small and medium sized tourism and travel enterprises should be adopted as a commitment of the government in order to develop and promote these enterprises in Afar to ensure the well being of the people.

- Long-term marketing and publicity programmes could also be devised for strategically positioning and branding the tourism products of Afar region in both domestic and international markets.

4. Integrated plan of action

- Afar region being a fragile ecosystem, all-possible care and mitigation plans have to be prepared and implemented to avoid environmental consequences. Unplanned and unsustainable use of natural resources have resulted in extensive land degradation, loss of habitat and genetic resources in Ethiopia in general and Afar region in particular. It is therefore essential to have a development strategy to ensure the maintenance of these resources so as to be utilize them on sustainable basis.

- The wild life resources of the region must be integrated with other forms of rural development and tourism activities when determining and planning long-term regional interests. The regional government must include and prioritize in its development programmes the protection and maintenance of selected areas of the main types of habitat.

- Modern farming and animal husbandry (including zero grazing) should be introduced to maximize yield and to reduce degradation of the natural environment.

5. Enabling environment and good governance

- Creating an enabling environment for investment is necessary.
- The good governance is also need of the hour.

6. Integrating Mechanism

- The creation of specialized micro financing institutions, such as cooperative banks, is of paramount importance for the development and promotion of small and medium sized travel and tourism enterprises in Afar.

7. Public awareness

- Public awareness should be crated in Afar about the conservation and the sustainable use of resources by using all means of communication; Pupils at the elementary schools, pastorlists, shops, offices markets, health offices should also be included.

- Local people must be made aware about how conservation can help improve their living standards. Pastoralists must participate from the initial stage of development planning to directly sharing the benefits that would accrue from the development of tourism

8. Cultural and Pale Anthropological aspects

- It is important to emphasize on the publicity of pale anthropological resources in the area so that Afar people can value their cultural resources.

Unless ecotourism actively incorporates the local society into service planning and provisions, and includes programmes to meet the fundamental needs of income and employment for people in the region, the special qualities of the region, i.e., its natural, cultural, pale anthropological resources may get irreparably damaged.

Conclusion

The international market for ecotourism is increasing at an alarming rate. There is an appeal to visit somewhat remote destinations with the natural environment as the principal allure. Many such places are in less developed countries like Ethiopia. Tourist's expenditure in such places can have a very positive effect on the social and economic wellbeing of local people. Even the Ethiopian Tourism Commission (ETC) has incorporated the development and promotion of ecotourism in its second five-year development program. But, detailed analysis should also be made to identify other areas where the above-mentioned measures could appropriated be taken for sustainable tourism development. Ecotourism, to be successful, must promote sustainable development by establishing a durable product base that allows local inhabitants and ecotourism service providers to enjoy rising standards of living. Finally, to sustain and enhance the overall attractiveness of natural, cultural and pale anthropological resources, the development and promotion of ecotourism is highly recommended.

References

Afar Forestry Action Program (2001). Wildlife Conservation, Vol.III, December Addis Ababa.

Boo, Elizabeth, *Ecotourism (1990). The potentials and pitfalls* (2 Vol.), Washington D.C., World Wildlife Fund.

Dianne Brouse (1992). *Socially responsible travel,* Transition Abroad January and February P.23.

Eagles J.F. Paul (1996). International Ecotourism Management: Using Australia and Africa as Case Studies, paper prepared for the IUCN World Commission on *Protected Areas in the 21st century: from Islands to Networks,* Albany, Australia.

Ethiopian Wildlife and Natural History Society (EWNHS): *Important Bird Areas of Ethiopia,* 1996, Addis Ababa.

Hillman J.C. (1993). Ethiopia – *Compendium of Wildlife Conservation Information,* EWCO, Addis Ababa.

Industrial Project Services: *Study on Tourist Attraction Potentials of the Afar Region,* Vol. III, 1998, Addis Ababa.

60

J. Molner (1992). *Ecotourism-with conscience as our guide*, *The Seattle Times* March, 24 Sunday, Final edition.

McIntosh/Goeldner/Ritchie (1995). *Tourism: Principles, Practices, Philosophies* 7th *edition*, John Willey and Sons, Inc., New York.

The International Ecotourism Society: Newsletter, 3rd Quarter, 2001.

Theodros Atlabachew (2000). *Sustainable Tourism Development and Ecotourism*, September 24, 2002, Addis Ababa.

Theodros Atlabachew: The promotion of small and medium sized travel and tourism enterprises in the least developed countries and their comparative advantages for sustainable development, paper presented in the *World Ecotourism Summit*, May, Quebec- Canada.

Travel Industry Association of America (1992). Tourism and the Environment, Washington D.C.

Sustainable Tourism Planning and Development, 61-77, 2006
Edited by Bagri, S.C.
Published by Bishen Singh Mahendra Pal Singh, Dehra Dun, India

Analysing Environmental Impact Assessment for Tourism and Developing a Framework for the Nilgiri Biosphere Reserve

M.R. Dileep

Faculty in Tourism, KITTS, Thiruvananthapuram

Abstract : Tourism generates different kinds of impacts on different spheres of life. Environmental effects of tourism development constitute an area which invites special attention. Discussions, meetings and summits have been held world over for a long time to evolve measures to mitigate environmental negative impacts due to tourism development and initiate effective measures for sustainable development of tourism, environmental impact assessment (EIA), environmental management systems (EMs), etc. are some of the results of them. The practice of EIA has been implemented in many industrial sectors of the developed countries and it is indispensable in tourism sector also. Nilgiri Biosphere Reserve was constituted in 1986 with the aim, mainly, to conserve and preserve the natural ecosystems and the traditional living of the indigenous people. Over the years, the NBR has experienced environmental degradation in an unbelievable manner and the reasons are many. Tourism also has significant contribution in it and the area is prone to further tourism developments. In these circumstances, EIA is one of the concepts that have to be considered seriously and to be practiced at the time of planning. Here an attempt has been made to explain the concept of EIA and to formulate a framework suitable for the NBR which can be considered at the time when tourism development activities take place. The framework demands that certain steps be followed at the time of doing EIA and also highlights some factors to be considered during the process.

Key Words : Nilgiri, environment, impact, biosphere.

Introduction

Tourism is no more considered an environment-polluting smokeless industry. The image of it as a clean industry with little impacts is now outdated. Different kinds of tourism activities effect the natural and built environment. Many studies have shown that tourism has an immense impact on the physical environment, and that little has been done to remedy or control the assault on the ecology. Any form of industrial development will impact the physical environment in which it takes place. In view of the fact that tourists have to visit the place of production in order to consume the output, it is inevitable that the tourism activity will be associated with environmental impacts. As soon as tourism activity begins to establish, the environment is inevitably changed or modified either to facilitate tourism or during the tourism process (Cooper *et al.*, 2000). Berlin Declaration (1997) concerns that while tourism may importantly contribute to socio-economic development and cultural exchange, it has the potential for degrading the natural environment, social structure and cultural heritage. In practice it is proved that tourism does destroy and protect natural environments. The increase in environmental impacts along with the growth of tourism has raised many eyebrows regarding the sustainability of tourism and the irrevocable damages it can do to the environment. The tourism industry very much represents 'a double edged sword for the socio-environmental movement, in that it is an activity which is both reviled and revered. It has become a focus of criticism, as a result of its impacts and a focus of promotion, as a means of achieving sustainable development (Mowforth and Munt, 1998).

Since 1960s, numerous meetings and summits have been held world over to discuss the environmental problems arising out of tourism and the means to minimize them sustainably. The emergence of various innovative concepts such as Environmental Impact Assessment (EIA), Environmental Management Systems, Environmental Indicators, Tourism Environmental Regulation and Policies, Code of Ethics, Sustainable Tourism Development of Tourism, etc. was the result of such discussions. This paper attempts to examine the concept of Environmental Impact Assessment and to introduce it as an inevitable step for preventing further degradation of environment in the of Nilgiri Biosphere Reserve area as part of tourism development.

Tourism and Environment—the complex relationship

The term environment can be defined as "the complex of external conditions surrounding an object, an organism or a community and the specific set of measurable phenomena existing during a specified period of time at a specific location". Every object will have some kind of relationship with the environment. All the destinations are partly a created environment. Tourism environments are considered as an amalgam of resources and facilities and such complementary support is vital for their effective support (Pigram, 2000). The environments whether natural or artificial, is the most fundamental and one of the vital ingredients of the tourism product. In general, impacts of tourism are the changes which occur as a consequence of the industry. The discussions on tourism impacts are mainly focusing on the changes in the destination areas (Wall, 2000).

Tourism generates different kinds of impacts on different spheres of life. Environmental impact refers to the positive as well as negative aspects of tourism organizations. As stated earlier, as soon as tourism activity takes place, the environment is inevitably changed or modified either to facilitate tourism or during the tourism process. Hughes (1994) comments that the case against tourism is well known which pollutes and disfigures, corrupts traditional cultures, and overburdens local resources. Man, one among the lakhs of species on the earth, has been destroying his own leisure habitats, never mind those of the animal kingdom, and the destruction of habitats leads to the destruction of the species. The negative environmental impacts were the highlights in major discussions in relation to tourism and the environment held world over since they were referred as posing threats to the life on earth and mostly they are irreversible. Tourism has made inroads into numerous spaces on the surface of the earth, encroaching into all types of ecosystems. The range of impacts identified encompasses a variety of items including changes in the floral and faunal species composition, pollution, erosion and related issues, natural resource depletion, littering, land taken out of primary production, change in hydrological patterns, congestion, deforestation, loss of natural beauty, maintenance and preservation of forest and other natural areas, etc.

During 1970s the OECD has set out a framework for the study of environmental stress due to tourism activities. It has pointed out four main categories of stress activities. First, the permanent environmental restructuring (it includes major construction works as highways, airports, roads, resorts, etc.). Second, the waste product generation (it consists of biological and non-biological waste which can damage aqua life, create health hazards, and destroy the attractiveness of a destination). Next is direct environmental stress due to tourist activities (like destruction of coral reefs, vegetation, breeding habits of animals, etc.), The last one is the effect on the population dynamics (migration, increased urban densities accompanied by declining population in rural areas, etc.). It has been stated that the environmental changes as a result of tourism development can be either tourist specific or industry generated. When tourist only perceives the consequence of his/her individual actions and ignores the cumulative effects of all tourists, the former case evolves. The industry generated changes occur when industry responds to demand without regard for the long term environmental consequences of their actions. The main factors towards the extent of environmental damage are intensity of site use, resiliency of the ecosystem where use and developments are occurring, time perspective of the developer and the transformational character of the developments (Gartner, 1996). Environmental impacts of tourism are often cumulative and recognizing the cumulative impacts can be just as beneficial to improving environmental performance as correcting the negative aspects (Peiyi, 2000).

When the World Tourism Organization (WTO) set up the environment committee to address the issues of conservation in 1979, the formal institutional recognition of the environmental issues due to the development of tourism was established. In 1982, it adopted a set of principles known as 'the joint declaration on tourism and environment' which seriously concerns the environmental issues. The Sustainability concept emerged during then. In fact the momentum for sustainable development of tourism came only after the introduction of the Brundtland Report-Our Common Future and the setting up of Agenda-21, a result of the Rio-Earth summit. Various discussions were held afterwards in this area. The concepts of carrying capacity (Swarbrooke, 2000), local peoples' participation and nature-culture preservation were the main themes of such discussions (Dileep, 2003). Environmental Impact Assessment (EIA), Environmental Management Systems, Environmental Indicators were evolved and implemented in the tourism sector during the era. EIA was introduced as a tool used in the planning process and the details are mentioned later. Environmental management is a concept that has been around since 1970s. Its development has been assisted by the introduction of legislation and the need for organizations to avoid prosecution for contravention of the legislation. EMS is a tool which a company can use to ensure that it is complying with the environment legislation and minimizing its impact on the environment. It is a management framework which includes the methods for structuring and processing the planning and day-to-day practices of a company or a section within a company (Tribe *et al.*, 2000). Environmental Auditing is a concept considered along with the EMS (Holden, 2000). Auditing is considered generally to compare the predicted outcomes with those outcomes that have already occurred (Hall, 2000). Environmental

Checklists and Environmental Indicators were formulated as part of increased urge for environmental preservation in tourism development. The World Travel and Tourism Council (WTTC) has published a study report on the "statistical indicators needed to monitor sustainable travel and tourism development" (WTTC 1992). WTO's Environmental Committee established a task force to examine the development of the indicators of sustainable tourism. They have suggested a range of performance indicators and further studies have recommended developing indicators by using the following categories to reflect differing policy needs. They are corporate indices, national level indicators and site or destination specific indicators. Thereafter more classifications were also formed (Hughes, 2002).

Environmental Impact Assessment

Many countries and regions have begun to use the environmental protection legislation, and EIA procedure is being increasingly applied throughout the world to all types of development, including tourism projects, to ensure that any negative environmental impact if identified in advance, analyzed and minimized. With the increasing concern about the environmental impacts of development, the EIA procedure has been set out to assess the impacts of the proposed development projects. EIA is considered as one of the primary tools for the environmental manager and a useful guide for decision making (Khoshoo, 1991).

Origin of EIA as a formal part of planning procedure can be traced back to the passing of the National Environmental Policy Act (NEPA) in the USA in 1969, which demanded the preparation of EISs (Environmental Impact Statements) by the federal agencies for all the major projects. Holden (2000) writes that it was not a coincidence that the adoption of NEPA was also accompanied by increasing vocality from the environmental groups over the environmental problems due to the development. EIA has been described as one of the foremost tools available to national decision makers in their efforts to prevent further environmental degradation (Sniffer, 1995). EIA process is seen as a means not only of identifying potential impacts but also of enabling the integration of the environment and the development (Green and Hunter, 1992). According to Middleton and Hawkins (1998), EIA is designed to prevent environmental degradation by giving decision makers better information about the likely consequences that the development actions could have on the environment. It thus informs planning decision and will ensure that decision makers take environmental issues into account while making development control decisions. It has been suggested that the assessment shall be undertaken by the planner working for the relevant public state policy.

EIA is defined as an analytical procedure for predicting and evaluating the environmental impact of the proposed development programmes and projects, terminating with a written report (environmental impact statement) to prescribe safeguards. It is also legally defined as administrative procedure to involve major interest groups in the decision making process, inform the public and resolve potential conflicts caused by multiple uses of the community's resources (Peiyi, 2000). Hence EIA can be considered as a procedure for bringing out the potential effects of human activities on environmental systems. The most significant benefit of EIA is the ability for the inter- comparison of the developmental options and the screening of the alternate sites for locating development projects. For getting maximum benefits, EIA must identify measures to minimize effects and evaluate both the beneficial and adverse environmental impacts of the development project (Khoshoo, 1991). Generally, the identification and measurement of potential impacts are assessed to varying degrees of precision, depending on the nature of the project and the data available. At the planning stage of a proposed project, the significant environmental impacts can be identified and examined, and measures suggested for the prevention or the mitigation. EIA is primarily done to identify risks, minimize adverse impacts, and determine environmental acceptability. Table-I gives the details of Green's Checklist of environmental impacts caused by tourism.

There is no set structure for the EIA process, but it is generally assumed that EIAs have to assess future levels of noise pollution, visual impact, air pollution, hydrological impacts, land use and landscape changes associated with the development. Holden (2000) states that most of the EIAs involve five stages such as identification of the impact, measurement of the impact, interpretation of the significance of the impact, displaying the results of the assessment and the identification of appropriate monitoring schemes. Checklists are widely used as a technology for conducting EIA. It is somewhat useful to have a preliminary assessment, but has limitations to be treated as a complete tool for the EIA. An example of a checklist suggested by Green *et al.* (1990) is given in Table-II.

Table I: Green's checklist of the Environmental Impacts Caused by Tourism

---

The Natural Environment

(a) Changes in the Floral and Faunal Species Composition
- Disruption to breeding habits
- Killing of animals through hunting
- Killing of animals in order to supply goods for the souvenir trade
- Inward or outward migration of animals
- Destruction of vegetation through gathering of wood or plants
- Change in the extent and/or nature of vegetation cover through clearance or planting to accommodate tourism facilities
- Creation of a wild life reserve/sanctuary

(b) Pollution
- Water pollution through discharges of sewage, spillage of oil/petrol
- Air pollution from vehicle emissions
- Noise pollution from tourist transportation and activities

(c) Erosion
- Compaction of soils causing increased surface run-off and erosion
- Change in risk occurrence of land slips/slides
- Change in risk of avalanche occurrence
- Damage to the geological features
- Damage to river banks

(d) Natural Resources
- Depletion of ground and surface water supplies
- Depletion of fossil fuels to generate energy for tourist activity
- Change in risk of occurrence of fire

(e) Visual Impact
- Facilities
- Litter

The Built Environment

(a) Urban Environment
- Land taken out of primary production
- Change of hydrological patterns

(b) Visual Impact
- Growth of the built-up area
- New architectural styles
- People and belongings

(c) Infrastructure
- Overload of infrastructure (public roads, railways, etc.)
- Provision of new infrastructure
- Environmental management to adapt areas for the tourist use

68

(d) Urban Form
  - Changes in residential, retail or industrial land uses
  - Changes to the urban fabric
  - Emergence of contrasts between urban areas developed for the tourist population and those for the host population.

(e) Restoration
  - re-use of disused buildings
  - restoration and preservation of historic buildings and sites
  - restoration of derelict buildings as second homes

(f) Competition
  - possible decline of tourist attractions or regions because of the opening of other attractions or a change in tourist habits and preferences

Source : Adapted from Green *et al.* (1990).

The checklist will give hints on whether further detailed EIA is necessary or not. Each value is evaluated in terms of possible types and extent of impact. Matrices will be a useful technique for evaluation which summarizes and synthesis as the impacts so that comprehensive evaluation can be made of all the factors. An example for the same is given in the Table-II.

Table II: Sample Evaluation Matrix for Environmental Impact

Type of Impact	Evaluation of impact				
	No Impact	Minor	Moderate impact	Serious impact	Comments impact
Air Quality					
Surface Water Quality					
Ground Water Quality					
Road Traffic					
Noise Levels					
Solid Waste Disposal System					
Archaeological and Historic Sites					
Visual Amenity					
Natural Vegetation					
Wild Animal Life					

Note : This list of types of impacts is only a sampling. There may be additional or different factors in an actual environmental analysis. After: Inskeep, 1991.

The matrices can have different arbitrary score of importance on the scale of 1 to 10 depending upon the seriousness of the issues. Apart from these, Systems and Network diagrams are also used which attempt to describe a little more comprehensively cause affect relationship listing impacts and how these are generated through effects on resources. In this context, modeling and computer simulation are sometimes utilized with mixed results. Map overlays which are also used in this context, that are intended to identify areas of lesser conflicts among resources use alternatives and environmental values. By superimposing maps depicting various uses for values, such as vegetation, water courses, unique wildlife habitats, etc., it is often possible to screen areas which have to be exempted in locating the projects. But this doesn't reveal relationships and is not good enough to differentiate among impacts. Delphi study is one of the techniques which can be used for EIA (Sharma, 2000). Adaptive Environmental Assessment and Management (AEAM) is another recently evolved tools used in the context of EIA. Cooper *et al.* (1996) argue that in spite of the apparent comprehensiveness of the above given checklist, it is clear that the primary focus is confined only to direct effects of tourism development. It is an inadequate approach since the indirect approaches have also to be assessed. In considering such views, they have formulated a process which consists of stages such as site selection and preliminary assessment, pre-feasibility report, detailed environmental assessment, feasibility study, modifications to proposals to minimize impacts, project physical planning and design, implementation of environmental protection measures, project implementation, environmental monitoring, project monitoring and evaluation. They state that the process should examine the environmental auditing procedures, limitations to natural responses, environmental problems and conflicts that may affect project viably and possible detrimental effects to people, flora and fauna, soil, water air, etc. either within the proposed project area or that will be affected by it.

The Nilgiri Biosphere Reserve—An Overview

The concept of biosphere reserve is a method whereby specific natural eco-systems are conserved and managed for prosperity. Biosphere reserve contains a set of unique ecosystems rich in biodiversity, such as medicinal plants, traditional landraces or crops and their wild relatives, ancient races of domestic animals and indigenous people. Biosphere Reserve Network Programme was launched by UNESCO in 1971 under its Man and

Biosphere Programme (Khoshoo 1991). The objectives of the programme are as follows:

- Conserve representative samples of eco-systems
- Provide long term *in situ* conservation of genetic diversity
- Promote and facilitate basic and applied research and monitoring
- Promote appropriate sustainable management of the living resources in the reserve
- Disseminate the experiences so as to promote sustainable development elsewhere; and
- Promote international co-operation.

In India, the creation of biosphere reserve has been put into practice since 1986. In a biosphere reserve, multiple land use is permitted by designing various zones, namely, core zone, buffer zone and manipulation zone. In the core zone no human activity is permitted. The buffer zone is the area where limited human activity is permitted. The manipulation zone is the area where a large number of human activities can continue. In a biosphere it is not only the wild population of plants and animals that are protected, but efforts are also made to keep intact the traditional life styles of tribes. There are fourteen identified biosphere reserves in India and only 9 are notified so far (Bharadwaj and Dev, 1998). Nilgiri Biosphere Reserve is one among the oldest reserves in India established in the year 1986. It is located in the Western Ghats and includes two of the ten bio-geographical provinces of India.

Total area of the Nilgiri Biosphere Reserve is 5520 sq.km. located between 76°-77°15'E and 11°15'-12°15'N. Site map of NBR is given in diagram 1. It spans in three southern states—Kerala, Tamil Nadu and Karnataka. The NBR encompasses many reserve areas such as the Mudumalai Wild Life Sanctuary, Wayanad Wild Life Sanctuary, Bandipur National Park, Nagarhole National Park, Mukurti National Park and Silent Valley National Park. The official conservation and management of the NBR is practiced by making the reserve into Core zone (1240 sq.km) and Buffer zone (4280 sq.km.). The buffer zone is again divided into manipulation zones like forestry, tourism and recreation zones. Most of the plantations are seen in the manipulation zone. Here, tourism activities can be possible in around 335 sq. km. The NBR comprises of substantial unspoilt areas of natural vegetation, ranging from dry scrub to evergreen forests and swamps, thus contributing to highest bio-diversity in India. The altitude and climatic gradients support and nourish the different vegetation types. The vegetation types there include moist evergreen, semi evergreen, thorn, savannah and woodlands, and sholas and grass lands.

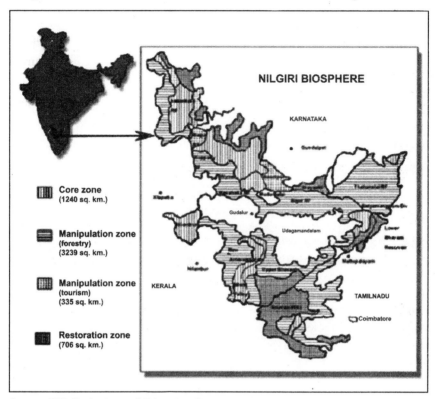

Source : CPR Environmental Education Centre

Fig.1: Site Map of NBR

The NBR is rich in plant diversity. About 3300 species of flowering plants can be seen here. Of these, 132 are endemic to the Nilgiris. The genus Baeolepis is exclusively endemic to the Nilgiris. Some of the plants entirely restricted to the NBR include species of Adenoon, Calacanthus, Baeolepis, Frerea, Jarodina, Wagatea, Poeciloneuron, etc. NBR includes around 157 species of Orchids out of which 8 are endemic to the NBR. These include endemic and endangered species of Vanda, Liparis, Bulbophyllum, Spiranthes and Thrixspermum. The sholas of the NBR are a treasure house of rare plant species.

The fauna of the NBR includes over 100 species of mammals, 350 species of birds, 80 species of reptiles and amphibians, 300 species of butterflies and innumerable invertebrates. Thirty nine species of fish, 31 amphibians and 60 species of reptiles endemic to the Western Ghats also occur in the NBR. Fresh water fish such as *Danio neilgheriensis,* *Hypselobarbus dubuis* and *Puntius bavanicus* are restricted to the NBR. The Nilgiri tahr, Nilgiri Langur, Slendor loris, Blackbuck, tiger, Gaur, Indian Elephants and marten are some of the animals found here.

NBR is one of the critical catchment areas of peninsular India. Many of the tributaries of the river Cauvery like the Bhavani, Moyar, Kabani and other rivers like Chaliyar, Punampuzha, etc. have their source and catchments areas within the reserve boundary. Many hydro-electric power projects are present in the Kundah, Bhavani and Moyar basins. The shoals and Grass lands play a very important role in retaining water and supplying it to the streams.

A variety of the human cultural diversity can be found in the NBR. Tribal groups like the Todas, Kotas, Irullas, Kurumbas, Paniyas, Adiyans, Edanadan Chettis, Cholanaickens, Allar, Malayan, etc. are native to the reserve. Except for Cholanaickens, who live exclusively on food gathering, hunting and fishing, all the other tribal groups are involved in their traditional occupation of Agriculture.

A variety of environmental problems are identified in NBR. Intensive tree felling and increase in influx of population from the surrounding areas led to the deforestation and consequent habitat destruction. Between 1990 and 1996, there has been a considerable decrease in the dense forest area. Almost 28.96 sq.km. of dense forest have become open forest and 22.67 sq.km of dense forests have changed into non-forest areas. This destroys the habitat of several species of animals and birds of the Nilgiris. Depletion of natural resources, erosion, degradation of environment are the results of the development activities. Monoculture is another issue in the Nilgiris. Intensive use of fertilizers and other chemicals for agriculture purposes degrade the quality of the soil. Agriculture enhances erosion also. Sholas were used for grazing the cattle. Destruction of shoals led to the perennial streams, causing soil erosion and micro climatic changes. Forest fires are common in the sholas and dry deciduous forests. Deliberate attempts are also there for creating wild fire. Extensive construction activities are being made inside and periphery areas of the NBR which creates different kinds of environmental problems.

It is stated that tourism also contributed towards the environmental degradation of the NBR. The NBR encompasses many tourism centers.

In all the wild life sanctuaries and national parks inside the NBR different kinds of tourism activities are being held. The Nilgiris are an important tourist centre of South India and attract a large number of tourists. Plenty of hotels, clubs, resorts, gardens and roads have emerged rapidly. All such developments have intensified the degradation of the environment over there. Extensive pollution and water scarcity are some of the results affecting the entire ecology of the NBR. Indiscriminate garbage disposal by tourism activities including those by the hotels have resulted in water pollution so much so that the Ooty lake in Ooty, the most popular hill station of South India has been ruined by accumulation of garbage and disposal of sewage into it- (Khoshoo, 1991, Bharadwaj and Dev, 1998, Negi, 1991).

A Framework

The environmental sensitivity and the fragility of the NBR have been mentioned in the above description. Already tourism has contributed in the overall environmental degradation of NBR in a big way. If the situation prevails and the tourism development proceeds without serious environmental considerations, the repercussions would be very serious. Internationally, EIA has been treated as one of the important tools used at the planning stage for identifying the potential impacts which will help in taking measures to mitigate the consequent environment degradation due to development. A framework, suitable enough for the Nilgiri Biosphere Reserve has been formulated which is elaborated in the following paragraphs.

The EIA of a site has to consider all factors that will become a reason for the environmental degradation. Sometimes, socio-cultural impacts are also identified using EIA. A comprehensive approach is essential for the same. But here, only environmental aspects are given much importance. For example, UNEP has set guidelines for tourism development in the convention biodiversity and tourism (UNEP/CBD 2001). In formulating the framework, such guidelines and declarations have been examined. EIA is usually undertaken at the time of planning process, and when it is used for a particular site, all the relevant national and international policies, regulations, code of conduct and other relevant issues are considered. NBR is a vast area covering more than five thousand sq.km and the environmental features vary from place to place. The site selection is very crucial since majority of the area is under the core zone. As per the national environment protection schemes no activities are possible inside

74

the biosphere reserve. Some parts are highly fragile like the Silent Valley National Park where, if any mass tourism development activities take place, it will ruin the ecosystem. Preliminary EIA process has to be followed after the site selection, usually as explained earlier. At the time of impact assessment, areas creating environmental degradation need to be taken into consideration. These include use of land resources for the construction of roads, railways, accommodation units and airports, and unsustainable use of natural resources like water, vegetation usage, pollution in water from sewage disposal, soil pollution due to solid waste, toxic substances and noise pollution from transportation and tourism entertainment activities, damage and destruction to eco-systems, risk of erosion, disturbance to floral and faunal species, changes in habitats, risk of fire, likelihood of change in animal behaviour, eutrophication of habitats, especially aquatic habitats, and other important environmental aspects.

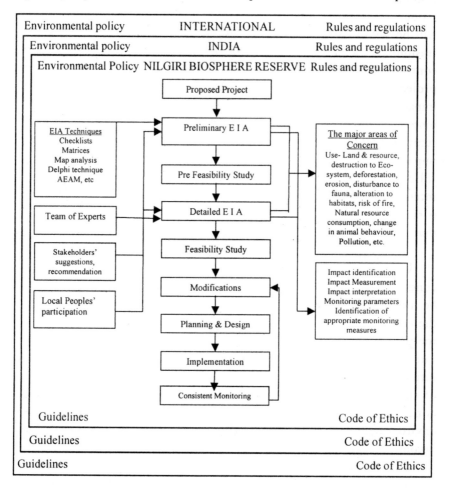

Care has to be taken in selecting the team of experts for conducting the EIA. Tourism is a multi-faceted activity which generates very complex impacts in different areas. An interdisciplinary approach is essential and the team must include ecologists, geologists, hydrologists, geographers and, possibly, sociologists and anthropologists. Suggestions and recommendations of the stakeholders relevant to the NBR, like forest department representatives, NGOs, researchers, developing agencies, etc. have to be involved for successful impact assessment. Apart from this, the local people, especially the indigenous communities, have to be consulted which will make available traditional knowledge that can be positively utilized for the impact assessment.

After the preliminary assessment, the pre-feasibility of the project could be found out. If the assessment indicates that the project will cause serious irreparable damages which cannot be controlled in the future, it will be better either to change the site or to avoid it. If the primary feasibility study shows positive signals and if the assessed impacts are controllable using various environmental management techniques, the project can be pushed ahead. Defended upon the seriousness of the impacts a detailed impact assessment can be undertaken afterwards using more relevant and better techniques. The EIA must contain the following steps as suggested by Andrew Holden. The major direct and indirect impacts have to be identified during the preliminary stage. It has to be followed by measurement of impacts and interpretation. After interpretation the results of the impacts have to be displayed and its parameters have to be fixed which can be utilized in the monitoring stage that comes later.

Using all the available data, a thorough feasibility study can be conducted and if the study results show positive signs, the project can be moved further. If needed, some modifications can be undertaken for the environmental sustainability of the project. After such modifications, the planning and design activities can be done and at this stage utmost care should to be taken to minimize environmental degradation since the future will depend on this decisions taken at this stage. Implementation of the project findings will be the next stage, when environmental concerns have to be taken care of. Consistent monitoring of the environmental issues has to be undertaken and if any modifications become necessary, steps can be taken to do so.

76

Conclusion

The ever increasing environmental problems have been under wide discussions since long and as a result many mitigating tools have been evolved. Tourism, though initially considered as a clean industry without negative impacts, is posing several kinds of threats to the environment, society and culture. Since 1970s different kinds of programmes were incorporated in the unplanned development process for minimizing environmental negative impacts due to tourism development, and environmental impact assessment is one among them. An attempt has been made here to look into the concept of EIA and on that basis a framework has been formulated which can be used for implementation at the time of tourism development in the Nilgiri Biosphere Region.

References

Berlin Declaration 1997, (2002). International Conference on Biodiversity and Tourism, in Suresh K.T., Syed Liyakhat and Roy Swaroop (eds.), *Indigenous Peoples, Wildlife and Ecotourism*, Equations, Bangalore.

Bhardwaj Subhash and Rao Dev (1998). *Ecology, Environment and Wildlife*, R.Chand and Company, New Delhi.

Cooper Chris, Fletcher John, Gilbert David and Wanhill Stephen (2000). Environmental Impacts of Tourism, in Rebeca Shepherd (ed.), *Tourism Principles and Practices*, Longman, Essex, England.

Gartner, C.William (1996). *Tourism Development-Principles, Processes and Policies*, Van Nostraud, Reinhold, ITP.

Dileep, M.R. (2003). Sustainable Tourism Development- a Framework of Kerala, *Review of Social Sciences*, 5(1) 35-43.

Green H. and Hunter, C. (1992). The Environmental Impact Assessment of Tourism Development in P.Johnson and B.Thomas (eds.), *Perspectives in Tourism Policy*, London Mansell.

Green, H., Hunter, C. and Moore B. (1990). Applications of the Delphi Technique in Tourism, *Annals of Tourism Research*, 17(4) 270-9.

Hall, C.M. (2000). *Tourism Planning. Policies, Processes and Relationships*, Prentice Hall-Person Education Centre, England.

Holden Andrew (2000). *Environment and Tourism*, Routledge, London.

Hughes (1994). Planning for Sustainable Tourism: the ECOMOST Project, Lewes, East Sussex: International Federation of Tour Operators.

Hughes, George (2002). Environmental Indicators, *The Annals of Tourism Research*, 29(2) 457-77.

Inskeep Edward (1991). *Tourism Planning- An Integrated and Sustainable Development Approach*, Van Nostrand Reinhold, New York.

Khoshoo, T.N. (1991). *Environmental Concerns and Strategies*, Ashish Publishing House, New Delhi,

Middleton and Hawkins (1998). *Sustainable Tourism Making Perspective*, Butterworth-Heinemann, Oxford.

Mowforth Martin and Munt Ian (1998). *Tourism and Sustainability, New Tourism in the Third World*, Rutledge, New York & London.

Negi, S.S. (1991). *Environmental Degradation and Crisis in India*. Indus Publishing Company, New Delhi.

Peiyi Ding (2000). Environmental Impact Assessment, In Jaffer Jafari (ed.), *Encyclopedia of Tourism*, Routledge, London. 299.

Pigram John (2000). Environment Tourism, in Jaffer Jafari (ed.), *Encyclopedia of Tourism*, Routledge, London.

Sniffer, J. (1995). UNEP Impact Assessment Meetings, Paris.

Sharma, J.K. (2000). *Tourism Planning and Development: A new Perspective*, Kanishka Publishers, New Delhi.

Suresh, K.T., Syed Liyakhat and Swaroop Roy (2002). *Indigenous Peoples, Wildlife and Ecotourism*, Equations, Bangalore.

Swarbrooke, J. (2000). *Sustainable Tourism Management*, CABI, Oxon, UK.

Tribe, Xavier Font, Nigel Griffiths, Richard Vickery and Karen Yale (2000). *Environmental Management for Rural Tourism and Recreation*, Cassel, London.

UNEP/CBD (2001). Biological Diversity and Tourism, UNEP/CBD/WS-tourism, Santo Domingo.

Wall, Geoffrey (2000). Impacts, in Jaffer Jafari (ed.), Encyclopedia *of Tourism*, Routledge, London.

WCED (1987). *Our Common Future*, The World Commission on Environment and Development, Oxford, New Delhi.

WTTC (1992). *Revised statistical Indicators needed to monitor the sustainable tourism and travel development*. Oxford.

Sustainable Tourism Planning and Development, 79-93, 2006
Edited by Bagri, S.C.
Published by Bishen Singh Mahendra Pal Singh, Dehra Dun, India

Ecotourism Complex Planning at Kalimath in Garhwal Himalaya

S.C. Bagri
Director & Dean
Centre for Mountain Tourism & Hospitality Studies
HNB Garhwal University, Srinagar Garhwal
bagri_sc@hotmail.com

Jitendra Mohan Mishra
Research Fellow
Centre for Mountain Tourism and Hospitality Studies
HNB Garhwal University, Srinagar Garhwal
jitendra@yahoo.co.in

Abstract : Kalimath is one of the sacred haunts of Hindu goddess *Kali* and being visited by tourists and pilgrims round the year. Besides pilgrimage it is surrounded by quite a large number of natural destinations known for rich flora and fauna. Incidentally, there is least participation of local people and much of the revenue from the tourist traffic goes to the hands of a couple of tourism professionals established hoteliers and resorts owners. In view of this an intensive survey was carried out in order to know the total financial requirement for the local involvement in ecotourism business. Ecotourism promotions in this region, may infure some economic activities with least destruction and damage to local habitat.

Key Words: Kalimath, Kedarnath Musk deer sanctuary, ecotourism.

The Problem

Kedarnath, since time immemorial, has been known as a religious center for Hindu pilgrimage. This abode of lord Shiva attracts lakhs of pilgrims for six-month in a year and provides income and livelihood to thousands of locals at various transit points. However, the locals complain about the seasonality of the pilgrimage as the major impediment to their overall income. There is ample scope for local persons to engage themselves in tourism profession round the year if Kedarnath Musk dear sanctuary is opened for ecotourism activities. Visitors and pilgrims though visit Kedarnath Sanctuary, the primary survey of pilgrims revealed that majority of them are not aware about the Musk deer sanctuary, which houses many rare and endangered species of the world.

Kedarnath Musk deer sanctuary, spread over an area of 967.25 sq.kms., was established in the year 1972 to protect the musk deer in its natural habitat. Besides grandeur of Himalayan wilderness, the sanctuary en-houses many important Hindu shrines such as Trijuginarayan, Rudranath, Tunganath, Madhamaheswar, Kalpeswar, Kalimath, Anusuya Devi and Kedarnath, abode of Lord Shiva. Existence of eminent pilgrim spots make this sanctuary an Eco-religious cum trekkers paradise. If properly marketed amongst the pilgrims coming to visit the abode of Kedarnath, this sanctuary can provide the locals with year round income besides generating income for the conservation of forest and its flora and fauna.

Objectives

- To identify the attractional base
- To identify tourist's preferences
- To forecast the financial requirement for developing ecotourism facilities.

Methodology

Data were collected from various stakeholders of ecotourism, like pilgrims, tourists, local people and service providers. Structured questionnaire method was adopted for the tourists and other visitors, while in-depth interviews were conducted for service providers during May and June 2004. Opinion leaders among the local people were interviewed for getting their perception about ecotourism.

Cultural background

Kalimath

Situated on the bank of river Saraswati Ganga, Kalimath is one of the famous *Shakti Pithas* of Garhwal (*Sakthi Pithas* are associated to Goddess *Shakti*, the other name of Parvati). The central courtyard en-houses a plethora of temples like *Mahakali, Mahalaxmi, Mahasaraswati, Gaurisankar, Bhairavnath* and *Sidheswar*. According to religious texts the *Devtaas* (God), when driven out of the heaven by the *Mahisasura* (the king of demons) rested here. Their prayers pleased goddess *Ambika* (One of the incarnations of Parvati) who later killed *Mahisasura*. The *Mahakali* temple is locally known as "*Khade Kalika*" (standing deity). Devotees feel grateful by getting blessings from the mother *Mahakali*. The numerous bells hanging in the courtyard are donated by the devotees. The large sword at the southern gate is also an attraction here. There is a *Ganesh* idol and *Akhand deepa* (everlasting candle) in this temple. A silver plate covers the round pit, which is worshipped daily. The *Kundi* (a bowl shaped structure) under the silver plate is washed once in a year during the *Navratras* (nine auspicious days during October) in the autumn season. The *Kundi* is washed after pouring the water into the river Saraswati Ganga. The water is deposited here during the whole year. During the *Navaratras* in the autumn, this holy place becomes centre of attraction for thousands of devotees. When asked about the *Kundi* the villagers remain salient. However, they reveal that the year they feel the touch of hair inside the *Kundi* brings natural calamities like landslides and earthquake take place. After pouring the water of the *Kundi* into the river, the *Kundi* is kept at its place with the chanting of *Vedic mantras* (hymns). Then the silver plate is covered over the *Kundi*. The whole process is done in complete darkness. After this, the idol of *Mahalaxmi* (the goddess of wealth) is brought to the *Mahakali* temple. Both the goddesses meet each other this day in a year. As per the tradition, during this occasion 15 - 20 persons with burning pine branches in their hand run around the temple. After this, they throw these branches at a red stone near the river. This is believed that the stone releases blood soon after these branches are thrown to it. People also believe that on this stone slab once the demon *Raktabij* was killed. However, nobody dares to adventure in the night to see this stone slab. In the morning, if one looks closely the bloodshed can be seen.

To the south of the *Mahakali* temple there is *Mahalaxmi* temple. This is built in polished stone, which is quite old. The temple is divided into three parts, viz. *Garbha Griha*, (sanctum) *Antarala* (gap), and *Mandap* (platform). There are 21 *Deepas* (clay lamps for lighting purpose) at the gate of the *Garbha Griha*. These light the temple all the time. There is also an ever-lasting fire in this temple which has been there since ages. The presiding *Laxmi* idol at this temple is built of bell metal. There are *Navduraga* (mother goddess Durga) idols and two *Brahma* idols here which is unique to this place. Rarely we can find the idol worship of *Brahma* in India. There is a huge *Havan kund* (bowl shaped structure used for pilgrims offerings) in front of the temple. Oblations are offered on special occasions. There is a *Shivalinga* behind the *Laxmi* idol. *Kali Mahatmya* (book written on the glory of Kali Goddess) describes that the water from this *Lingam* is very pious which gives immortality to the human. There is an 18-line stone inscription in green colour in front of the temple. This slab is 1.5 ft in length and 8 inch width. In front of this, there are *Gauri Sankar* (Shiva Parvati) and *Maha Saraswati* (goddess of knowledge) temple.

The *Maha Saraswati* idol has 8 hands (*Astabhuja*). The hands of idol holds sword, bow, *trishul* (trident), *bhala* (spare), *barcha* (sharp pointed weapon), *mala* (Garland), *khadga* (sword), *nagphans* (an auspicious rope) and *gada* (mace). Right to the *Maha Saraswati* there is a *Linga* of *Maha Sidheswar* which is of green colour. Apart from that there are icons of *Nandis, Simhas, Nagarajas, Shringi, Bhringis* and lord *Ashutosh*. Mother *Parvati* sits on the lap of Lord *Ashutosh*. There is also a *Bhairav* temple where there are numerous copper idols. It is believed that *Bhairav* watches the temple with a stick on his hand.

Another legend tells a different story. After killing a number of demons like *Rakta-bija, Mahisasura, Sumbha, Nishumbha, Mata Ambika* became furious with persisting anger and frustration. While walking in the street unconsciously, she stepped on her husband lord *Shiva*. She bit her tongue for this sin and beheaded herself repenting for this sin. The head flew in the river and stopped near Srinagar Garhwal (85 km down toward Rishikesh), where she is called *Dharidevi* (this place is 15 km from Srinagar Garhwal and is visited by a large number of devotees round the year). Here one can see only the head portion of the female goddess made of black granite). The remaining body is called *"Chhinna masta"* who is worshipped near *Kalimath* in a village called *Kundjethi*. Other places connected with this legend are *Maikhand, Rondlake* and *Mansuna,* which used to be the capitals of *Mahisasura, Rakta bija* and *Shumbha-Nishumbha.*

At present, river *Kaliganga,* that flows from *Kaligarh* (Kalisila), meets the *Sarswati* here. There is a *Siva Linga* here at the confluence called *Kaleswar Mahadev.* There is a reference of this place in *"Kali Mahatmya"* (religious Significance of goddess Kali). After this confluence, the river is named as Kali Ganga. At a small distance from Kalikshetra (region of

Kali goddess) there is a temple dedicated to *Draupadi* (the wife of Pandavas in the *Mahabharat*). Kalimath has also historical lineage with *Kalidas* who used to be one of the *Navaratnas* (nine noble laureates) in the court of Chandragupta Vikramditya, ruled Dharanagiri in central India located near Ujjain. It is believed that goddess *Saraswati* blessed *Kalidas* with the supreme knowledge at the place. The virgin climate with clear water stream is an ideal place for concentration and meditation. Perhaps this would have been the reason why *Kalidas* had selected this place for contemplation. Kalimath is one of the base points for trekkers going to *Madhmaheswar* (one of the Panch Kedars).

The stone *Kalishila* (Auspicious rock related to goddess kali) here is of copper ore and has magnetic power. Locals here believe that although it is polished one does not slipover it because of the divine magnetic power. When sunrays fall here, it seems as if thousands of candles are lighted. It is believed to be unholy to walk around the stone. However, it is said that a saint known as Bratibaba has done it thrice. The *Kalishila* has some grass on its centre without any soil on the slab. The stone is also believed to change its colour from time to time. Below this *Kalishila* there is a village called Kundjethi. There is a temple of *"Chinna masta"* (head Portion) where there is a *Yantra (Instrument)* depicted on a stone slab. There is a *Sivalinga* here too, which emits little smoke when water is poured on it. There is a *Kund* called *Daitya kundi* (place for demons offerings) and a temple called *Kailapuri Jagadamba* (Kailapuri goddess). There are two big stones of 200 ft. hight and 100 ft. width in a village called *Byomkhi*. These are known as *Bhimsen ka chullha* (cooking stove of Bhima). In front of this, there is a *Ranachandika* temple. *Kaliganga* river emerges from here which later merges into the *Saraswati* near *Kalimath*. The place *Kalimath* has been the centre of attraction since ages for knowledge seekers, philosophers and persons in search of salvation. *Chaukhamba, Trisul Kantha, Nanda devi, Nilkantha* and *Kedarnath* peaks are visible from here. At present, this place comes under Rudraprayag district. Between *Ukhimath* and *Guptakashi* this is located in the *Madhmaheswar* valley and the trek to *Madmaheswar* starts from here. Table-I gives the details.

The trek is of five-days duration from *Guptakashi* to *Madhmaheswar* and back. *Kalimath* is connected by road from *Guptakashi* and is the base point for the trekkers to *Madhmaheswar*, which is one amongst the five *Kedars* of the region.

Table I: Approach to Madhmaheswar Trek

From	To	Distance
Guptakashi (1319 m)	Kalimath (1463 m)	17 km Road
Kalimath	Ransi (1765 m)	7 km
Ransi	Gaundhar (3073 m)	6 km
Gaundhar	Madhmaheswar (3490 m)	11 km

Discussions and Interpretation

In the process of data interpretation, Uttaranchal Tourism Statistics and Government records could not be taken into consideration as much of the available information was not factual and authentic. Whatever data have been compiled by the authors were obtained from local hoteliers and villagers. Moreover, the owners of the existing accommodation units, in order to avoid being taxed, tend to give wrong details. Hence, the authors felt that the records of the local temple and perceptions of locals were more reliable in comparison to the government records. Since the policy has to be formulated for the locals, their perception regarding the business viability has been taken into consideration.

In 2003 around 1.8 lakhs domestic visitors visited the destination in four-month tourist season and there were only 1000 international visitors during the same year. However, there were a large number of uncountable daily visitors from nearby villages and towns reaching here round the year. Kalimath has not been considered for pilgrimage tourism promotion and as such there is paucity of suitable hotel accommodation. At present people opt to stay in the newly built lodges or the temple *dharmashala*. The trekkers prefer to stay in the camps that constitutes 20% of the total inflow. remaining 30 per cent visitors return back or proceed further. Table-III projects the details.

Table II: Tourist Arrivals in 2003

Nature	Numbers per year	Season
Domestic	1.8 lakhs	4 months
International	1000	3 months

Source : Data collected from the local people

Table III: Visitors stay

Unit	Per cent share
Hotel	-
Lodge	25
Ecolodge	-
Dharamshala	25
Camp	20

Source : Data collected from the local people

There are five main villages around Kalimath which are sparsely populated at isolated places. However, the education standard is quite high. The local people were quite inclined in tourism seasonal jobs. Since the area comes under Kedarnath Sanctuary, constructions are not allowed. Table-IV gives brief profile of surrounding villages.

Table IV: A Brief Profile of Surrounding Villages

Name of the village	Existing Population	Educated per cent (10th standard)	Are villagers Interested in seasonal jobs	Availability of land	Road Accessi-bility	Bank/ ATM	Water	Drainage
Kundjethi	600	50	Y	N	N	Y	Y	N
Byomkhi	450	60	Y	N	N	Y	Y	N
Kabiltha	800	65	Y	N	N	Y	Y	N
Kalimath	700	75	Y	Y	N	Y	Y	N
Sashugarh	400	65	Y	N	N	Y	Y	N

Source : Data collected from the locals: Y: available N: not available.

Local people consider that personal security and safety, friendly and interesting people, provision of sanitation and culture and history are the prime factors required for promotion of ecotourism. It was analysed that a large number of population was not aware of the conceptual meaning of ecotourism and intermixed its meaning with mass tourism. Despite of this, maximum people feel safety and security to be the prime requirement for further tourism development. Local transport facility, escorting, guiding services and shopping facilities do not exist at all while in other areas it scores good or average. Table-V gives a brief picture.

Table V: Local perception about Ecotourism Promotion

Sl. No.	Quality of Service	Score (Out of 10)
1.	Personal Security and Safety	09
2.	Friendly and Interesting People	09
3.	Comfort	06
4.	Variety of Food	05
5.	Communication System	05
6.	Local Transport Facility	00
7.	Tourist Attractions	05
8.	Culture and History	09
9.	Adventure Activities (river rafting)	04
10.	Wildlife	04
11.	Cleanliness	04
12.	Escorting	00
13.	Guide Services	00
14.	Health Service	06
15.	Sanitation	09
16.	Shopping Experience	00
17.	Accommodation	05
18.	Food & Beverages	05

Score 7- and above stands for excellent, 5-6 stands for good, 3-5 for fair and below 3 stands for poor.

Source : Data collected from locals

Tourists opine the place is primarily important for pilgrimage, snow peaks, dense forest, climate, culture history as well as one of the major transit points for Madhmaheswar. Table-VI undoubtly makes an interpretation to show this as pilgrimage centre. But in view of its natural surroundings and local people intention to involve themselves in tourism profession there are bright chances of promoting ecotourism.

In the name of tourism development only a few eateries and lodges are functioning whereas there is acute shortage of proper infrastructure and it mainly includes hospital, private medical practitioner's, electricity, paying guest houses, post office, bank and also a couple of good restaurants. Table-VII projects brief picture and gives the details of required numbers of employees and business turn over of the supporting infrastructure, pilgrimage and outdoor recreation. Further, the basic amenities are not commercial by nature. The researchers intend to create small-scale entrepreneurship for promoting ecotourism ventures.

Table VI: Resource Interpretation

Existing Tourism Attractions/ Nature of Tourism	Grades		
	A	B	C
Pilgrimage	A		
Complete Sightseeing		B	
Adventure Sports			C
Wildlife			C
Snow Covered Himalayan Mountain Peaks	A		
Dense Forest (Oak, Deodar Forests)	A		
Climate	A		
Local Culture and History	A		
Transit Point	A		
Transportation			C
Any other attraction (Potentiality of a bath pool)	A		

Note : Researchers' own interpretation based on tourist' perception
A = Prime, B = Existing C = Rare

Primarily the existing accommodation units are sufficient to meet the current tourist flow. Further, in view the fragile landforms here new proposal for constructions can be avoided. The excess of the tourists at the end of year 2014 or in between may be accommodated in ecolodges or prefabricated structure. Table VIII projects the details of further requirements.

On an average 10 rooms have been assumed for each hotel in which all rooms are double bedded.

Eateries play significant role in ecotourism promotion and can provide maximum business to local people. As of now a couple of eateries are running at Kalimath but the poor quality of food and beverages do not prove this business beneficial to the involved personnel. However in order to meet the requirement of increased visitors there would be additional need of eateries as table-IX reveals the details.

Table VII: Existing Infrastructure: Facilities and Amenities

Amenities & Facilities	Number of Units	Number of Employees Roll direct/ indirect	Approximate Annual Business Turnover per unit (in Rs.)	Approximate Per Day Turnover per unit	
				Seasonal	Non-seasonal
Eatery	04	Self managed	24000	70%	30%
Hotel	N	-	-	-	-
Restaurant	N	-	-	-	-
Lodge	02	4 x 2	48000	80%	20%
Petrol Pump	N	-	-	-	-
Govt. Hospital	01	12	-	-	-
Private Medical Practitioner	N	-	-	-	-
Electricity	Y	2	-	-	-
Paying Guest House	N	-	-	-	-
Post Office	Kalimath	2	-	-	-
Bank	N	-	-	-	-
Fax	N	-	-	-	-
Telephone STD	N	-	-	-	-
Cooking Gas	N	-	-	-	-
Internet @ Rs.25 an hr.	N	-	-	-	-
Beauty Parlour	N	-	-	-	-
Video Game Parluor	N	-	-	-	-
Tourist Office	N	-	-	-	-
Grocer	02	4	@120,000	60	40
Tourist Guide	N	-	-	-	-
Handicraft Emporium	N	-	-	-	-
Available Handicraft	N	-	-	-	-
Yoga Centre	N	-	-	-	-
Tour Operator	N	-	-	-	-
Tourist Taxi Operator	N	-	-	-	-
Tourist Literature/Books	N	-	-	-	-
Photo Studio	N	-	-	-	-
Coffee Shop	N	-	-	-	-
Fast Food Restaurant	N	-	-	-	-
Chemist	01	-	-	-	-
Camping Site	N	-	-	-	-
Tent Colony	N	-	-	-	-
Bar	N	-	-	-	-
Folk Culture Centre	N	-	-	-	-
Pony and Horse Operator	10	5 Seasonal workers	@75000	60	40
Cycle Safari	N	-	-	-	-

Note : Researchers' own interpretation based on primary survey
Y= Available N= Not available

Table VIII: Accommodation Requirements

Year	Day Visitor			Stay in nearby Hotel @5%	Existing Accommodation (Lodge)			Additional Requirement		
	Total	PDV	Cumulative Stay		No. of Unit	No. of Rooms	No. of Beds	No. of Unit	No. of Rooms	No.of Beds
2004	180000	1200	NIL	60	02	20	80	-	-	-
2005	187200	1248	NIL	62	02	20	80	-	-	-
2006	194688	1297	NIL	65	02	20	80	-	-	-
2007	202475	1350	NIL	67	02	20	80	-	-	-
2008	210574	1403	NIL	70	02	20	80	-	-	-
2009	218997	1460	NIL	73	02	20	80	-	-	-
2010	227757	1518	NIL	76	02	20	80	-	-	-

Note : Growth has been assumed to be 4% over the previous year. Tourist season is of 4 months in which 80% of the total number of visitors visit. So per day visitors (PDV) = Total nos. X 80% X 1/120. All the visitors stay overnight. 5% of the visitors prefeared to stay in ecolodges ecolodges or prefabricated hotels other than paying guesthouses (PGH).

Table IX: Requirement of Eatery

Year	Per Day Visitor	People dine in eateries @50%	Existing Eateries		Additional Requirement of Eateries	
			No.	Capacity	No.	Capacity
2004	1200	600	4	360	3	270
2005	1248	624	7	630	-	-
2006	1297	648	7	630		
2007	1350	675	7	630		
2008	1403	701	7	630	1	90
2009	1460	730	8	720	-	-
2010	1518	759	8	720		

Note : Per Day Visitors = As per table No. 8
As 90% of the visitors visit the place in 3 months i.e. 90 days. The capacity of an eatery = 10 tables X 1 person who can be served in an hour X 9 hrs a day = 90 (It is assumed that an eatery, on average runs its business for 9 hours duration. Most of the business establishments normally shut own their operation after 8 PM).

Kalimath and its environment, if developed as sustainable ecotourism destination, needs all possible amenities and facilities with complete projection by 2010. Table-X makes the projection of such products and services that are not only possible for operation but also liked by ecotourists worldwidely. Such amenities are environment friendly and are capable to involve local people on nominal capital investment in view of growth of tourist arrivals. The project has been made in such a way that the visiting tourists may get complete satisfaction of available products and services.

The basis of proposing above ecotourism facilities is based on authors hypothetical vision. It depends on the funds available for developing these facilities with private participation. Further the expenditures have been estimated with suggestions from the specialists in the area concerned.

Table X: Forecast of other Tourism Plant Facilities

Activities	2005	2006	2007	2008	2009	2010
Yoga and Meditation Centre	-	1	-	-	-	-
Ayurvedic Treatment Centre	2	-	2	-	-	-
Camping Site	1	2	-	2	-	-
Trekking Equipment Operator	3	1	2	1	2	1
Photographer	4	-	4	-	4	3
Pony/Mule Operator	2	3	-	2	3	-
Paying Guest House	2	2	2	2	2	-
Health Tourism Complex	1	-	1	-	1	-
Rural Tour Package Operator	2	-	-	2	-	1
Fax/ PCO / Courier	2	-	1	-	2	-
Handicrafts Emporium	2	-	-	1	-	1
Ecofriendly Restaurant	3	-	-	1	-	-
Tent Colony	1	-	-	2	-	2
View Point	2	-	2	-	1	-
Vegetable Shop	1	-	1	-	1	2
Escorting/Guiding	3	-	3	3	-	1
Private Health Centre	1	-	-	-	-	-
Garbage Treatment Plan	1	-	-	-	-	-
Paid Public Toilet	5	-	-	-	-	-
Provision of Garbage Bin	5	-	-	-	-	
Provision of Sign Board	5	-	-	-	-	
Provision of Maintenance Staff	1	-	-	-	-	-

However, this may vary with the place and time since transportation is a major factor in determining the funds needed for constructions. This may be taken, as a model (may not be with strict adherence) for calculating the funds requirements. A standard rate of 20 per cent may be given to the beneficiaries as subsidy.

A detail estimation has been proposed for developing the above facilities. The estimation of cost is based on the prevailing cost of construction in district Chamoli whereas financial requirement for other products and services are projected after making consultation with existing operators running such nature of businesses in the higher altitude of Garhwal Himalaya. Table-XI gives the details of total financial requirement.

Table XI: Total Financial Requirement for the period 2004-2010

Units	Total Units/ Numbers	Allocation for each unit (Rs. in lakh)	Total Budget (Rs. in lakh)	Possible Subsidy @ 20% (in Rs.)
Yoga and Meditation Centre	01	2.00	2.00	0.20
Ayurvedic Treatment Centre	04	3.00	12.00	2.40
Camping Site	05	2.00	10.00	2.00
Trekking Equipment Operator	10	1.00	10.00	2.00
Photographer	15	0.20	3.00	0.60
Pony/Mule Operator	10	0.50	5.00	1.00
Paying Guest House	10	1.00	10.00	2.00
Health Tourism Complex	03	3.00	9.00	1.80
Rural Tour Package Operator	05	2.00	10.00	2.00
Fax/ PCO / Courier	05	0.50	2.50	0.50
Handicrafts Emporium	04	2.00	0.50	0.10
Ecofriendly Restaurant	04	1.00	4.00	0.80
Tent Colony	05	3.00	15.00	3.00
View Point	05	0.50	2.50	0.50
Vegetable Shop	05	0.20	1.00	0.20
Escorting/Guiding	10	0.20	2.00	0.40
Private Health Centre/ Clinic	01	1.00	1.00	0.20
Garbage Treatment Plant	01	1.00	1.00	0.20
Paid Public Toilet	05	0.50	2.50	0.50
Provision of Garbage Bin	05	0.10	0.50	0.10
Provision of Sign Boards	05	0.10	0.50	0.10
Provision of Maintenance Staff	01	0.15	0.15	0.03
Total funds outlay			104.15	20.83

Conclusion

The current research paper is a sincere effort by the researchers to identify the tourists' perception and developing facilities in and around Kalimath. The proposed facilities have been earmarked in such a way that the local people of surrounding villages like Kundjethi, Byomkhi, Kabitha Sashugarh and Kalimath may involve themselves in the proposed amenities. The local people however and need know how as well extensive training of operating identified ecotourism plant facilities. The training may be arranged by local NGOs at such locations where tourists prefer to enjoy ecotourism products and services. The villagers not only require knowledge of tourist perception but also they are expected to make themselves skilled in product business management and business skills. There are a number of village entrepreneurs involved in ecotourism business in Anapurna area of Nepal, Sikkim and Western Ghat in India and a field tour of local people may be arranged to make them aware in ecotourism business management in these locations. The dearth of financial assistance is another hindrance depriving a large number of enthusiastic young personnel since long. To avoid such expected difficulty the state govt. should persuade bankers to grant financial assistance on easy terms and condition. State Bank of India has introduced Travel Plus Scheme under which financial assistance of Rs. 2 lakh is admissible for tourism and travel related business. Planning and promotion of ecotourism is figuring in official papers of Uttaranchal tourism but how to involve the local people and in what way the local people be generated financial assistance has hardly been incorporated in the State Tourism Policy 2002. Tourism is an amalgam of many components and its promotion is jointly managed by many segments of public and private sectors; be it transport, hydel, telecom, health or forestry. There is wide variation in the nature of nodel agency looking after the tourism affairs. It is a sad paradox that ecotourism is the subject matter of Ministry of Rural Development and Forest and Environment whereas it is the entire responsibility of Ministry of Tourism. In view of this Uttaranchal State Govt. should persuade Department of Forest and Environment to promote ecotourism in the higher reaches of the Himalaya or in and around the national parks and sanctuaries. But much of the flora and fauna treasure house of the state exist in remote and far away locations werein it is ardous to transport potential buyers of ecotourism products.

Kalimath is a sacred haunt of pilgrimage tourism but its surrounding places are full of natural attractions and activities. This place needs to be promoted in such a way that it may pave way for economic benefits to local people receiving pilgrimage since long but seldom find any gain from visiting tourists. The findings of the present research paper can be of significance for the local people if the projected amenities are implemented on phase wise basis.

Acknowledgement

Authors would like to acknowledge ICSSR for funding the major research project on "Ecotourism Planning in Kedarnath Musk Deer Sanctuary". The current paper is a part of the project carried out by the authors. In addition, the support and participation of the service providers, Tourists and locals of the Kalimath are acknowledged with obligation.

References

Bagri S.C. (2003). "Trends in Tourism Promotion: - Emerging Issues", BSMPS Publishers, Dehradun, pp. 303-330.

Bagri S.C. (2004). "Ecotourism Planning in Uttaranchal Circuit" project submitted to Agricultural Finance Corporation, Mumbai.

Sustainable Tourism Planning and Development, 95-100, 2006
Edited by Bagri, S.C.
Published by Bishen Singh Mahendra Pal Singh, Dehra Dun, India

The Changing Trends of Pilgrimage Tourism in India

Ravi Bhushan Kumar

Reader
Department of Tourism, Kurukshetra University
Kurukshetra - Haryana

Abstract : India is a land of diverse faiths and beliefs. A number of shrines have been established across the country for offering prayers and performing rituals through ages and such practices are still dominant in society. But with the availability of fresh moving transportation system and affordable products and services, the concept of pilgrimage has changed immensely.

Key Words: Pilgrimage, India, tirtha, tourist, accommodation.

India is country of vast cultural diversity with a number of sects and faiths. Each faith is followed by millions of persons and they visit a number of sacred haunts round the year. The largest segment of domestic tourism market is pilgrimage tourism, where without any publicity unprecedent number of visitors gather at a given location for solace and salvation. Earlier, the routes of pilgrimage were ardous and unknown, and were not well-defined. The means of transportation were very poor and undeveloped. Accommodation, food, etc. were not easily available. The journey was infested with dense forests, mountains, wild animals and robbers. So it was very difficult to visit and even return home. In such adverse situations only old persons, who had completed all worldly duties, could think of pilgrimage. But today all means of transportation are well-developed. Routes are well defined. Several travel agencies, tour operators or bus operators are offering the whole package of journey. Accommodation and food are easily available. So the journey has become easy and pilgrimage can now be undertaken by process of all age groups.

In this changing scenario, there has also been changes in values of pilgrimage and spiritual aspects. The modern age pilgrims emphasize on luxuries, comforts and entertainment rather than on hardships. Pilgrims are not going to wash the sins of their life and improve the next life but are inclined to opt for physical gains in the life. The importance of pilgrimage has changed. Some have emerged to be very popular and several notable practices have lost their importance and values.

India is a holy place where gods, goddesses, *gurus*, *seers*, *pirs* and *saints* have appeared. There are still so many living religious leaders, *gurus* who have a large number of followers and devotees within and outside India. It appears that Indians are very devotional in nature. They are god-fearing. Hinduism is a way of life. It is not like other religions which are based on a single religious book. In Hinduism every one is free to accept any way of world's philosophy and a person has liberty to follow any faith and is free to analyse the religious book by his own theory and method. According to Hindu philosophy man is an exposition of '*atma*', (soul or spirit). The body and mind are the means equipments to facilitate the meeting of soul with the great soul or God (*Paramatma*). In Hinduism, spirituality covers religiosity, philosophy, moral and ethical values, ideals, yoga, meditation and *ayurveda*. So Hinduism is not based on a particular religious book, but it is a way of life which reflects in every person's day to day activities. It is believed that a number of gods, goddesses, saints etc. have played to pivotal role at a number of sacred places. Wherever they lived, acted and performed '*leela*' (performances), the place is considered sacred place or '*Tirtha*' (pilgrim place).

Some *tirthas* are very old, which are mentioned in holy books such as the *Ramayana*, the *Mahabharta*, *Puranas*, etc. Some were established/set up or associated with some known religious saints and reformers, e.g. Adi Guru Shankaracharya, Guru Nanak, Chaitanya Mahaprabhu, Saint Thiruvalluvar, Ramanujacharya, Sai Baba, etc. Some *tirthas* are related to some holy events such as birth/death anniversary of some saint or solar or lunar eclipses, *Kumbh mela*, etc. Some are located on natural setup, e.g. Amarnath, Gangotri, Yamunotri, Badrinath and Kedarnath and some are located in densely populated cities like Varanasi] Ujjain, Puri, Dwarika and Mathura. So, there can be several criteria for classification of pilgrimages. Whatever may be the class and criteria but there is no doubt that millions of devotees gather in such places without any publicity or media blitz. In the year 2000, during Kumbh mela around 7.2 crore people took the holy dip at Allahabad. This was the largest gathering on earth at any particular place. One can just imagine the quantity of food, water, transportation, accommodation and other services needed to feed such a large gathering. About fifty lakh pilgrims visit Vaishno Devi in

Jammu and about one crore devotees visit Tirupati every year. The number of pilgrims to Amarnath, Mansarovar, Shabrimala, Ganga Sagar, etc. are increasing year by year despite adverse weather conditions and poor services. Almost all places, villages, rivers, mountains and forests claim to be holy places, which are directly or indirectly related with some gods, goddesses or saints. Such sacred places are supposed to have some super natural power's, which can do miracles. They are worshipped by locals. Some holy places transcend the boundary of villages, caste and ethnic groups. They become popular *tirthas*. Unlike other tourist destinations, Indian *tirthas* became very popular.

It also appears that religiosity is increasing everywhere and every year. The number of visitors to temples and *tirthas* is increasing day by day. Thousands of *Kanwarias* are carrying water from the holy Ganga (or any river/lakes) to temple of Shiva, especially from Sultanganj to Deoghar in Jharkand, and from Haridwar to different places in the north. There are several other reasons for popularity of a pilgrim center and in includes temple architecture (eg. most of south Indian temples), location (Himalayan, coastal, hill station such as Vaishno Devi, Haridwar, Mt. Abu, Puri-Konark, Rameshwaram, Kanyakumari), and celebration of fairs and festivals (Kullu, Mysore, Allahabad, Ujjain, Varanasi). In almost all *tirthas* there are poor means of transportation facilities, and accommodation in Amarnath and Mansarovar, pilgrims face severe cold, snowfall, slippery trails, and landslides whereas in Shabrimala and Ganga Sagar, mass tourist arrival causes a large number of accidents. Inspite of such ardous conditions pilgrimage tourism is the largest segment among all the types of tourism and is increasing day by day.

Today, the whole scenario has changed. These changes are in the field of social, political and technological arena. Education, literacy, electronic and print media have increased awareness among the people about the outer world. The means of transportation has revolutionized the time of journey. There is a common acceptable currency. The language barrier is low. The income of people has increased. The facility of hotels, food, transportation, travel agencies is available almost everywhere. As a whole, the magnitude of journey has increased several folds. The growth rate of domestic tourists is very high. The *Hindu* philosophy believes in the cycle of birth after death and according to this philosophy, a person gets rebirth according to his performance or *karma*. The birth of man is best, because he can rectify his past *karma* and he can make his life better. There ultimate goal is *'moksha'*, that is going beyond the cycle of birth, ultimate achievement of god or the supreme soul. The average human age is considered as 100 years which is divided into four *'ashrams'*. In the first 25 years a person remains bachelor, gains knowledge as he prepares for practical life. In the next 25 years he leads a family life, which is the hub of society. In this period he gets married, gets children, earns money. In the later phases he gradually detaches himself from worldly desires and pleasures and devotes himself to god. The last two phases are most important for pilgrimage. After completing his worldly duties, such as marriage and settlement of children, a person starts to move for his next birth. It is said that there was a ritual of *Kaashivaas* (settlement in Kashi) in which old persons spent their last days at Kashi which is belived to be located on the trident of Lord Shiva. It is one of the holiest place where if a person dies certainly attains *moksha* (Salvation). So the main motivation of pilgrimage was to attain salvation. As mentioned earlier, the journey was very difficult in earlier days, especially for aged persons. It was almost impossible to return to their original place. So a person had to perform all rituals before planning for a long pilgrimage.

Today's pilgrimage is not so difficult. Modern Pilgrims uses modern shoes, packed with warm clothes, keeps food of all variety and taste, medicine and stays in tent or good accommodation. It is not like old age when pilgrimage was undertaken on bare foot (whether to Badrinath, Kedarnath or anywhere else), unsuitable clothes (dhoti or saree), with no prior provision of food, water and medicine. Today a pilgrim is young or middle aged person and often without completing his worldly desires and duties. So the concept has changed. The change can be observed not only in mode of journey but also in the method of journey. Earlier most pilgrims were moving on bare foot as it was considered disgraceful to walk on the earth with shoes. When Dr. Rajendra Prasad, the first president of India, visited Kurukshetra to inaugurate the Kurukshetra University, he put off his shoes at the railway station because the whole Kurukshetra, according to him, was a holy place. Earlier people, were using simple, pure, vegetarian, self-made food, staying with *pandas* or at *dharmasala* or under open sky. Today they are travelling in modern comfortable luxury vehicles, staying in modern luxurious hotels and eating all types of foods. The pilgrimage is not totally a sacred journey, but it also includes entertainment. The entertainment factor has added value to those pilgrim centres which are located in beautiful locations. Now the pilgrim centres located in the Himalayas or at coastal regions, forests, etc. are more popular than others and allure visitors from all walks of life.

The services in pilgrim centres are also now different. Earlier in the traditional *Panda* system the local *Pandas* were designated priests. They were performing *pooja* and *Yajnas*, providing food and accommodation and acting as guide. Now luxurious accommodation are constructed everywhere from Vaishno Mata to Rameshwarm. At several places necessary provision of ticket system for *darshan* of deities have been made. The importance of *panda* system is diluted. Due to changing values, now people do not give importance to austerity or religious performance. The materialistic and selfish approach is visible everywhere. In several temples there are different types of *darshans* - from simple to expensive and special *darshans*. So today pilgrimage tourism is not only a religious performance but a commercial business too.

Conclusion

Pilgrimage tourism is the base of India's domestic tourism. According to the Annual Report of Department of Tourism, Govt. of India (2003), there were 275 million domestic tourists in India in 2003 alone and their number is expected to increase further in the near future. Out of the total domestic tourist 75% tourists go for pilgrimage tourism and their journey is determined not by prevailing facilities and amenities but by the internal faiths and beliefs. Apart from Badrinath, Kedarnath, Gangotri, Yamunotri, Amarnath, Mansarovar, India's fiftyone *Sakti Pithas* (abode of Durga) attract lakhs of pilgrims round the year for *puja* and *darshan*.

The religious places do not enjoy enough amenities. However, faith and belief are such strong motivating elements that sizeable share of visitors visit these places of cultural values of benign past. Incidentally, it is noticed that the upcoming generation is changing its visiting perception and has become more inclined towards facilities and quality of services. In view of this, local entrepreneurs have redesigned their products and services as per visitors preferences and expectations. Kedarnath, Vaishnodevi, Tirupati have been connected by air services. Haridwar, Ujjain, Allahabad, Nasik, Varanasi enjoy star hotel units. The *puja* is now being conducted under parameters of business skills. In Badrinath alone there are five types of *puja* being extended to customers depending upon money and time factors. The affluent pilgrims can be offered elite puja package. However, the puja product is free of cost for budget pilgrims and its takes upto 2 hrs to 1 day waiting time. India's population is getting the feeling of pilgrimage on a wider-scale. The per capita income is increasing and every third person of India's urban area can afford a computer now. In view of this, there is wide scope for pilgrimage tourism not only for visitors but also for the people involved with this business. Most of the pilgrimage tourism markets exist in urban areas whereas a large number of attractions of pilgrimage interest are in rural areas. The main problem of rural areas is to provide jobs to people. Therefore, pilgrimage tourism if promoted in India can not only solve the problem of unemployment but will also be helpful to satisfy visitors of urban area as well as make the people of rural India self reliant.

References

Ahmad, E. (1978). *Social and Geographical Aspects of Human Settlements*, Classical Publication, New Delhi.

Allchin, F. R. (1969). *Cultural Tourism in India: Its Scope and Development*, Department of Tourism, Government of India, New Delhi.

Banerjee, Anukul Chandra (1973). *Buddhism in India and Abroad*, The World Press (P) Ltd., Calcutta.

Bagri, S.C. (1992). *Buddhist Pilgrimages and Tours in India.* Trishul Publication, Nodia.

Brown, Percy (1976). *Indian Architecture* (Buddhist and Hindu Periods), Bombay.

Cunningham, A.R. (1924). *Ancient Geography of India*, Calcutta.

Diwakar, R.R. (1980). *Bhagawan Buddha*, Bharatiya Vidya Bhawan, Bombay.

Fielden, Bernard M. (1982). *Conservation of Historic Buildings*, Butterorth & Co, London.

Gupta, S.P. and Lal Krishna (1974). *Tourism, Museums and Monuments of India*, Oriental Publishers, Delhi.

Singh, R.L. (ed.) (1971). *India*, National Geographical Society of India, Varanasi.

Singh, T.V. (1975). *Tourism and Tourist Industry in Uttar Pradesh*, New Heights, Delhi.

Sustainable Tourism Planning and Development, 101-116, 2006
Edited by Bagri, S.C.
Published by Bishen Singh Mahendra Pal Singh, Dehra Dun, India

Tourism in Kumaon Himalaya:
A Study of Tourist Traffic and Visitors Profile of Nainital and Almora

Anjana Sharma

Department of Management (Tourism)
Maharaja Surajmal Institute of Management & Technology,
Indraprastha University, C-4 Janakpuri, New Delhi

Abstract : The Tourism profile of Kumaon Himalaya reveals that a large number of tourists visit Nainital and Almora during summer season and helps the local economy to a large extent. A number of books and articles have been written on Kumaon Tourism Resources but much of them are devoted only on scenic attractions. There is hardly any authentic document published and prepared by any organization that may be consulted to know the tourist trends and their life style patterns. Extensive information on visitors trends and pattern may be useful for integrated planning and promotion.

Key Words : Tourism, Kumaon, Nainital, Almora, traffic, profile.

A Brief Scenario

Kumaon Himalaya is known for its diverse attractions including wide ranges of snow-capped mountain peaks to well known hill stations and National Parks. It attracts quite a large number of tourists from far and wide. There are so many beautiful hill regions in India but very few of them can be compared with Kumaun Himalaya famous for lush green land and landscape. Shimla, Mussoorie, Darjeeling and Ooty become by and large noisy in summer and are no longer an ideal places where people can be with nature. Nainital in Kumaon is not very different but there are many beautiful places nearby where people could enjoy the beauty of nature. Kumaon is a wide, gently sloped valley that comprises of a large number of attractive destinations.

The term Kumaon has its origin from the word '*Kamdeo or Kurma*'. According to mythology, Lord Vishnu in his tortoise incarnation is said to have dwelt for three years on Kamdeo, a peak in *Patti* Charal to the east of Champawat district or *Kurmanchal. Kurma* means tortoise and *Achal* means mountain. The region is also known as Kedarkhand or Uttarakhand in Puranic literature. Situated between latitude 28⁰44' and 30⁰49' N and 78⁰45' and 81⁰10' E Kumaun region is spread over 21035 sq km area. The altitudinal range varies from 204 mt to 7436 mt above sea level. Kumaon can be visited throughout the year. In fact, the crowded summer months are perhaps the worst time. The monsoon period is not too good but the rain tends to clear after a few hours. The best times are spring and autumn when the air is clear and the mountains look most beautiful. In winter, the air is crisp and clean and it is surprisingly warm in the bright sunshine while a blazing fire dispels the cold of the evenings. This beautiful region offers something for everyone. Serious trekkers can find a huge variety of low and high altitude treks to the Pindari glacier, Munsiari and other places. The less sporty can find many excellent treks and walks as well as great opportunities for bird watching, photography and fishing in the sparkling Kosi, Kali, Saryu or Sarda rivers that now also offer river rafting. And golfers can also have a great time. Lovers of history and religion can visit many exquisite temples including Jageshwar, Bageshwar, Baijnath and Pithoragarh, dating from the 8th to 14th centuries-AD. Jageshwar, an hour's drive from Almora, has some 100 exquisite temples in a deep *deodar* forest and has one of the 12 *Jyotilingas,* where Lord Shiva is believed to have emerged in his original form to another world. There are many interesting shrines of popular deities throughout Kumaon.

Nainital, at an altitude of 1950 metre, with its exquisite deep blue lake, is the social capital of the region. The passing view of honeymooners, holiday-makers and sociolizers at the boat-house club is one of general revelry. There is facility of horse riding, sailing and boating at Nainital for those who are fond of soft adventure and want to see mountain views from China top or Kilbury. A visitor can move easily from the pretty lake resorts of Nainital, Bhimtal, Sat-tal, Naukuchiatal to acquaint colonial towns like Almora and Ranikhet or go to Ramgarh or Mukteshwar, at over 2250 m, for spectacular mountain views. Kasauni or Binsar offer even better views of the spectacular snow-clad Himalayan peaks like Trishul and Nandadevi soaring to 7500 metre. As they are connected by excellent roads, it is especially appealing to motorists who can enjoy a wonderful driving from the pretty lakes to some of India's most spectacular mountain views in just an hour or two. Except at peak summer, good accommodation is available in a large number of small and big hotels, resorts and guest-houses. The *Kumaon Mandal Vikas Nigam* also has a chain of adequate small hotels at most of the tourist spots. Tourists can get accommodation in Government rest houses or forest rest houses on reasonable rates.

Many veteran travellers do not bother to book in advance as they can usually find good places to stay without too much trouble. Consumerism has also made available medicines, cosmetics, toiletries, chips, colas, biscuits, noodles even at the most remote little towns. Getting around Kumaon from Delhi takes about 6 hours by road via Moradabad, Rampur and Rudrapur and is an hour drive by road from the railhead of Kathgodam. There is a daily Ranikhet Express from Delhi and a Shatabdi train ply on Sundays in summer. Kumaon can be visited throughout the year.

During the last ten years tourist arrivals in Kumaon has been increasing but there is no uniformity in the growth rate. Table-I shows the tourist traffic in Uttaranchal and Kumaon, and percentage share of Kumaon in Uttaranchal tourist traffic.

Table I: Tourist Traffic in Uttaranchal and Kumaon

Year	Tourist Traffic in Uttaranchal (in lakhs)			Tourist Traffic in Kumaon	% share of Kumaon
	Indian	Foreigner	Total		
1995	139.83	0.41	140.24	42.73	30.47
1996	160.53	0.47	161.00	51.49	31.84
1997	181.40	0.52	181.92	59.01	32.44
1998	192.47	0.56	193.03	63.37	38.83
1999	193.60	0.64	194.24	72.64	37.39

Source: Uttaranchal Tourism, Dehradun.

Among all the tourist centres of Kumaon, Nainital is presently the most popular tourist destination both for domestic and foreign tourists because of its being a key recreational destination of national and international importance and easy accessibility. The other locations, especially Almora, Ranikhet, Kausani, Corbett National Park have less appeal comparatively to Nainital and are attracting about less than one lakh domestic tourists annually. Tough comprehensive data of foreign tourists was not available, overall inflow is almost negligible

and limited to 1000-2000 in numbers except Nainital town and
Corbett National Park. It is clear from Table-II that Nainital town
received maximum number of tourists in the years 2000 and 2001.

Table II: Tourist Traffic at Major Tourist Centers in Kumaun Region in
2000 and 2001.

Name of the Place	2000			2001		
	Indian	Foreigner	Total	Indian	Foreigner	Total
Nainital	250947	7589	258536	356941	5793	362734
Almora	64989	3633	68622	67108	1664	68872
Ranikhet	62487	342	62829	65747	663	66410
Kausani	67460	722	68182	66577	733	66310
Pithoragarh	63929	504	64433	70805	444	71249
Champawat	33820	91	33911	33171	90	33261
Kathgodam	40642	266	40908	42899	251	43150
Corbett National Park	57877	3624	61501	57113	3775	60888
Udham Singh Nagar	61673	86	61759	62203	207	62410
Total	70382414	16857	720681	822564	13620	836140

Source : Uttaranchal Tourism, Dehradun.

While there has been increasing trend of growth in tourist arrivals at
Nainital and Ranikhet, Almora saw some fluctuation due to less
development facilities. Ranikhet received more tourists than Almora
because of being a military sanatorium. It is more developed than Almora.

Table-III gives details of the annual Tourist Traffic from 1995 to 2001
at Nainital, Almora, and Ranikhet.

Tourists Traffic in Corbett Tiger Reserve

Considering the pace of growth in the tourist traffic in the Tiger
Reserve over last three decades, it is evident that the inbound tourist
profile to some extent is encouraging. In 1965-66 the park visitation was
merely 3,900 of which 3,343 were Indians and 553 were overseas visitors.
The number of visitors increased to 18,092 in the year 1982-83, out of
which 1,057 were foreigners. This figure went up to 49,942 in the year
1996-97. However, year-wise break down of tourist traffic from 1990-
91 to 1998-1999 is indicated in Table-IV below:

Table III: Tourist Traffic (from 1995 to 2001)

Name of the place	Year	Indian	Foreigner	Total
Nainital	1995	188381	1514	189895
	1996	187424	3163	190587
	1997	224406	4421	228827
	1998	214051	4045	218096
	1999	211011	3579	214590
	2000	250947	7589	258536
	2001	356941	5793	362734
Almora	1995	64877	949	65826
	1996	59940	1138	61078
	1997	60728	1281	61009
	1998	52452	857	53309
	1999	54907	1554	56461
	2000	64989	633	65622
	2001	65747	663	66410
Ranikhet	1995	57745	747	58492
	1996	60843	859	61702
	1997	61312	955	62267
	1998	71040	857	71897
	1999	54252	776	55028
	2000	62487	342	62829
	2001	66577	733	67210

Source : Uttaranchal Tourism, Dehradun.

Table IV: Tourist Traffic in Corbett Tiger Reserve

Year	Indian Tourists	Foreign Tourists	Total
1990-1991	36161	2917	39,078
1991-1992	30277	2770	33,047
1992-1993	28480	3483	31,963
1993-1994	37265	6199	43,464
1994-1995	37459	4771	42,230
1995-1996	41283	5415	46,698
1996-1997	45019	4923	49,942
1997-1998	52514	2215	54,729
1998-1999	66718	2513	69,231

Tourism in Kumaon Himalaya is expected to grow in the coming years. However, it depends on economic growth and proportional disposable income of people. Focus on promotion of adventure tourism on National and international level will provide additional impetus to several locations in the circuit which have high worth for adventure tourism. The share of foreign tourist arrivals which is very low in this region, may rise in the coming years. Therefore, there is need to regulate and develop year round tourism as far as possible. The tourism development process must be applied to other lesser known destinations of Kumaon also where suitable facilities have been made available. This may help to increase tourist traffic to Kumaon region.

Visitors Profile

Tourist information regarding their origin, purpose of visit, age-sex structure, length of stay, mode of transport and accommodation used, etc. are some of the main factors to determine the standard of tourist traffic and their behavioural characteristics. These characteristics are the determinants of tourism development that play a significant and crucial role in further planning and promotion. Measuring tourist is difficult and rather complex as it needs competent researchers and involves various research methods. To understand general characteristics of tourist arrivals, a detailed field survey was conducted at Nainital and Almora towns. Several information with specific purposes were acquired through questionnaires filled up by surveyed tourists. Some 150 tourists were interviewed at Nainital and Almora. On the basis of visitors analysis some salient characteristics of tourist behaviour are summarized below:

Origin of Tourist

The survey reveals that 89 per cent tourists come to Kumaon from urban areas, and the rest from rural areas. If we distinguish tourist flow state wise, it is noticed that maximum tourists come from Delhi, West Bengal, Uttar Pradesh, Maharashtra, etc. Tourists from West Bengal generally come to Almora and Nainital in winters during the months of October and November specially on the occasion of *Durga Pooja*. Locally this season is often termed to be the *Season of Bengali Tourists*. Due to climatic preferences autumn season attracts maximum foreign tourists from USA, Germany, England, Australia, France, etc.

Demography

Demographic details of tourists is an essential aspect through which accommodation preferences, food habits, and recreational interests, age-sex ratio can be identified. For example young children always requires milk supply, parks, play grounds, etc. Adults need more recreational opportunities, and sporting facilities etc. while old persons need avenues for peace, rest and relaxation. To know the age-sex structure of tourist, a field survey was conducted at Nainital and Almora and the result of the survey is depicted in Table V below.

Table V: Kumaon Himalaya: Visitor's Demographic Structure

Place	Age structure	%	Male	%	Female	%
Nainital	Below 30	36.25	16	55.2	13	44.8
	30-50	48.75	23	58.97	16	41.02
	Above 50	15.00	08	66.66	04	33.33
	Total	100.00	47	58.75	33	41.25
Almora	Below 30	20.00	09	64.28	05	35.72
	30-50	42.85	17	56.66	13	43.34
	Above 50	37.15	15	57.69	11	42.31
	Total	100.00	41	58.59	29	41.42

Source : Personal survey.

Since Nainital is a recreational place, most tourists come here for recreation and holidays. Comprises of young and middle-aged persons. It is obvious from the above Table that 48.75% tourists were in the age-group of 30-50 years. Tourists below 30 years were represented by 36.25% share. Only 15% tourists were above 50 years and they had come alongwith their family members to rejuvenate their health and to have a *darshan* of Naina Devi also. On the basis of sex wise distribution of tourists it is noticed that majority of tourist were male accounting to 58.25% share of the total tourists in which female tourists had the share of only 41.25%. As regards Almora, it was found that the middle aged persons between the age group of 30-50 years were in dominant position and 43% tourists belonged to this age group. Tourists below 30 years of age mostly come with their parents and their share was only 20%. As Almora is very popular for its well known temples - Nanda Devi, Surya Temple, Kasar Devi Temple, Jageswar and many others most of the tourists prefer to visit Almora for religious purpose and account 38% of total tourists.

Purpose of visit

It is not very easy to assess the purpose of visit of tourist arrivals because most of the respondents had more than a single purpose. In the present survey it was noticed that there were five categories of visitors as per their preferences which reflects the tourist behavioural pattern.

Since Nainital is very popular for its majestic natural beauty and bracing climate, enjoying natural beauty and rest and recreation are the most prominent purposes for visit. Approximately 37.5% and 32.5% tourist visit Nainital for natural beauty and rest and recreation, respectively. The percentage of tourists coming to Nainital for religious or business oriented activities is very low and represents only 11.25% or 3.75%, respectively. Only the young generation seems interested in adventurous persuits and 15 per cent tourists come under this category.

Almora is famous not only for its natural beauty but also for its temples. The temples which are worth visiting for their sacredness and holy past are Jageshwar, Chitai temple, Gananath temple, Kasar Devi temple, Vrinda Devi temple and the most popular Nanda Devi temple. Almora can offer a lot to those who wish to travel this region for the purpose of pilgrimage. So the purpose of visit to Almora does not need much explanation. It is clear from Table-VI that large number of tourists come to Almora for recreation, fun and pilgrimage. In comparison to Nainital the number of tourists were much more for religious purpose in Almora and registered the share of 31%. The people who visited Almora for natural beauty secured the share of 40% and about 22% people visited Almora for rest and recreation. Very few people visited Almora for business purpose and secured the share of only 7.31%. It is worth mentioning here that Almora is known for copper ware and its utensils are famous worldwide.

Duration of Stay

Length of stay is an important measurement for the tourism industry. Earnings from tourism are primarily dependent upon the total nights of the tourists stay and secondly on the number of tourist arrivals. The average duration of stay is closely related to the cost of accommodation. During visitors survey when people were asked about the duration of their stay at Nainital, most of the visitors said that they would like to stay over here just for two to four days to enjoy the beauty of Naina lake and to go around several beautiful places of Nainital. As regards Almora the duration of stay was only for two to three days.

Table VI: Purpose of Tourist Visit

S.No.	Place	Purpose	Percentage
1.	Nainital	Natural beauty	37.50
		Adventure Activity	15.00
		Rest and Recreation	32.50
		Religion	11.25
		Bussiness /others	03.75
		Total	100.00
2.	Almora	Natural Beauty	40.00
		Adventure Activity	00.00
		Rest and Recreation	22.00
		Religion	31.00
		Bussiness /others	07.00
		Total	100.00

Tourist Typology

The tourist trend during 2000-2001 of Kumaon reveals an appreciable percentage of tourists belong to high income group. Tourist according to their monthly income have been categorized into four groups, i.e. middle income group (below Rs.10,000), high income group (Rs. 10,000 to 20,000), higher income group (Rs. 20,000 to 50,000) and highest income group (above Rs. 50,000).

The majority of tourists who visited Nainital during 2000-2001 were Government employees. Therefore most of them belong to high income group (Rs.10,000 to 20,000) and their share was 57.5%, whereas people who belonged to higher income group (Rs.20,000 to 50,000) and highest income group (above Rs.50,000) shared only 15%, and 5% respectively. About 22.5% people belonged to middle income group (below Rs.10,000). During the survey of Almora majority of tourists who visited Almora belong to high income group and accounted the share of 52% followed by middle income group (29%), higher income group (15%) and highest income group (0.5%).

Table VII: Tourist Typology

S. No.	Place	Income group	Percentage
1.	Nainital	Middle income group (below Rs.10,000)	22.50
		High income group (Rs.10,000 to 20,000)	57.50
		Higher income group (Rs.20,000 to 50,000)	15.00
		Highest income group (above Rs.50,000)	05.00
		Total	100.00
2.	Almora	Middle income group (below Rs.10,000)	28.57
		High income group (Rs.10,000 to 20,000)	51.42
		Higher income group (Rs.20,000 to 50,000)	15.01
		Highest income group (above Rs.50,000)	5.75
		Total	100

As regards to profession-wise distribution of tourists in Nainital, about 43.75% of the total tourists were government employees and 25% were involved in business. The share of persons who were engaged in agricultural pursuits and studies were 3.30% and 12.5%, respectively and the rest 15%, tourist were involved in other professions such as lawyers, engineers, doctors, executives, etc. In Almora government employees registered 54.28% share of the total tourists followed by students (21.42%), businessmen (10%), and others (14.30%). The details are projected in Table-VIII.

Table VIII: Distribution of Tourist on the basis of Profession

S.No.	Place	Profession	Percentage
1.	Nainital	Government Service	43.75
		Business	25.00
		Agriculture	3.75
		Studying	12.50
		Others	15.00
		Total	100.00
2.	Almora	Government Service	54.28
		Business	10.00
		Agriculture	3.30
		Studying	21.42
		Others	11.00
		Total	100.00

Repeat Visits

When asked about their previous visits to Nainital Town about 61.25% tourists replied in the negative, while 33.75% said that it was their second visit. Some 5.25% tourists replied that they had visited this town three times and have a desire again in next year due to its divine natural beauty surmounted by beautiful lake. About their frequency of travel to Almora, about 65% tourists were first timers. Almost 23% tourists were on their second trip while approximately 13% tourists confessed that they had already visited Almora three to four times earlier. Some tourists expressed their eagerness to visit this town again as they were deeply impressed on seeing its uncothed beauty and calm prevailing around.

Table IX: Distribution of Tourist on the basis of Previous Experience

Sl. No.	Place	Frequency of Travel	No. of Tourist	Percentage
1.	Nainital	For the first time	49	61.25
		Twice	27	33.75
		Thrice and more	04	5.00
		Total	80	100.00
2.	Almora	For the first time	45	64.30
		Twice	16	22.85
		Thrice and more	09	12.85
		Total	70	100.00

Accommodation Preferences

During the entire survey it was noticed that majority of tourists preferred to stay in unclassified hotels. In Nainital the percentage of visitors staying in unclassified hotels were 47.5%. Approximately 32.5% tourists liked to stay in Tourist Bungalows, Tourist Rest Houses, Tourist Lodges, Forest Rest Houses, etc. because of their less tariff. About 13.75% upper class tourists stayed in classified hotels (star category) with western comforts and facilities and only 6.25% tourists liked to stay in budget and supplementary accommodation such as *dharamshalas*. As regards distribution of tourists on the basis of accommodation at Almora it was noticed that most tourists preferred to stay in hotel. Approximately 43%

tourists stayed in such hotels at Almora. The next choice of tourists at Almora was Tourist Rest Houses, Tourist Bungalows, Tourist Lodges, and it share was 35%. About 10% tourists stayed in resorts and classified hotels and some 12.87% tourist stayed at other cheap accommodation units. Table-X shows the distribution of tourists on the basis of accommodation preferences at Almora and Nainital.

Table X: Distribution of Tourists on the basis of Accommodation facility Used.

Place	Category of Accommodation	Percentage
Nainital	Classified Hotel (Star Category)	13.75
	Hotel	47.50
	Tourist Lodge/Tourist Rest House/Tourist Bungalow	32.50
	Others	6.25
	Total	100.00
Almora	Classified Hotel (Star Category)	12.87
	Hotel	42.28
	Tourist Lodge/Tourist Rest House/Tourist Bungalow	34.28
	Others	10.00
	Total	100.00s

Mode of Travel

The following Table-XI indicates the mode of travel of visitors who stayed in Nainital and Almora.

Table XI: Visitors Travel Preference

Name of the place	Mode of travel	Percentage
Nainital	Bus	56.25
	Rental car	23.75
	Own vehicle	20.00
	Total	100.00
Almora	Bus	55.80
	Rental car	28.20
	Own vehicle	14.00
	Total	100.00

In view of the above, it can be concluded that the mode of travel used by tourists to reach Nainital and Almora was almost the same. Most of the tourists reached Haldwani/ Kathgodam/ Ramnagar by trains and they used bus, rental cars and other modes of travel as per to their convenience and budget. About 56.25% and 55.80% tourists used bus to reach Nainital and Almora, respectively. Approximately 23.75% and 28.20% tourists travelled by rental cars and about 20% and 14% tourists reached Nainital and Almora by their own vehicles respectively.

Motivational Factors

Most of the tourists visited Kumaon hills through self decisions. Add to this some tourists were visiting Nainital and Almora, on being inspired by their friends and relatives besides getting information from travel literature including magazines, guide books, newspapers, journals, etc. It was noticed that foreigner notified these places through travel guide books.

Means of Recreation

Kumaon Himalaya is well endowed with beauties and bounties of nature and culture and because of this the region is favoured for tourism and recreation by tourists. It was noticed that more than 70% tourists preferred boating in Nainital as a large number of them agreed that this is the best means of recreation in Nainital followed by trekking to China peak and horse riding.

Shopping Pattern

About their shopping experiences at Nainital most tourists were interested to purchase decorative candles, woolen clothes, pine cones, cane sticks and bamboo baskets. Some tourists were least interested in shopping because of having other priorities. Some tourists expressed their intention of buying photographs of scenic beauty of Nainital, particularly of the lake and its surrounding areas. As regards shopping at Almora, majority of them denied having any such intention as they prefer to have shopping at Nainital because of wider choice and availability of wide variety of souvenirs and handcrafts.

Season

Nainital has two popular tourist cycles : Summer cycle (May to June) and Autumn cycle (Sept.-Oct.). In the month of May and June when mercury shoots up in plains, Nainital gets too busy in dressing its tourism shops. The hotel cafe and restaurant owners, the porters, the taxi drivers, the *coolies* all look towards a good business. The second half of May and the first half of June constitute the peak period when thousands of tourists flock Nainital to get relief from scorching heat of plains. Sport lovers from all over the world come here for Polo, Hockey, Football, Golf, fishing and, above all, Yatching and Kayaking, etc.

The second tourist cycle is associated with autumn festival. In this season mostly those tourists come here who normally do not like to visit Nainital during the summer rush due to high-cost holiday. Fun seekers who do not like the noise pollution, generally come in this season. Some people come here when rain gives a fresher, greener and brighter look to Kumaon Himalaya. Enthusiastic tourists generally come in this season to enjoy water sports, trekking, hiking, etc. Autumn festival, a revival of the British traditions, is the main attraction to those who come to Nainital in the month of Sept.-Oct. For Almora also there are two popular tourist seasons: i.e. summer and autumn season. Thousands of enthusiastic visitors going on different expeditions to Milam, Pindari, Kafni, Mrigthuni glaciers normally pass through Almora. Though, majority of tourists come to Almora in the month of May and June, nature loving tourists come in the month of September and October. Among such tourists *Bengalis* are dominant who visit Almora, Ranikhet and Kausani during this period. However, tourist normally make their way to Ranikhet and Kausani especially during the months of March to June and September-October.

Tourism and Local Community

Community development is the prime concern of tourism activities in any tourist regions. Normally local people are benefited from tourism activities be they associated with mountain treks or historic monument tourism business. Majority of the local people were satisfied with the nature and type of tourism flourishing in Nainital and Almora and its surroundings. Whereas some people emphasized that there was enough opportunities to develop different forms of tourism and it includes event tourism, adventure tourism, and farm tourism, etc. As regards to the role of tourism in enhancing of air, water, noise pollution, etc. in Nainital and Almora, approximately 85% local people opined that tourism is responsible for increased litter and garbage trails, thereby contributing to ecological deterioration. Most of the respondents said that unplanned and unmanaged tourism promotion had led to downfall of quality tourism and admitted that excessive tourism activities had encroached upon flora and fauna of Corbett National Park and Binsar Wild Life Sanctuary. On the other hand some people admitted that tourism created mass awareness of local traditions and culture and therefore tourism is responsible for changing the life style and making them more informative.

Local people were agreeful to the fact that tourism had promoted robbery and cheating in Nainital and Almora districts. They also confessed that increased tourist traffic have over burdened the residents of the region. They found tourism for crimes, prostitution, gambling, smoking, drinking, drug-addiction, and other social abuses and negative activities. The tremendous influx of visitors during the peak tourist season caused over-crowding, traffic congestion, noise and inflated prices of goods and services. Tourism creates more jobs for local people in tourist season and promotes seasonal dependency on hospitality industry, but simultaneously produces utter frustration among the local people due to low paid jobs. It is because of this that the community area needs integrated planning and management with local participation.

Conclusion

Tourism development contributes to the benefits and burdens of a region received from visitors directly and indirectly. There are several tourist places like Bangkok, Goa and Paris where tourists have created numerous problems. Kumaon Himalayas two prime destination undoubtedly are fascinating tourist attractions having all possibilities of tourism development. But the way the present nature of tourism has taken shape is hardly going to help local people. The primary aim of planners and professionals should be to introduce quality tourism so that it benefits all stakeholders, be they local people or hoteliers and eateries owners. Ecotourism and sustainable tourism have become tourism buzz words of modern tourism. Almora is a small town having very low physical space to accommodate tourist traffic. The roads and lanes are very narrow and if a group of 100 tourists reach there it would be difficult for them to cross the roads easily. Binsar Wildlife Sanctuary, 35 km from Almora,

116

is ideal for ecotourism, but the restrictions placed by the Department of Forest, Govt. of Uttaranchal, would hardly benefit any stakeholder. Proposals are being made for the beautification and landscape designing of Almora, Nainital and its environs in order to meet the requirements of increased number of visitors. But to what extent the increased tourism traffic would offer job opportunity to the local people and check their out migration is a subject that should be debated openly.

References

Bisht, D.S. (1982). *Guide to Garhwal* and *Kumaon Hills,* Trishul Publication, Dehradun.

Fonia, K.S. (1978). *Uttarakhand: The Land of Jungles, Temples and Snows,* Lancer Books, New Delhi.

Jayal, N.D. (1990). Himalaya Our Fragile Heritage. In the Proceeding of *Nehru Institute of Mountaineering 25 Years Conference,* Uttarkashi.

Kaur, J. (1982). Pilgrims Progress to Himalaya Shrines. T.V. Singh (ed) *Studies in Tourism Wildlife Parks and Conservation,* Metropolitan, New Delhi.

Kaur, J. (1985). Himalayan Books, New Delhi. *Himalayan Pilgrimages and the Neo Tourism.*

Kumar, G. (1989). Impacts of Tourism on Mountain Environment: a Case Study of Nanda Devi National Park. In Singh, S.C. (ed.), *Impacts of Tourism on Mountain Environment,* Research India Publication, Meerut.

Negi, S.S. (1982). *Environmental Problems in Himalayas,* Bishen Singh and Mahendra Pal Singh, Dehradun.

Shrestha, Tirtha B. (1995). *Mountain Tourism and Environment in Nepal,* International Center for Integrated Mountain Development, Kathmandu.

Singh, J. (1986). The Joys of Trekking, *Travel Times,* The Times of India, New Delhi, March 29.

Travis, Antony S. (1982). Managing the Environment and Culture, Impacts of Tourism and Leisure Development, *Tourism Management* 3 (4).

Sustainable Tourism Planning and Development, 117-124, 2006
Edited by Bagri, S.C.
Published by Bishen Singh Mahendra Pal Singh, Dehra Dun, India

Tourism Entrepreneurship Development in Uttaranchal : A Case of Tourist Guest House Project of Uttaranchal Tourism

S.K. Gupta
Reader, Center for Mountain Tourism and Hospitality Studies,
H.N.B. Garhwal University, Srinagar Garhwal
&

Sanjay Dhyani
Co-ordinator, Tourist Guest Houses
Centre for Mountain Tourism and Hospitality Studies
H.N.B. Garhwal University, Srinagar Garhwal

Abstract : Uttaranchal Tourism Development Board plays a decisive role in accommodation sector and is responsible to provide a favorable framework for the development of tourism. Tourist Guest House Project (previously branded as *Raen Basera)* is an example of public sector investment in accommodation sector, and its all units are the properties of Uttaranchal State it has been established with the purpose of catering to the budget tourists. All properties of this project are presently being operated by the Hemwati Nandan Bahuguna Garhwal University and the dividends earned are equally divided among operators and promoters. The present paper makes an indepth analysis of the benefits achieved by university since the inception of the project.

Key Words : Uttaranchal, tourism, Raen Basera, TGH Group.

Background

Uttaranchal is a tiny state in the Himalayan region. Its adverse geographical conditions have given Uttaranchal a remarkable heterogeneity to its entire natural and cultural environment. The diverse and yet extensive and virgin plethora of tourist places offer immense opportunities for the development of religious tourism, leisure tourism, adventure tourism, natural environment and ecotourism across the region. These resources of Uttaranchal make it land of diversified attractions and offer tremendous scope for developing tourism in the region. For this, development of tourism infrastructure is an essential part and accommodation and catering sector is one of thrust areas for further planning. Tourist attractions serve as prime motivators, but factors like accommodation, transportation, catering, etc. serve as satisfiers. The experiences of the tourists depend to a great extent on the existence of good combination of both motivators and satisfiers. It is important that attractions of the region should be backed by amenities and facilities. Hence building of basic infrastructure and proper staffing should be the first priority for the development of a viable tourism industry. Tourist Guest House project of Uttaranchal Tourism is one such entrepreneurship project.

The project across the state was established in the mid-nineties under the patronage of Uttar Pradesh Tourism Department. It was recognized that the public sector had become sluggish as well as expensive to sustain the emerging competition at a number of tourist places. The need of the hour was to trim the public sector and thereby reduce their financial burden on government exchequer. In view of this, the Govt. of Uttaranchal signed a Memorandum of Understanding with the H.N.B. Garhwal University on 24th May, 2002 to run the Tourist Guest House properties under the joint collaboration of Uttaranchal Tourism and H.N.B. Garhwal University. The project started with handing over of 22 units by the Uttaranchal state government to H.N.B. Garhwal University. The university, under its well-established Center for Mountain Tourism and Hospitality Studies, set-up a co-ordination office for the overall management of Tourist Guest House units as well as to ensure easy sharing of information with State Tourism Development Board. The overall philosophy behind this venture was to promote tourism, innovate professionalism and encourage business entrepreneurship among young tourism professionals in the state having limited economic opportunities.

Aims and objectives

The main objectives of this project are:

❑ Opening new vistas for the budding tourism professionals in various fields of tourism and travel sector;

❑ Providing an opportunity to tourists/pilgrims to avail themselves of environment friendly professional ambience within limited budget;

□ To check out migration of professionally trained youths;

□ Stimulate business opportunities for the local youths to acquire seasonal jobs.

Business operation

In order to manage TGH units after their inception in 2002, the TGH Co-ordination office invited applications from young, energetic and skilled persons of the state to undertake the responsibility of TGH units as an operator. Starting with the small family of limited number of operators, today the number of TGH operators has increased to 106, out of which 36 are management professionals working as unit incharge and the rest are helping hands. Today, the group comprises of well-qualified professional managerial staff at all the operating units. All the units are staffed with two operators with three supporting staff to ensure better services and functioning. The supporting staff are mostly from the surrounding villages, thereby contributing towards the economic upliftment, employment generation and community involvement. The TGH group is widely spread out in various destinations on *Badri* and *Kedar yatra* routes along with some lesser known destinations in *Pauri* district. Operationally, the physical distribution of TGH Group comprises of the following:-

□ *Badrinath* route group

□ *Kedarnath* route group

□ Lesser known destinations group

As **Badrinath and Kedarnath** are major destinations for tourists visiting Uttaranchal, this route has been well fortified with accommodation units of TGH Group at various important transit stopovers starting from *Rishikesh* as may be seen in Table I below:

The *yatra* route to Kedarnath is bifurcated at Rudraprayag. In the Kedarnath route the following units are located at various stopovers starting from Agastyamuni.

Table III gives the detail of Lesser Known destinations of Garhwal with bed capacity of accommodations breakup.

Table I: TGH Units on Badrinath yatra Route

Tourist/ Transit Point	Location	Bed Capacity	Types of Rooms
Rishikesh	TGMOUL Bus Stand	70	TB-13, Dor-3
Muni-ki-Reti	Kailash Gate	30	DB-6, FS-I, Dor-2
Swargashram	Near Chaurasi Kutia	30	DB-1, Dor-2
Shivpuri	Shivpuri	30	Dor-3, DB-I
Devprayag	Near B.K.T.C	30	Dor-3
Kirtinagar	Near Police Chauki	50	DB-3, FS-3, Dor-2
Srinagar	Near New Bus Stand	30	DB-5, Dor-2
Nagrasu	Near *Gurdwara*	30	DB-6, SB-2, TB-2, Dor-2
Gauchar	Near GREF Camp	30	DB-7, Dor-3
Kaldubagar	Kaleshwar	70	DB-10, Dor-5
Nandprayag	Near GMVN, TRH	30	DB-1, Dor-2
Joshimath	Upper Bazaar	70	Dor-5
Badrinath	Near Parmarth Niketan	30	TB-5, FS-1, Dor-2

TB- Triple beds, DB- Double beds, Dor- Dormitory, FS- Family suite

Table II: TGH Units on Kedarnath Route

Tourist/ Transit Point	Location	Bed Capacity	Accommodation Breakup
Agastyamuni	Near Girls College	50	DB-3, TB-2, Dor-5
Rampur	1.5 km from the Market	70	FS-10, Dor-2
Soneprayag	Near *Zila Panchayat*	70	DB-4, TB-I, FS-5, Dor-4
Gaurikund	Near *Zila Panchayat*	70	FS-4, Dor-8

TB- Triple beds, DB- double beds, Dor- Dormitory, FS-Family suite

Table III: TGH Units in Lesser Known Destinations of Garhwal

Name of Destination	Location	Bed Capacity	Accommodation Breakup
Devprayag	Bah Bazaar	30	FS-6
Kunjapuri	Near Temple	30	Dor-4
Danda Nagraja	Near Temple	30	Dor-4
Satpuli	Near Treasury	30	Dor-4
Dugadda	Near Bus Stand	30	Dor-4
Paithani	Near Temple	30	Dor-4
Tahilisani	Near Main Market	30	Dor-4

TB- Triple beds, DB- Double beds, Dor- Dormitory, FS- Family suite

A few more units are under construction and are expected to be completed by the end of 2004. The upcoming units shall be functioning as Spa Centers and TGH units with diversified purposes at different locations of the state as indicated in Table IV below:

Table IV: Upcoming Units

Spa Centre	TGH Units	
Gaurikund	Rambara	
Badrinath	Pipalkoti	
Tapovan	Kedarnath	Chamoli
Sheraghat (Kumaon region)	Gyansu	Govindghat
Madhkot (Kumaon region)	Kund	Neelkanth

Project Interpretation

The TGH project was started with an allotment of 16 units for a period of 10 months from June 2002 till 31st March 2003. As these units were handed over to the unit operators from the mid tourist season of 2002, the overall business performance could not achieve the expected level of benefit. Furthermore, a number of other factors including poor publicity and lack of suitable promotional measures had also contributed to the poor performance of TGH units. But due to the hard work, innovative ideas and professional skills, all young entrepreneurs were able to harness due profits and placed the brand image of TGH units in the minds of inbound visitors. As per the MOU signed with HNB Garhwal University, Uttaranchal Tourism is also receiving 25% share of the total profit generated by the TGH project. Had these units been in the hands of public sector, they would have failed due to their nature and designing. Today all units are not only generating employment, but have also created a positive image of Uttaranchal Tourism as well as of the University.

Garhwal Himalaya is a tourist destination of 5-6 months duration and it remains effective from May to November every year. But on an average the exact tourist season is of 120 days and the remaining period of tourist season is hampered either by rains or landslides occurring from time to time. Under such circumstance the economics of TGH units do not yield expected benefits. Figure-I projects its operators performance with overall recorded occupancy of units, except the Kaldubaggar unit, which could not start its operation due to lack of sufficient supplies.

Muni-ki-Reti, Rishikesh, Soneprayag, Gaucher and Srinagar units have performed well. But in view of revenue generation, Agastyamuni achieved a significant position and generated better revenue in comparison to Goucher and Srinagar and was at par with Soneprayag. Rishikesh and Muni-ki-Reti receive tourists round the year but the performance of both the units was not satisfactory, the reason being competition with other accommodation properties and *Dharmshalas*.

Table V and Table VI give details of the overall performance of TGH units for 2002-2003 and form April 2003 to November 2003.

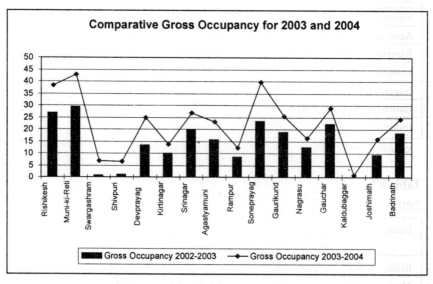

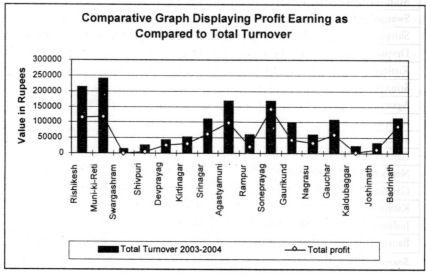

Table V: Performance of TGH units from 20th June 2002 to 31st March 2003

Name	Max\Min Occupancy (%)	Gross Occupancy (%)	Turn over (in Rs.)	Profit (in Rs.)
Rishikesh	42/7	27.22	1,18,000	60,000
Muni-ki-Reti	62.3/12.47	29.60	1,22,000	67,000
Shivpuri	8.5/1.22	03.45	19,700	2,700
Devprayag	32.3/9	18.00	34,000	13,590
Kirtinagar	25/3.88	09.70	46,980	24,300
Srinagar	53.6/3.76	22.90	98,700	46,500
Agastyamuni	45/8.3	19.40	1,07,200	70,000
Rampur	13.2/1.25	03.70	20,000	1,500
Soneprayag	49/17	28.00	91,070	65,000
Nagrasu	17/1.67	09.20	26,000	8,300
Gauchar	44.62/6.76	19.25	76,000	40,215
Joshimath	32.5/6.32	18.80	42,812	16,514

Source: Tourist Guest House Group Annual Report, 2003-2004

Table VI: Performance of TGH units from 1st April 2003 to 30th November 2003

Name	Max\Min Occupancy (%)	Gross Occupancy (%)	Turn over (in Rs.)	Profit (in Rs.)
Rishikesh	58.9/12	38.32	2,12,790	1,15,160
Muni-ki-Reti	88/20.11	42.95	2, 41,010	1,18,728
Swargashram	24.6/.66	6.94	15,500	00
Shivpuri	12.43/2.23	6.68	27,355	4,802
Devprayag	40.15/15.66	24.84	43,010	25,910
Kirtinagar	30.66/5.42	13.81	51,790	30,140
Srinagar	67/2.22	26.87	1,09,531	61,404
Agastyamuni	50/13	23.12	1,67,972	97,902
Rampur	32.4/2.32	12.23	60,728	21,638
Soneprayag	78.8/14.4	39.60	1,67,652	1,42,002
Gaurikund	49/10.25	25.50	99,220	42,465
Nagrasu	43.33/2.77	16.25	58,860	34,410
Gauchar	67.77/9.11	28.85	1,07,940	59,230
Kaldubaggar	10/.22	0.77	23,847	2,347
Joshimath	28.11/7.61	16.14	33,945	12,635
Badrinath	42.2/6.63	24.32	1,11,615	86,815

Source: Tourist Guest House Group Annual Report, 2003-04

Conclusion

Joint venture operation and privatization of public sector units have been accepted for effective business promotion worldwide. A number of public sector units, such as ITDC hotel units and 49% equity share in aviation sector have been included in such schemes. The HNB Garhwal University through its Centre for Mountain Tourism and Hospitality Studies has made sincere efforts and has allotted all TGH units to efficient and dedicated young persons having enough trade experience and related business skills. The findings of the TGH project reveal that joint venture operations is the need of the hour as it not only generates employment for local youths but also reduces financial burden on the state exchequer. The aims and objectives of tourism are to generate employment and revenue as well as to keep visitors informed and satisfied. TGH Group is playing a significant role in this field and its four major stakeholders: Government, University, Operators and Visitors are satisfied with its operation. The Group is a pioneering effort in infrastructures planning and is playing a pivotal role in community-oriented tourism. The group is expected to achieve new heights in the years to come as the Govt. of Uttaranchal proposes to construct more such units across the state.

References

Gupta, S.K. (2002). *Tourism and Heritage Resources in Garhwal Himalaya; An Approach to Planning and Management*, Kaveri Books, New Delhi.

IGNOU, Study material MTM-8, Managing Entrepreneurship and Small Business in Tourism, New Delhi.

Mishra, S.K. (1998). Public-Private Partnership, New Ways of Managing Tourism in India, *Journal of Tourism*, Vol.3.

Tourism for Local Community Development in Mountain Areas: Perspectives, Issues and Guidelines, ICIMOD, Kathmandu, 1995.

WTO Newsletter, Issue No. 2, 2000.

WTO Newsletter, Issue No. 4, 1997 p.14.

Sustainable Tourism Planning and Development, 125-136, 2006
Edited by Bagri, S.C.
Published by Bishen Singh Mahendra Pal Singh, Dehra Dun, India

Sustainable Tourism Development: Present Scenario of Sustainable use of India's Tourism Resources

Rakesh Dhodi
Centre for Mountain Tourism & Hospitality Studies,
H.N.B. Garhwal University, Srinagar Garhwal

&

Rashmi Dhodi
Centre for Mountain Tourism & Hospitality Studies,
H.N.B. Garhwal University, Srinagar Garhwal

Abstract : The environmental and social impacts of the unprecedented tourism boom call per an eventual shift of a comprehensive strategy that sets limits to growth in order to sustain socially and environmentally compatible tourism. It is the "Sustainable Tourism Development" which need to be more promoted to pamper international tourism. Sustainable implies permanence and conveys to use the resources optimally, with the involvement of the surrounding and local population. Sustainable tourism encourages an understanding of the impact of tourism on the natural, cultural and human environment. In Indian context various tourism promotional development like new outdoor activities, rural tourism, adventure tourism, fairs and festivals, water sports and many other leisure activities are being promoted. For infrastructure and product development Department of Tourism (DOT) Govt. of India is taking initiatives to improve the quality product and providing central financial assistance to the state Governments for various destinations. The DOT, has provided 100% financial assistance for destination development of different states like Karnataka, Delhi, Haryana, Rajasthan, Tamil Nadu and Uttaranchal. The development should be based on master plan and be promoted in a sustainable way.

Key Words: Sustainable development, tourism, travel circuit, regional planning.

Introduction

Since the term 'sustainable development' was coined by the Brundtland Report (Our Common Future) in 1987 and Internationally agreed at the Rio Earth Summit in 1992, it has been much debated by the UN and international forums by academics, scientists, NGOs, public sector institutions and agencies, and increasingly by private businesses. Most emphasis has been focused on the environmental aspects of sustainability since the global effects of misuse and over using the earth's natural resources are hard to ignore. However, even in its initial formulation, the concept of 'sustainable development' has always been broader and more far-reaching and stresses the interdependence of the natural environment with economy and society. In this wider sense, sustainability is a comprehensive and inclusive approach, and an on going process. The triple-bottom-line framework encompasses a broad spectrum of issues, which includes for example, natural, economic, social and cultural diversity, equity and human rights, globalisation and localisation, and corporate and individual citizenship and responsibility.

Sustainable tourism development is not happening on a mass scale. Although tourism development can provide employment and associated benefits to the local community, too often it has ignored their needs and rights. Sustainable tourism refers to a type of tourism which optimises the benefits and limits the negative impacts. The unsustainable consequences of tourism include: over consumption of natural resources and environmental degradation, exploitation of cultures and labour, displacement of people from their land, lack of consultation with local communities, and above all high foreign exchange leakage which reduces local economic benefits. As there is a number of increase in tourist flow all over the world the economy of many countries also having positive impacts of tourism. In India tourism may play a vital role to give economic support as it has a number of tourist attractions potential for tourism but there is serious need to make sustainable development planning. Due to lack of proper sustainable development planning approach India is receiving very less number of arrivals in comparison to the world.

Why Sustainable use of tourism resources?

Tourism continues to grow at a great rate worldwidely and the increasing pressure of tourist traffic naturally aggravates the degradation of the environment and social milieu. There are two extreme conditions to work on: whether to promote tourism at the cost of environment degradation or to preserve environment for "no tourism" through a forceful, well conceived and defensible manner the problem that often accompanies tourism is when it is too "successful" i.e. many tourists visit a destination, it can destroy the very attraction that initiates the tourism. When this occurs, usually the tourism business is not the only thing lost, but financial resources, social cultural aspects of communities, and natural landscapes, may be disrupted as well. When tourism development is not socially appropriate it can result in negative feeling on the part of the on-site populations and regions. Communities and families can become divided or disintegrate. Negative sentiments may be passed on tourists who may experience harassment, crime or violence in the extreme cases. It is possible that the tourist will simply perceive some sort of ill will from the on-site residents. When this severe reaction by the on-site pollution occurs, the local tourism industry will be negatively receive massive environmental degradation which will eventually threaten our generation. For example health cost due to water and air pollution is costing the country around Rs. 24,500 crore every year.

The Benefits of Sustainable Tourism

The following are some of the benefits a tourist destination normally receives from sustainable tourism (WTO; 1993):

☐ Sustainable Tourism encourages an understanding of the impacts of tourism on the natural, cultural and the human environment.

☐ Sustainable Tourism ensures a fair distribution of benefits and costs.

☐ Sustainable Tourism generates local employment, both directly and indirectly in tourism sector and in various other support and resource management sectors.

☐ It stimulates benefits to domestic industries like hotels and other lodging facilities, restaurants and other food services, transportation systems, handicrafts and guide services.

☐ It helps to generates foreign exchange for the country and injects capital and new money into the local economy.

☐ Sustainable Tourism diversifies the local economy, particularly in rural areas where agricultural employment may be sporadic or insufficient.

☐ Sustainable Tourism seeks decision making among all segments of the society, including local population, so that tourism and other resource users can co-exist. It incorporates zoning and planning which ensure tourism development appropriate to the carrying capacity of the ecosystem.

128

- Sustainable Tourism stimulates improvement to local transportation, communications and other basic community infrastructure.

- It creates recreational facilities, which can be used by local communities, as well as domestic and international visitors. It also encourages and helps preservation of archaeological sites, and historic buildings.

- Sustainable Tourism encourages productive use of lands, which are marginal for agriculture, enabling large treks to remain covered in natural vegetation.

- Sustainable tourism enhances local community esteem and provides the opportunity for greater understanding and communications among people of diverse backgrounds.

- Environmentally sustainable tourism demonstrates the importance of natural and cultural resources to a community's economic and social well being and can help to preserve them.

- Sustainable tourism monitors, assesses and manages the impact of tourism, develop reliable methods of environmental accountability, and counter any negative impacts.

Sustainable use of India's tourism resources: Present Scenario

Until the late eighties tourism was not recognized as an industry in many of the Indian states. But due to sustained effort by public and private sectors a remarkable development in tourism has been noticed in recent past. This has resulted in various tourism promotional developments like targeting particular foreign markets and segmentation of tourism products like new outdoors activities, adventure tourism, fairs and festivals, water sports, winter skiing, ballooning, cycle safaries, rock climbing, trekking, aero-sports motor rallies and mountaineering. This had to be developed despite the popular cultural and heritage tourism potential.

The increasing participation of Indian middle classes in domestic tourism enhanced the variety of tourism products in several famous and already over-crowded destinations like Kashmir, Goa, Delhi, Rajasthan, Kerala, and Agra. For the first time the importance of domestic tourism and the need of one of its main component, Pilgrimage Tourism is also formally recognized by the Indian Government. This is important because

250 millions domestic tourists go for Tourism and pilgrimage every year in India. India is now slowly picking ecotourism. This has led to the mobbing of some of the virgin coastal landscape such as of Goa, Kerala, Lakshwadeep, Tamil Nadu, Orissa and mountain attractions like Sikkim, Uttaranchal, Himachal Pradesh, Karnataka, Jammu and Kashmir, Assam, West Bengal and several other states of eco importance. As most of the Eco cultural tourists travel from the most developed countries, the benefits of tourism hardly percolates to the indigenous people of the third world, and India is no exception (Bagri; 1997).

In destinations like Goa and Kashmir, the so-called nature based mass tourism sparked discontent among the locals. A few years back a militant radical local elite group of Goa state has taken altogether strange stand of inhospitality bordering on rudeness (a rare phenomenon in the great sub-continent) and declared a five point declaration against the promotion of nature based mass tourism. The predominantly dominant Roman Catholic community had also resented the fall in the normal standards of the beaches. The unprecedented construction of Five Star hotels and convention centers at places like Goa, Kashmir, Uttaranchal and Kerala have sent land values out of common reach. This has led to non-locals taking possession of indigenous and tribal enclaves. Places like the Nilgiris and Kodaikanal (Blue Mountains) in Tamil Nadu are famous hill resorts, which were developed by the Britishers to respite from the summer heat of the plains. These have been exploited beyond their carrying capacity. Another strange phenomenon of the Indian hill resorts is the dominance of plantation agriculture over the native ecology. The North Indian summer resorts Nainital, Darjeeling, Mussoorie, and Kullu Valley are having similarly characteristics.

Gulmarg, Shimla and Srinagar have been under considerable stress and the strain of mass-ecobased domestic tourism. These resorts have been providing winter sports opportunities to domestic tourists during winter months. Gulmarg's T-ban Ski lift takes the skiers to the amateur slopes. The locals also resent the highly promoted Himalayan car rallies in recent years. Even the tourism promotional activities in Ladakh have been found wanting in many sphere of true development. After several episode of discontent, the 1992 National Action Plan for Tourism had accepted the integrated spatial planning approach for the development and preservation of the tourist's destinations as well as travel circuits of India (Bagri; 2003).

130

The New Tourism Policy and Sustainable Tourism Development

The Ministry of Tourism prepared a draft National Tourism Policy with the objective of positioning tourism as a major engine of economic growth and to harness its direct and multiplier effects for employment and poverty eradication in an environmentally sustainable manner. Department of Tourism 2002 this draft was circulated to all the stakeholders in the Tourism Sector, the Private Sector, the Industry Associations, the State Governments, Departments and Ministries of Government of India. After detailed interaction with all concerned, the National Tourism Policy was announced in the year 2002. The Policy document seeks to enhance employment potential within the tourism sector as well as to foster economic integration through developing linkages with other sectors. Broadly, the policy paper aims to:-

❏ Position tourism as a major engine of economic growth;

❏ Harness the direct and multiplier effects of tourism for employment generation, economic development and providing impetus to rural tourism;

❏ Focus on domestic tourism as a major driver of tourism growth;

❏ Position India as a global brand to take advantage of the burgeoning global travel å trade and the vast untapped potential of India as a destination;

❏ Acknowledge the critical role of private sector with government working as a pro-active facilitator and catalyst;

❏ Ensure that the tourist to India gets physically invigorated, mentally rejuvenated, culturally enriched, spiritually elevated and "feel India from within".

❏ Create and develop integrated tourism circuits based on India's unique civilisation, heritage, and culture in partnership with states, private sector and other agencies;

Regional Tourism Promotion

It is planned to take up a circuit in each region. Accordingly, the following circuits have been identified for development in 2002-2004:

❏ Eastern Region - (Buddhist Circuit)

❏ Bodhgaya-Rajgir-Nalanda-Varanasi

- Northern Region - (Himalayan Circuit)
  Route I-Chandigarh-Bilaspur-Kullu-Manali-Rohtang-La-Keylong-Sarchu-Upshi-Leh
  Route II -Shimla-Sangla-Kaza-Chatru-Keylong-Sarchu-Yashi-Leh

- Central Circuit-(Heritage, Nature & Wildlife Circuit)
  Gwalior-Shivpuri-Chanderi-Orchha-Khajuraho-Jhansi-Bhopal-Sanchi and surrounding Buddhist areas - Bhimbetka-Pachmarhi-Kanha, Jabalpur (Bedaghat)

- Western Circuit - (Konkan Riveria Circuit)
  Mumbai-Alibagh (Mandva)-Muradjanjira-Ganapatipule-Vijayadurg-Mithibad-Kunkeshwr-Mochetmad-Sindhudurg-Tarkarli-Shiroda-Savantwadi-Amboli-Goa-Bekal

- Southern Circuit - (Backwaters and Beach Circuit)
  Cochin-Kumarakom-(Backwaters)-Kottayam-Quilon-Thiruvananthapuram (Kovalam)

- North-East Circuit - (Ecotourism Circuit)
  Shillong- Guwahati - Kaziranga - Tezpur - Bhalakpung - Tawang (Arunachal Pradesh)-Majuli-Sibsagar-Kohima

Destination Development

The focus under this scheme will be on improving existing products and developing new tourism products to world class standards. For infrastructure and product development, the Department of Tourism has been providing Central Financial Assistance to the State Governments. It has resulted in strengthening of the infrastructure and product development in the country. This scheme has now served its objectives and it is now important to restructure it to meet the present day infrastructure requirements. It is therefore being revamped in the Tenth Plan. The past experience has been that a large number of small projects have been funded under the Scheme, spreading the resources very thin, which at times has not created the desired impact. The focus in the Tenth Plan would be to fund large projects of infrastructure or product development. In the Ninth Plan, assistance was provided in the following fields:

- Construction of Budget Accommodation
- Tourist Complex

- ❑ Wayside amenities
- ❑ Tourist Reception Centres
- ❑ Refurbishment of Monuments
- ❑ Special Tourism Projects
- ❑ Adventure and sports Facilities
- ❑ Sound and Light Shows and Illumination of Monuments

Separate allocation has been made for each one of these schemes as indicated earlier. But this allocation would suffice for the initial few months only for the old projects. All these works would be taken up under this new scheme. The focus would however shift to integrated destination development which would be selected and based on the tourism potential. Master planning of these destinations will be undertaken so as to develop them in an integrated holistic manner. The Master Plan will tie up all backward and forward linkages, including environmental considerations. Realising the importance of destination development, the total outlay for this sector is being increased substantially. An important tourist destination in each state in consultation with the State Government would be taken up for development. This would include all activities ranging from preparation to implementation of the Master Plans. The destinations would be selected in consultation with the State/UT Governments. After identification of the project, the State Government/Executing Agency would be requested to furnish a detailed proposal along with the detailed estimates. The implementing agency would also be identified at this stage in consultation with them. The maximum amount that could be sanctioned under this scheme would be Rs. 5 crores. The channelisation of funds to the executing agencies would also be decided in consultation with the State Governments. State-level Monitoring Committees would be set up under the Chairmanship of the respective Secretary (Tourism). This Committees would comprise of a nominee of the Department of Tourism, Government of India and a nominee of the executing agency. All activities will be funded on a 100% basis of the cost that would be borne by the Department of Tourism. Govt. of India. However, the State/ UT Governments will be fully responsible for running all the components of the project as explained under integrated development of tourist circuits. Quite a large number of destinations have been identified in each State for development under this scheme in consultation with the State Governments. So far, works have been sanctioned at the following destinations. The unique feature of these destinations would integrate elements of Tourism, Culture and Good Governance.

Karnataka : Hampi

Delhi : Red Fort

- ❑ Cleaning / washing of city wall
- ❑ Upgradation of Tea House - Electrical work
- ❑ Upgradation of Tea House - Civil work
- ❑ Toilets and parking on rear side of Red Fort
- ❑ Illumination of front side of Red Fort
- ❑ Illumination of remaining rear side of Red Fort
- ❑ Development of lawn in front of Red Fort

Haryana : Kurukshetra

- ❑ Renovation of Jyotisar, Kurukshetra - Provision of sub-station, DG set, path lighting, internal EI & split type AC unit (new)
- ❑ Providing lighting arrangement at Brahm Sarovar (East & West and North)
- ❑ Development of Tapovan Park A (Phase II) and shifting of service road

Rajasthan : Mewar

- ❑ Sound and Light show at Kumbhalgarh Fort
- ❑ Sound and Light show at Chittaurgarh Fort
- ❑ General lighting of Kumbhalgarh Fort

Tamil Nadu : Mahabalipuram

Uttaranchal : Haridwar and Rishikesh

- ❑ Development of Green Great Vista for Haridwar
- ❑ Landscaping and parking development along the Ganga at Rishikesh

Rural Tourism

Rural Tourism is one of the few activities which can provide a solution to these problems. Besides, there are other factors which are shifting the trend towards Rural Tourism like increasing levels of awareness, growing interest in heritage and culture and improved accessibility, and environmental consciousness. In the developed countries, this has resulted in a new style of tourism of visiting village settings to experience and live a relaxed and healthy lifestyle. This concept has taken the shape of a formal kind of Rural Tourism. Under this scheme, thrust will be to promote village tourism as the primary tourism product to spread tourism and its socio-economic benefits to rural and its new geographic regions. Key geographic regions would be identified for development and promotion of Rural Tourism. The implementation would be done through a Convergence Committee headed by the District Collector. Activities like improving the environment, hygiene, infrastructure, etc, would be eligible for assistance. Apart from providing financial assistance, the focus would be to tap the resources available under different schemes of Department of Rural Development, State Governments and other concerned Departments of the Government of India.

Each State/UT Government would be requested to furnish one proposal for promotion of Rural Tourism. Based on the merits and after a joint inspection by the Department of Tourism and the State/UT Government, ten proposals would be identified for implementation in the country. After short-listing the proposals, the State/UT Governments would be requested to draw up a detailed plan of action. The thrust area would be to achieve convergence between the different schemes of the Government of India and the State Governments. It should be ensured that at least 50% of the project should be implemented through achieving convergence of different schemes. Assistance up to Rs. 3 lakhs would be provided to the State Government for engaging an expert for preparing the project report.

Resources are required for India to upgrade its ecocultural destinations to international standards. Although India has the scientific skills to implement the integrated planning approach. However with growing incentives, it is very doubtful how this can be achieved without a uniform policy concerning sustainable tourism development. Although Australia is three times larger than India geographically it may have a one federal policy. This may not be so in India for the simple reason that India not only have different ecological regions but is culturally different also. Japan has offered Rs. 100 crore (A $ 43,000,000) financial assistance to India to tune up the facility in Buddhist Travel Circuit to enable Japanese tourist to enjoy their pilgrimages. This should not mislead India tourist destination operation like of Belize as nearly 90% of all coastal development in Belize is now in foreign hands.

Another area where these nature based tourism promotional efforts will run into rough weather is Indian culture. Although there is mass tourism towards Khajuraho, these world famous *Kamasutra* sculptures have become one among the tourism icons of India. They are generally disassociated from general Indian morality. India does not live in its past anymore but at the same time it can not be disassociated completely its 5000 years old cultural mooring to fill up its depleted coffers. Goa, alone should be an eye opener to the tourism planners in India.

Statistics have proved that nearly 92 % of tourists who visit India falls under the non-packaged category. Indian tourism planner could develop models of destination development that could be useful to both the middle class overseas as will as domestic tourists. This is a Herculean task, but ought to be investigated for the sake of future of Indian sustainable tourism. However, it is really laudable to think of planning the river running tour packages in Ladakh, Garhwal Hills, Teesta (Sikkim), water sports in Goa, Andaman Islands, Kovalam and Dal and Nagin lakes of Kashmir, winter skiing in Gulmurg, and Manali, Balloning in Thar desert, Kangra Valley, Safaris in Jaisalmer and Jodhpur, Rockclimbing in Sonamorg (Kashmir), Chamundi Hills in Karnataka and trekking in the Himalayas and in its majestic glaciers. But it is more precedent to estimate how much substance these efforts have brought to these regions and to the people in particular. Watching a speeding foreign car rally does not make sense to the poorer section of the society of the operational area.

Conclusion

Tourism is a very complex activity that requires planning and coordination at every step with great sense of responsibility. Careful study of Tourism in comparison to Sustainable tourism reveals that to extract maximum profit from the tourism and it is essential to preserve and conserve various destinations of tourism. So in this respect planning, coordination and implementation is very essential that must starts at the introductory stage of any destination while implementing a tourism plan proposal So tourism can be enjoyed and the profit and nature may remain within its boundaries.

References

Annual Report (2002). Department of Tourism, Govt. of India, New Delhi.

Ascher, B. and Cooper, C. (1994). The positive and negative impact of Tourism, are Theobald, W.F. (Ed) *Global Tourism,* Butterworth and Heinemann: Oxford.

Bagri, S.C. (2003). Issues and Trends in Tourism Promoter, Bishen Singh Mahendra Pal Singh, Dehradun.

Bagri, S.C. and Bhatt A.K. (1997). Sustainable Tourism Planning and Development, Report of the Conference on Sustainable Tourism Planning and Development, August 8-10, 1997, IITTM Gwalior.

World Tourism Organisation (1993). Sustainable Tourism Development: Guide for Local Planners, Madrid, Spain.

World Tourism Organisation (1996). WTO News, No. 2, Madrid.

Sustainable Tourism Planning and Development, 137-146, 2006
Edited by Bagri, S.C.
Published by Bishen Singh Mahendra Pal Singh, Dehra Dun, India

Sustainable Tourism in Developing Countries : Relevance and Challenges

Surender Pal Singh

UGC Research Scholar
Department of Tourism Management, Kurukshetra University, Kurukshetra
E-mail : surindermorwal@yahoo.co.in

Abstract : This paper presents an analysis of the relevance of and challenges to Sustainable Tourism Development (STD) in developing countries and suggests timely remedies. STD offers a much broader approach to the reform of tourism practices and a built-inability to control the rate of growth and sale of tourism product. The normative offers the principles but the question of accountability; affordability; dual pricing of destination; long run vs short run focus; high value-low volume proposition and to ensure tourism education and awareness are some of the challenges ahead. Although, the principles of STD are beneficial, their implementation is an enormous task to achieve owing to the prevailing socio-economic and political conditions in developing world. The success of sustainable tourism largely depends upon the financial and technical assistance by the developed world and international organizations like International Monetary Fund (IMF) and World Bank.

Key Words : Sustainability, tourism, tourist, development, local people.

Introduction

The last five decades have witnessed a growing recognition of the importance of the sustainability, imperative for the survival of mankind. Sustainability means "the average well-being of global population over time". Sustainable development is defined by United Nations World Commission on the Environment and Development (1987) as the "Development that meets the needs of the present without compromising the ability of future generations to meet their own need". Writers generally trace the origin of the term sustainable development back to 1987 World Commission on Environment and Development report entitled "Our Common Future" (also know as Brundtland Report) in order to attempt the smooth and transparent integration of economy, society and environment-the three-dimensional 'sustainability-trinity'. Sustainable tourism, which is derived from the general concept of sustainable development, is an approach that has arisen because of the need to avoid environmental, social and economic pitfalls. The World Tourism Organization (WTO) has defined STD as that which meets the needs of present tourists and host regions while protecting and enhancing opportunity for the future. It is envisaged as leading to the management of all resources in such a way that economic, social and aesthetic needs can be fulfilled while maintaining cultural integrity, essential ecological processes, biological diversity and life support systems. The Pressure Group on Tourism Concern has defined sustainable tourism as "Tourism (and associated infrastructure) that operates within the capacity of natural resources to ensure their viability for future generations, recognizes the contribution of local people and their culture, accepts that these people must have an equitable share in the economic benefits of tourism, and is guided by the wishes of local people and communities in the destination areas".

The concept of sustainability applies to all sectors of economy including tourism. Tourism is a multi-beneficial industry in terms of foreign exchange earning, generating employment and revenue, boosting the local economy and preserving the fragile environment and has proved 'indispensable' for the development of any region or country. The significance of sustainability in tourism is recognized by developing countries keeping in view the negative impacts of mass tourism. The National Tourism Policy of India (2002) emplanning rests on the sustainable principles. Thus Sustainability should serve as a guiding force for the new policy. The development and management strategies should be so worked out as to ensure that tourism largely acts as a smokeless industry and its ecological footprints remain as soft as possible. No one should be allowed to secure short-term gains by resorting to what has been called the darker side of tourism. Neither over-exploitation of natural resources should be permitted nor the carrying capacity of the tourist sites ignored.

Greater emphasis should be laid on ecotourism whose parameters should be broader than those of nature tourism alone. It must rap in eliminating poverty in ending unemployment, in creating new skills, in enhancing the status of woman, in preserving cultural heritage, in encouraging tribal and local crafts and in improving and facilitating overall environmental growth of a more than just and fair social order. For developing countries, sustainable tourism in the Journal of Tourism Management (2001) relies on:

a) Meeting the needs of the host population in terms of improved standards of living in the short and long term;

b) Satisfying the demands of increasing tourist numbers and continuing to attract them to achieve this; and

c) Safeguarding the environment to achieve the two foregoing aims.

The environment considered above encompasses the broader sense of socioeconomic and natural phenomenon as well as biophysical elements.

Relevance of Sustainable Tourism

Developing countries seem to suffer generally because of having less use of advanced technology, poor economy, under-utilization of major resources, external indebtedness and poor quality of life. Under these circumstances, sustainable tourism can play a vital role in balanced development not only in the present scenario, but also to meet the needs of coming generations of the world, particularly for developing countries.

The comparative advantage the developing countries seem to enjoy is unspoiled nature and other tourist products. Cohen (1978) suggests that "as unspoiled nature becomes rare and competition fore is stiffer, developing nations are better placed to impose the terms of its exploitation on the developed nations who seek it". Negative impacts due to unruly mass tourism is the major concern of the existing and potential tourist destinations worldwide. For the success of sustainability it is necessary that the outcomes related to negative impact should be minimum. Findings of field studies reveal that Alpine ecosystem, destination of Himalayas (Shimla, Manali, Mussoorie, Nainital) are under stress due to overcrowding and pollution. Over 1,300 years old Magdalenian cave paintings in France have miserably suffered from visitors' breath and moisture. In Egypt, the constant pounding of visitors' feet is destroying the ancient sites. In India, incidents of landslides in the Himalaya, high temperature on hill stations, disturbance at beaches of Goa are some of the negative impacts reported. Thailand, Singapore, Sri Lanka and some other countries are struggling with the problems of child abuse, prostitution and cultural shook. Going beyond the carrying capacity is the major cause for these unwanted situations. Tourism must be planned according to the sustainability and optimum carrying capacity of touristic areas for future need. Hawkes and Williams (1993) state that the concept of sustainable tourism embodies a challenge to develop the world's tourism capacity and the quality of its products, without adversely affecting the environment that maintains and nurtures them. Developing countries have still time to take hold over the present situation and take necessary steps to avoid further deterioration of existing and future prospects in order to establish it as "A forever a green industry".

Sustainable tourism can contribute to the overall sustainable development. The 1992 United Nations Conference on Environment and Development (UNCED), the Rio Earth Summit, identified Travel and Tourism as one of the key sectors of the economy, which could make a positive contribution and which is economically, ecologically and more socially sustainable because it has lesser impact on natural resources and the environment than most other industries. Secondly, tourism is based on enjoyment and appreciation of local culture, heritage and natural environment and, finally it strives to play a positive role in increasing consumer commitment to sustainable development principles through its unparalleled consumer distribution channel. According to Curry and Mooveridi (1992) "the potential for sustainability in tourism lies within the principles of sustainable development. Hence, any tourism policy should reflect concern for the environment and provision of an economic resource base for future generation with the concept of sustainability, depending upon the persistence or desirability of a system's productivity under known or possible conditions, and consumption not exceeding resources". Developed countries can bring uniformity between tourism policy and overall development in order to find their future 'qualitative and quantitative' safe and favorable. Michael Hall (1992) suggests that "the vital recognition of the social dimension of the relationship between tourism development and the environment has been absent in ecotourism in the South-West Pacific, thus compromising sustainability". Balanced planning of different sectors may help to achieve common development objectives. It is worth mentioning here that tourism industry itself is a blend of a number of major industries of an economy.

Sustainability can be used as a gimmick for tourism promotion by the developing countries this being a 'catchy word'. Wight (1993) observes that some businesses and tourism promotional agencies have attempted to cashin on the growing interest in nature- based tourism by adopting an ecotourism label as a promotional gimmick, a ploy to attract consumers. On the other hand, travellers also understand the need of ecofriendly tourism and spend more. A U.S. Travel Data Centre Survey (1992) revealed that "travellers, on an average, would spend 8.5% more for travel services and products, provided there are environmentally responsible suppliers (including transportation, accommodations, food services, attractions and sightseeing tours)". The developing nations have enough natural and fresh tourist resources, which is an advantage for USP and destination positioning.

Sustainable and strategic tourism planning is Hobson's choice for the developing countries to stay competitive in long run. Developing nations have full prospects as these regions abound in unique biodiversity, ranging from tropical to *savana* grassland and secluded beaches fringed with corals. According to Pearce *et al.* (1989) "a major problem in the past has been that environmental considerations have not been incorporated in models or measurements and thus not in decisions making". The environment was externally treated as 'free' goods. Tourism planning in these countries is still in its nub. It is high time to formulate a comprehensive tourism development plan keeping in view the tourism (is a golden chicken which lays golden eggs) for the coming generation. It is effective sustainable tourism planning which prolongs the life cycles of destinations and also fosters the notion of developing satellite destinations. It is strategic planning which can turn this industry from good to the best. Precise data on sustainable tourism earnings are not available. A World Wide Fund for Nature (WWF) study estimates that out of $55 billion earned through tourism by the developing countries in 1988, about $12 billion was the result of Ecotourism. Dominica, Costa Rica, Kenya, Zimbabwe and Bhutan are some of the set examples of successful sustainable tourism for other developing countries.

Tourism education and interpretation is another important ingredient of sustainable tourism. Active participation of local community in sustainable tourism activity provides an opportunity to get the exposure of external environment in widening the perspective, knowing the technological advancement and, most importantly to remove the social and cultural frictions with the guests so as to achieve international peace and understanding. In developing countries, local people often earn low benefits as underpaid labour forces but they have to bear major costs. Tourism education may help the locals to recognize the benefits and true nature of tourism to ensure awareness of destination environment and positive attitude towards the guests.

Challenges to Sustainable Tourism

The positive contribution of sustainable tourism is significant but there are a number of challenges to be met if the potential of sustainable local development and poverty alleviation through the localization of benefits is to be realized. The question of accountability is a major challenge from planning level to achieving results from STD for developing countries like India. Erlet and Dekadt (1992) suggest that operation of "the market will not itself lead to sustainable tourism practices. A more proactive role needs to be taken by the relevant organizations, associations, governments and institutions". The key participants in tourism industry like accommodation sector, transport sector, regional development groups, stakeholders, destination planners and local community have their own interest(s) and agenda(s). It is difficult to provide them a set-stage of harmony in order to achieve the desired objectives due to fact that the interests of these players are conflicting and incompatible. According to Kripendorf (1987) "everybody wants more business; a larger share of the market; use of well-contrived methods to reach their respective goal". The priority of private sector is to stay competitive and to cash on the opportunity of tourist resources to the maximum extent, trespassing the notion of sustainability. It is crystal clear that holiday producers are not charitable institutions but commercial undertakings. The tourism policy of developing countries use sustainability as an ideal word but hardly discloses how to achieve it. The complex tourism industry hints to the difficult solution of such a situation. The research study conducted by Planning Department of East Sussex County Council in UK (1997) reveals that "despite the willingness on the part of the small business to engage itself in sustainable activities, those engaged in the tourism business have little understanding of the concept of sustainability. The vague principles do not easily translate into workable-place". How to ensure accountability of the key players is a big question in itself.

The question of affordability for sustainable destination development is one of the major issues. How can the developing world which is struggling with the basic problems of food, health, shelter, education and poverty develop projects of sustainable tourism? Clark (1991) also endorsed this view, suggesting that "there is some poverty level below which sustainability becomes an unaffordable luxury. Vast numbers of impoverished people throughout the world face this dilemma every day of their lives". STD is possible with advanced technological know-how, managerial efficiency and financial assistance in which these countries are lagging behind. It is estimated that on an average, a five star hotel consumes as much water as five local villages and 28 times more electricity per day than a local village. Hundreds of gallon water is required to sustain a golf course. It is unaffordable for a developing country to sustain its tourist attractions where people are dying due to the scarcity of food and water. Heavy pumps are being buried to sustain the tourist resources, but the local community is suffering from the problem of low water-table and other natural calamities which surround almost all the developing countries of the world. Sustainable tourism can be successful if it is economically viable. The destination should be at least self-sustaining. The findings of cost-benefit analysis and feasibility study (environmental and social) should be favourable. How can the developing countries afford destinations, which are not economically viable and further investments for their sustainability? Developing countries, which have been successful in developing sustainable tourism, are able to do so because of timely assistance by the developed world. Erlet Cater and Lowman (1994) discloses that the "British Govt. helps by giving £12 million within a large multidoner project to improve the management of Kenya Wildlife Service". The earnings should meet at least the fixed and variable costs of the destination to survive for sustainable tourism growth. Developing countries posses significant affordability for various attractions like national parks, reserve areas, entertainment centres, and golf courses.

It is a general belief, that by increasing the price of the destination, the influx of tourist can be controlled. Developing countries, which are generally democratic and populist in nature, have to tackle the problem of price-discrimination for the same destination. For instance, in India, the system of dual entry fee at Golkunda Fort and Taj Mahal at Agra have become controversial. For domestic tourists it is nominal while for foreign tourists it is many times more. The authorities are facing criticism on this issue of tourism organizations, experts, planners and other social and pressure groups in and outside the country. In order to avoid this backlash, it is advisable that developing countries should set their price at a level which could be an 'accepted price' for all the segments of travel trade. Developing countries are in the dilemma of short-run vs long-run focus of tourism development. Developing countries like India have chronic and severe macro-economic problems such as high rate of unemployment, rapid growth of the working age population, high rate of inflation, etc. Thus, developing world does not have any other option than to support current tourism development, which is impairing the environment, socio-cultural sanctity of the destinations and obvious

144

dangers. The economies of some developing countries like Singapore, Malaysia have improved drastically because of tourism, but at cost of environmental degradation, social and cultural malpractices. It is a major conclusion that STD is an enormously difficult task to achieve in developing countries without the collaboration of the international tour operators and donor agencies, such as World Bank and IMF. It will be quite impressive if developing countries evolve consensus on the sustainable use of their tourist resources considering their common (social, cultural, environmental and economical) conditions, avoiding inter-competition for international tourist arrivals and receipts. Financial and technological know-how can be impressively used not only to retrieve the past losses but also for future games to balance tourism development with social and cultural bonding. World Travel and Tourism Council statistics points out that the tourist arrivals and receipts will increase in the developing world, indirecting a positive nod to support sustainable tourism.

As case studies conclude high value-low volume is not the synonym to sustainable tourism, rather it is the degree of impacts that matters. For example, the environment of Andaman & Nicobar is deteriorating, though the carrying capacity of all the islands is fixed. This misconception can lead to the danger fall in tourist arrivals and loss of earnings. The form and scale of international tourism is largely shaped by international tour operators. The Department of Environment (1992) states that "the tourism industry should flourish in response to the market while respecting the environment which attracts visitors but also has far wider and enduring value". Intense competition between identical tourist destinations in terms of price and wider supply of services increase the dependency of destination countries on the international tour operators. This high level of market dependency puts the developing countries in a position of haphazard and mass tourism, ignoring 'value and volume' proposition.

Ensuring community participation and tourism education for sustainable tourism is another problem of developing countries with the facts that they have low literacy rate, dearth of tourism educational institutes and research, poor means of information technology, etc. When local community does not understand the significance and benefits of tourism, the approach of sustainable tourism cannot be successful. It is mandatory to adopt different and more interactive methods to spread tourism education and interpretation. The success of Thenmala

Ecotourism project in Kerala can be sited here as an example, which is being developed in accordance with internationally accepted principles of ecotourism and where education and interpretation is a major component and local people are benefitted.

Conclusion

Sustainable tourism is not just the creation of a healthy all-time prosperous tourism. It is much more. It means accepting a commitment to provide healthy long-term tourism thoroughly integrated with other elements of economy, environment and society in such a manner that a policy change in one does not unduly interfere with the optimal functioning of any of the others. World Development Report (1992) says that there is a growing consensus that policies for economic efficiency and for environment management are complementary. Good environment policies are good economic policies and vice-versa. Till date, the lesser tourist flow can be taken as boon that has left resources unspoiled but damage might have been done by lack of upkeep of destinations. Efforts can be made now onwards to promote or use them with sustainability in mind. Sustainable tourism should not be executed on experimental basis to a limited number of sites but should be an integral component of all tourism planning. Tourism should not be developed without this additional and essential dimension.

References

Berry, S. and Adele, L. (1997). Sustainable Tourism: a Regional Perspective, *Journal of Tourism Management*, Vol. 18 (7), p.p. 433-440.

Clark, C.W. (1991). Economics Biases Against Sustainable Development, in Costanza, R.(ed) *Ecological Economics*, Columbia, New York.

Cohen, E. (1978). The impact of tourism on the Physical environment, *Annals of Tourism Research*, p.p. 215-237.

Curry, S. and Mooveridi, B. (1992). Sustainable Tourism: Illustrations from Kenya, Nepal and Jamacia, in cooper, C.P. and Lockwood, A.(eds) *Progress in Tourism, Recreation and Hospitality Management*, Belhaveh, London.

Dekadt, E. (1992). Making the Alternative Sustainable: Lesson from Development for Tourism, in Smith, V.L. and Eadington, W.R. (eds) *Tourism Alternation*, University of Pennsylvania Press, Philadelphia.

Department of Environment (1992). *Policy Planning Guidelines 21*, HM 50, London.

146

Erlet Cater and Lowman, G. (1994). *Ecotourism : A sustainable option?* John Wiley and Sons Ltd., p. 88.

Hall, C.M. (1992). *Issues in Eco-tourism: From Susceptible to Sustainable Development in Heritage Management; Parks, Heritage and Tourism,* Royal Australia Institute of Parks and Recreation, Hobart.

Hawkes, S. and William, P. (1993). *The Greening of Tourism from Principles to Practice,* Globe'92.

Journal of Tourism Management (1998). *Beyond the Rhetoric of Sustainable Tourism,* Vol. 19 (3), p.p. 201-212.

Kripendorf, J. (1987). *The Holidaymaker.* Butterworth Heinemann, London.

Mohan Lal, K.G. (2001). Ecotourism in Kerala, *Journal of Sajosps,* p. 104.

Pearce, D.W., Markandya, A. and Barbier, E.D. (1989). *Blueprint for a Green Economy,* Earthscan, London. WWF Ecotourism.

UK Pressure Group on Tourism Concern (2002). *In Beyond the Green Horizon : Principles of Sustainable Tourism. National Tourism Policy of India* 2, No. V. VI.

US Travel Data Centre Survey (1992). *Travel Industry Association of America,* p. 43.

Wight (1993). Sustainable : Balancing Economics, Environmental and Social Goals within an Ethical Framework. *Journal of Tourism Studies,* Vol. 4 (2), p.p. 54-66.

World Commission on the Environment and Development (1987). p. 42.

Word Tourism Organization (1995). *Planning for Sustainable Development : National and Regional Tourism Planning, Methodologies and Case Studies,* Madrid.

Sustainable Tourism Planning and Development, 147-151, 2006
Edited by Bagri, S.C.
Published by Bishen Singh Mahendra Pal Singh, Dehra Dun, India

Temporal Distribution of Tourists in Goa

S.M. Ambli

S.P. Chowgule College, Margao-Goa

Abstract : Tourism as a phenomenon in the context of Goa has been a post-liberation experience. Tourist arrivals in Goa are neither ubiquitously nor spatially distributed throughout Goa over a period of time. There is a strong bias of the tourists to come to Goa particularly in the months of November to February. This is observed almost every year that the winter months are attracting more than 60% of the total arrivals of both domestic and international tourists. The months in rainy season are the lean months for tourist arrival. The paper will take into account the secondary data available from the Tourism Department and analyse the same – monthwise, seasonwise, yearwise.

Key Words : Goa tourist, Season tourist.

Introduction

The state of Goa has emerged as one of the most sought after holiday making areas in the world. The hospitality industry has contributed to the economy of the state in terms of earnings, and employment generation besides helping to improve the living standards of the people, infrastructure development, such as hotels, lodgings, paying guest houses (1893), travel agents (146), tour operators (91), tourists guides (59), dealers (20), tourist taxi operator (2710), and tourist boat operator (11) as an recorded till 2004. Accordingly, there is a positive change in the economic aspects of the state of Goa which accounts for 10% of the employment in Goa.

Objectives

The article aims at analysing the temporal distribution of tourist arrivals in Goa, yearwise, monthwise and seasonwise – The article refers to the basic concepts, such as distribution of tourists in relation to who, when, how, why, etc.

Methodology

All the data used in the article are taken from the published records (secondary data) of the Department of Tourism, Govt. of Goa and the methodology involves simple cartographic representation of data and analysis of the same.

Location

The state of Goa has an area of 3702 sq kms, enjoys tropical maritime location lying between north latitude 14^0 53' 57" and 15^0 27' 59" and east longitudes from 73^0 40' 54" to 74^0 20' 11" in the west coast of India, i.e. "Konkan". Flanked by the Arabian Sea in the west and the Sahyadris in the east, it has numerous streams in its area. The state of Maharashtra to the north and the state of Karnataka to the east and south form the boundary of Goa.

Climate

The climate of Goa is influenced by its location, i.e. maritime tropical in the West Coast of India. The summer temperature is around 35^0 Celsius, i.e. between March and May. The rainy season experiences precipitation of about 250 cms of rainfall, i.e. between June and September. The mild winter season is experienced between November and February. The transition between rainy season and the winter season is in the month of October, i.e. autumn and parts of February and March form the transition of spring.

Heritage

The state of Goa is known both for its natural and cultural heritage. There are over 29 beaches in the 105 km long coastline of Goa. The deciduous and evergreen Sahyadris also present a pleasing tropical forest area with four important wildlife sanctuaries. The cultural heritage reflects historical influences and, therefore, they exhibit a composite culture of different ages of Goa's history. It said that Goa is bestowed with the best of the east and the west. It is therefore has churches, temples, fairs, festivals, *jatras* (Pilgrimage) which exhibit societal harmony. These form the important pull factors for the tourist arrival.

Tourist Arrivals

Goa has been attracting, from ancient times many foreign travellers besides domestic tourists who have left their record and observations. The post-liberation (December 1961) period has seen a tremendous increase in arrival of the foreign tourists. The following diagrams indicate the tourist arrivals from 1997 to 2002 and 1962 to 2002 respectively.

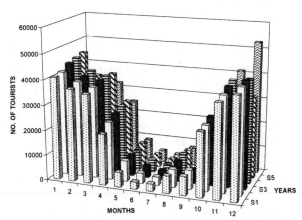

MONTHWISE ARRIVAL OF FOREIGN TOURISTS(1997-2002)

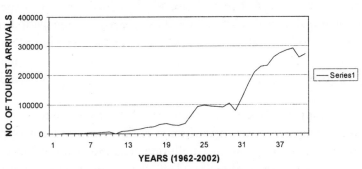

FOREIGN ARRIVALS IN GOA (1962-2002)

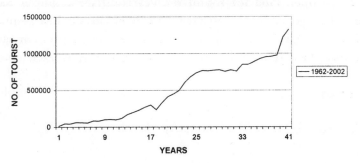

DOMESTIC TOURIST ARRIVALS IN GOA(1962-2002)

The diagrams clearly indicate slow arrivals of tourist during 1960's which increased rapidly 1970 onwards. The year 1970 witnessed the first lakh tourist arrivals, second lakh 1975, third lakh in 1978, fourth lakh in 1981, fifth lakh in 1983, sixth lakh in 1984, seventh lakh in 1985, eighth lakh in 1986, ninth lakh in 1993, tenth lakh in 1994, eleventh lakh in 1995, twelfth lakh in 1998, thirteenth lakh in 2001 and fifteenth lakh tourist visited Goa during 2002-2003 – it is reported that over 20 lakh tourists have visited Goa in 2004.

Nationality

Tourism is a leisure activity which involves tourists' attitude, leisure, money and resourcefulness of the destination area. These attributes are best represented by GDP, their world ranking. They are basically from North America, Europe, Far East and South Africa with their world ranking forming important push factors besides the winter weather conditions.

Monthwise Distribution

The table of tourist arrivals, both domestic and foreign, and the graphs indicate dominance of winter months in attracting tourists to Goa. The movement is more like the migration of birds during winter but the international arrivals show extremities is arrivals. Lean period in the rainy season of Goa while the peak period in during the winter.

Observations

There is lot of scope for promotion of rural ethnic tourism in Goa. However, for sustainability of tourism it is the prime concern of public and private sectors to keep Goa pollution free and make it a preferred destination for tourist worldwide. Goa Tourism in its vision document planned to open Goa for round the year tourism activities but the parameters suggested for the carrying capacity of Goa's tourist destinations should also be taken into consideration in order to keep visitor satisfied and to place Goa Tourism Board in the world tourism market.

References

WTO (1993). WTO News, No. 5, Sept./Oct. Madrid.

WTO/UNEP (1992). Guidelines: Development of National Parks and Protected Areas for Tourism, Joint Technical Reports Series, Paris.

UNEP (1989). Asia/Pacific Consultative Meeting on Conservation of Critical Ecosystem and Economic Development. UNEP Regional Office for Asia and the Pacific, Bangkok.

UNEP (1992). *Industry and Environment.* July-December, Paris.

Sustainable Tourism Planning and Development, 153-161, 2006
Edited by Bagri, S.C.
Published by Bishen Singh Mahendra Pal Singh, Dehra Dun, India

Environmental Codes of Conduct for Sustainable Ecotourism Development in India

Tarun Roy

Sustainable Tourism Consultant, New Delhi

Introduction

Sustainable development emphasized economic development, social development and environmental protection at the local, national, regional and global levels as well as poverty eradication and human development. In the Plan of Implementation of the World Summit on Sustainable Development' 2002, emphasis was given on protection and management of the natural resources base for economic and social development as human activities are having an increasing impact on the integrity of ecosystems that provide essential resources and services for human well-being and economic activities. Special focus of the implementation plan was given to promote sustainable tourism development and it includes ecotourism as an emphasis, taking into account the spirit of the International Year of Ecotourism' 2002.

Key Words : Ecotourism, sustainable tourism, environment.

Scope of Ecotourism development

India is a vast sub-continent and have enormous tourism potential with greatest biological diversity (India ranks as the 12th mega biodiversity country in the world) and natural heritage. India possesses a wide coverage of 1,50,809.6 sq. km. protected areas and includes 89 National Parks, 500 Wildlife Sanctuaries, 27 Tiger Reserves, 14 Elephant Reserves, 9 Biosphere Reserves, 3 Natural World Heritage Sites, 183 Wetlands, 19 Ramsar Sites with infinite variety of flora and fauna. The 7,000 km coastline includes breathtaking beaches, mangrove and coral reef areas, and superb islands are also potential for ecotourism. "The mighty Himalayas" – world's highest mountain range, covers 2,500 km in length and 250 km in wide cradles with verdant valleys, glacial lakes, wild rivers, alpine meadows, water falls, frozen glaciers, snow-capped peaks that are a great attraction to ecotourists. All these can make India an outstandingly year-round diversified ecotourism destination.

Ecotourism Development

Considering the vast potential and scope and importance of sustainable tourism, ecotourism has been recognized for sustainable tourism development in the country. The Ministry of Tourism, Govt. of India has already drawn up a Policy and Guidelines' 1998 for the growth of Ecotourism in India. In the *National Tourism Policy 2002*, emphasis had been given to (a) impart dynamism and speed to the process of sustainable development as well conservation, and also the socio-economic advancement of the local communities, and the communities in the neighborhood, (b) Promote sustainability which should serve as a guiding star for the new policy in which over-exploitation of natural resources should not be permitted nor the carrying capacity of the tourist-sites ignored, (c) it must help in preserving cultural heritage with overall improvement of environment, and (d) Promotion of rural tourism and with tourism development in small settlements should not endanger the lives of ethnic minorities.

Ecotourism Products

In the competitive global tourism market, consumer trends are also changing towards new products. The modern tourists seek off-beaten-track destinations that are remote and lesser known. It demands the market of Special Interest Tourism – culture, ecology, trekking, river rafting, wildlife safaris, bird watching, flora and fauna, etc. which are generally treated and presumed to be the major components of ecotourism. There is enormous opportunity and prosperity for sustainable ecotourism in India and expected to meet the growing demands of the global ecotourism market.

Sustainable Ecotourism Development

It has been always observed that mass tourism is more or less destructive and very unfortunately our domestic tourists' attitude is so negative and vulnerable that it greatly effects our environment. Environmental conservation is the key factor and basic instrument for the growth of sustainable ecotourism development. WTO, WTTC, PATA, UNEP and Ecotourism Society have already given priority to environmental conservation in formulation of strategic policy, scientific planning and effective management for sustainable tourism development. Environmental conservation highlights the need for air, soil and water conservation, maintaining essential ecological processes and life support systems. The UNDP has also strongly emphasized environmental protection for poverty elimination, for linking the management and maintenance of the country's floral and faunal wealth, and of the fragile ecosystems. The UNEP and Ecotourist Society have already prepared new guidelines for ecotourism Principles, Practices and Policies for Sustainability. Environmental protection was emphasised in the 9th Five Year Plan and in the 10th Five-Year Plan.

Environmental Codes of Conduct for Ecotourism

Environmental codes of conduct are the guidelines based on the Do's and Don'ts - the keys of environmental conservation for control of the growth of sustainable Ecotourism. Awareness plays an important role in promoting conservation in the tourism industry. Awareness develops an appropriate and positive attitude among people, by removing any wrong perceptions they had and fostering better understanding about tourism. Awareness can be created through campaigns, training, exhibitions, seminars/conferences, fairs/carnivals, publicity materials/activities, etc. The Department of Tourism, Govt. of India has evolved certain environmental guidelines and pledges as Environmental Codes of Conduct in the Ecotourism Policy & Guidelines' 1998 for sustainable ecotourism development. These guidelines are based on the PATA Code of Environmentally Responsible Tourism, Environmental Guidelines of the World Travel & Tourism Council, Global Code of Ethics for Tourism as adopted by the World Tourism Organization, Himalayan Code of Conduct prepared by the Himalayan Tourism Advisory Board and Ecotourism Guidelines by the Ecotourism Society and United Nations Environment Programme. The following are the environmental codes of conduct categorically drawn up by the Ministry of Tourism, Government of India:

The Government

❑ The management Plan for each area should be prepared by professional landscape architects and urban planners in consultation with the local community as well as others directly concerned.

- Integrated planning should be adopted to avoid inter-sectoral and cross-sectoral conflict.

- The architectural programme for ecotourism centres should include controlled access points and cabins, roads, self-guided nature trails, transportation options, interpretive centres, signs, observation towers and blinds, adequate but unpretentious lodging and dining facilities, docks, garbage disposal facility and other utilities as per requirement. If needed, suitable living quarters and facilities for project personnel have to be provided.

- Structures creating visual pollution, unaesthetic values and non-compatible architecture, should be controlled and temporary structures using local building material and befitting the local environment should be encouraged.

- Exclude developments in geologically unstable zones and define development and buffer zones after proper environmental impact assessments.

- Establish standards, building codes and other regulations.

- Specify environmental, physical and social carrying capacities to limit development activities.

- Ensure continuous monitoring of adverse effects of tourism activities and initiate suitable corrective measures.

- Recognise and award quality labels to ecotourism operators.

- Provide visitor information and interpretation services covering particularly – (i) what to see, (ii) how to see, (iii) how to behave. It can be by way of brochures, leaflets, specialised guides, and visitor information centres.

- Prepare and widely distribute codes of conduct to all visitors.

- Launch training programmes on ecotourism for tourism administrators, planners, operators and general public.

Developers, Operators and Suppliers

- Respect and follow the planning restrictions, standards and codes provided by the government and local authorities.

❑ Implement sound environment principles through self-regulation.

❑ Practice environmental impact assessment for all new projects and conduct regular environmental audit for all ongoing activities leading to development of environmental improvement programmes.

❑ Be sensitive to conservation of environmentally protected or threatened areas, species and scenic aesthetics, achieving landscape enhancement wherever possible.

❑ Ensure that all structures are unobtrusive and do not interfere with the natural ecosystem to the maximum extent.

❑ Recognise the optimal environmental capacity and sociological use-limits of the site in creating tourist facilities. They should also take into account safety and convenience of tourists.

❑ Buildings should be designed strictly on functional and environmental considerations and avoid overconstruction.

❑ Local material and designs should be used in all construction to the extent possible.

❑ Physical planning, architectural design and construction of tourist facilities should employ eco-friendly techniques like solar energy, capture and utilisation of rain water, recycling of garbage, natural cross-ventilation instead of air-conditioning, a high level of self-sufficiency in food generation through orchards, ecological farms, aqua-culture and such.

❑ Energy and water-saving practices should be employed to the extent possible. Fresh water management and controlled sewage disposal also should be practiced.

❑ Control air emissions – both chemical pollutants and noise.

❑ Control and reduce environmentally unfriendly products such as asbestos, DFCs, pesticides and toxic, corrosive, infectious, explosive or flammable material.

❑ Respect and support historic or religious objects and sites.

❑ Provide information and interpretive services to visitors, especially on attractions and facilities, safety and security, local customs and traditions, prohibitions and regulations and self-conduct and behaviour.

❑ Ensure adequate opportunities to visitors for mixing with nature and native cultures.

❑ In marketing ecotourism products, customers should be given correct information, as the visitors who appreciate ecotourism products usually belong to environmentally aware groups.

❑ Training and research programmes of the company should include environmental issues.

❑ Prepare tourists to minimise possible negative impacts while visiting the tourist places.

❑ Ensure safety and security of visitors and inform them of precautions to be taken.

❑ Exercise due regard for the interest of the local population, including their history, tradition and culture and future economic development.

❑ Involve the local community to the extent possible in various activities and vocations.

The Visitors

❑ Help to conserve habitats, those of flora and fauna and any site of natural or cultural interest which may be affected by tourism.

❑ Make no open fires and discourage others from doing so. If water has to be heated with scare firewood use as little as possible. Where feasible, use kerosene or fuel-efficient wood stoves.

❑ Remove litter, burn or bury paper and carry back all non-degradable litter.

❑ Keep local water clean and avoid using pollutants such as detergents in streams or springs. If no toilet facilities are available, try to relieve yourself at least 30 metres away from water source and bury or cover the waste.

❑ Plants should be left to flourish in their natural environment and avoid taking away cuttings, seeds and roots.

❑ Leave the campsites clean after use. Remember that another party will be using the same camp site after your departure.

❑ Help guides and porters to follow conservation measures. Do not allow cooks/porters to throw garbage in streams or rivers.

- Respect the natural and cultural heritage of the area and follow local customs.

- Respect local etiquette and wear loose clothes. Kissing in public is disapproved of.

- Respect privacy of individuals and ask permission and use restraint in taking photographs of local inhabitants.

- Respect holy places – do not touch or remove religious objects.

- Strictly follow the guidelines for personal safety and security and always take your own precautions and safety measures.

The Destination Population/Host Community

- Realise and respect the value of the environment, the flora and fauna, the monuments and the cultural heritage.

- Practice conservation of nature and culture as a way of life.

- Establish guidelines to protect valuable local resources and foster tourism management.

- Realise and react to the potential threat of investors who see opportunities in development but lack sensitivity to local values.

- Become effective nature guides and conservationists of natural areas by enhancing the practical and ancestral knowledge of the natural features of the area.

- Be friendly with visitors and help them to practice ecotourism codes.

Non-Governmental Organisations/Scientific & Research Institutions

- Create awareness amongst all concerned about the importance of sound eco-practices in tourism development.

- Motivate the local community to increase their involvement in sustainable tourism activities.

- Organise training programmes to prepare the local people for taking up various vocations relating to ecotourism.

Role of Youth in Sustainable Ecotourism Development

Youths are the backbone of a nation. One of the objectives of the India's National Youth Policy' 2003 was to promote a major participatory role for the youth in the protection and preservation of natural resources to channelise their abundant energies in community service so as to improve the environment and foster a scientific, inquisitive reasoning and rational attitude in the younger generation. Considering the importance of community involvement in preservation of the environment, the policy also advocates motivating the youth to develop respect for nature and to lead lifestyles that are less resource consumptive and more source conservationist. Promotion and support of youth participation in programmes and activities for the achievements of sustainable development by encouraging their establishments where they do not exist, was emphasized in the broad plan of implementation of the United Nations' *"World Summit on Sustainable Development' 2002"*. UNEP also places great emphasis on communicating with the youth of today and educating today's youth about the environmental needs of tomorrow. With great importance of the role of youth, it is imperative that participation of the youth should be emphasized in all programmes and activities for sustainable tourism development in the country where the youth can share the responsibility for promoting environmental conservation and changing the negative and vulnerable attitude of the domestic tourists and local communities.

Conclusion

Ecotourism development has vast opportunity and possibility of further promotion in India with environmental conservation and development of positive attitude of the domestic tourists. It needs scientific planning and implementation of the existing National Tourism Policy and the Tourism Action Plans for sustainability of ecotourism. However, it is only possible if the following points are considered for further tourism development.

❑ Promotion of environmental and conservation with ecotourism awareness.

❑ Uniform environmental codes of conduct for all natural sites/places.

❑ To develop positive attitude of the domestic tourists/visitors.

References

Department of Tourism, Govt. of India (1998). Eco-tourism Policy & Guidelines, New Delhi.

Department of Tourism, Govt. of India (2002-03). Annual Report, New Delhi.

Ministry of Environment & Forests, Govt. of India, New Delhi (1988). National Forest Policy, New Delhi.

Ministry of Environment & Forests, Govt. of India (2000). National Forestry Action Programme-India Executive Summary, Vol-1, New Delhi.

Ministry of Tourism & Culture, Govt. of India, National Tourism Policy (2002). New Delhi.

Ministry of Environment & Forests, Govt. of India (2002). Environment News, (2002) Vol. 6, New Delhi.

Ministry of Environment & Forests, Govt. of India (2002-2003). National Wildlife Action Plan, 2002-2016, New Delhi.

Ministry of Environment & Forests (2002-03). Annual Report, Govt. of India, New Delhi.

Ministry of Youth Affairs & Sports, Govt. of India (2004), National Youth Policy (2003). New Delhi.

United Nations Environment Programme (2001). Annual Report, Paris.

World Travel & Tourism Council (2001-02). Annual Report, New York.

Sustainable Tourism Planning and Development, 163-167, 2006
Edited by Bagri, S.C.
Published by Bishen Singh Mahendra Pal Singh, Dehra Dun, India

Food and Beverage Industry in Garhwal Himalaya: A Case Study of Srinagar Garhwal

Saurabh Dixit

Institute of Tourism and Hotel Management
Bundelkhand University, Jhansi

Abstract : The hospitality industry is one of the fastest growing economic sectors and it is already the world's largest industry, employing over 15 million people. This is the only industry that generates maximum number of indirect employment. Food and Beverage (F&B) sector is one of the major constituents of the hospitality industry and comprises of a number of F&B units and services. Accommodation sector is mainly responsible for arranging rooms for tourists and other traveller.

Key Words : Food, beverage, service, hospitality, Srinagar.

Introduction

The simple definition of Food and Beverage Service is the provision of food and drinks ready for consumption away from the home. This however fails to differentiate the Food and Beverage Service industry from the retailing industry – a distinction that is becoming increasingly difficult to identify in view of the growth in takeaway restaurants, convenience stores and fast food outlets. However a F&B establishment is defined in these terms:

❑ The goods sold are usually consumed on the premises.

❑ The buyer is able to determine the quantity of goods purchased in retail shop but in a catering unit the caterer determines quantity, i.e. portion size.

❑ The caterer also determines quality as in most cases the customer orders the meal without seeing it before the order is placed.

❑ The caterer is processor of materials as well as a retailer of goods.

❑ While discussing food and beverage service one cannot ignore food and beverage production.

❏ The prime concern of these outlets is not how the food is prepared but how it is served.

Background

Srinagar is one of the important towns of Garhwal Himalaya since time immemorial. During 18th and 19th century this was the capital of Garhwal rulers. Situated on the left bank of river Alaknanda, it is located between 78⁰44" longitude to 30⁰08" N latitude at an altitude of 579 mts. It sprawls into a spacious valley (8 km long) with low hills (1500 mts) in the environ and fertile flood plains and river terraces. It is also an important transit point leading to *yatra* routes to Badrinath, Kedarnath, Valley of Flowers, Hemkund, Roopkund, Nanda Devi Biosphere Reserve, Auli etc. inviting a wide range of tourists, naturalists, scientists, mountaineers from India and abroad. Srinagar is one of the biggest educational centres housing an university, which offers a wide ranges of regular and professional courses, along with a polytechnic and a industrial training centre. Population of the town, according to 2001 census, within the municipality was approx. 45,000. But being a big educational center its population varies drastically with each session of colleges and institutions.

Methodology

In order to know the profile of the hospitality industry of Garhwal Himalaya as a whole and Srinagar in particular, an intensive survey was conducted during May and June 2004. In this survey an attempt was made to make the field study of visitors and hospitality operators at Srinagar Garhwal, which is an important transit point of the tourists proceeding to Badrinath, Kedarnath and Hemkund Sahib. Around 50 foreign and 100 domestic visitors, along with major hospitality operators at Srinagar were surveyed. Interviews were mainly conducted at different accommodation units comprising of Hotels, Garhwal Mandal Vikas Nigam (G.M.V.N.) tourist bungalows, guest houses, restaurants, and eateries.

Profile

Garhwal region has sufficient number of accommodation and food and beverage units catering to the needs of economy class tourists and pilgrims. These units are catering only to the basic requirements of provision of rooms and food for the tourists. The Garhwal region has a large number of hospitality units located at different tourist centers and intermediary stations.

However in order to ascertain the detailed profile of the hospitality industry at Srinagar Garhwal the researcher distributed questionnaires, (prepared in English) in Srinagar in June 2004. The following Table-I gives the details of existing food and beverage units at Srinagar.

Table I: Existing Food and Beverage units in Srinagar

F. & B. Unit	Number of Units	Employees roll direct/ indirect	Average Monthly Sales Tax	Monthly Turnover of each unit (average)	Per Day Average Turnover of each unit	
					Seasonal	Off seasonal
Eatery	30	300	-	Rs.55000/-	Rs.2000/-	Rs.800/-
Restaurant	10	45	Rs.260/-	Rs.1,20,000/-	Rs.4500/-	Rs.2000/-
Hotel	06	75	Rs.340/-	Rs.1,80,000/-	Rs.6000/-	Rs.2500/-
Resort	01	04	Rs.280/-	Rs. 150.000/-	Rs.5,000/-	Rs.2,000/-
Guest House	02	10	-	Rs.100.000/-	Rs.3300/-	Rs.800/-
G.M.V.N. Tourist Bungalow	02	22	Rs.480/-	Rs.1,25,000/-	Rs.8000/-	Rs.4000/-

Source : Author's Field Survey conducted in May 2004.

It is evident from the above table that most of the F&B Units did good business only during the tourist season where as lean period shows less tourist traffic. The following Table II depicts average percentage break up of expenditure during tourist season on major heads. This table also suggests major proportion of the food and beverage units expenditure made on wages, salaries, allowances, electricity, gas and fuel.

Table II: Food and Beverage units: Average Percentage break up of Expenditure

Expenditure	Eatery	Restaurant	Hotel	Resort	Guest House	G.M.V.N. Tourist Bungalow
Wages, Salaries, Allowances	40%	43%	43%	23%	20%	29%
Food & Beverages Costs	30%	29%	37%	35%	37%	28%
Administrative Expenses	1%	1%	.2%	4%	5%	8%
Repairs & Maintenance	3%	1%	1.8%	5%	7%	10%
Electricity, Gas & Fuel	26%	26%	18%	33%	31%	25%

Source : Author's Field Survey undertaken in May 2004.

Table-III gives the average monthly percentage break up of revenue of the food and beverage units. The table also reveals that there is quite a good scope for F&B services in Srinagar to become an year round business activity as these generate major revenues for hotels, resorts, guest houses and G.M.V.N. Tourist Bungalow. If we look into the survey more deeply, it is noticed that during the peak season most of the units having accommodation rely on sales of rooms, whereas during off-season hoteliers depend largely on Food and Beverage sales.

Table III: Food and Beverage Units: Average Monthly Percentage Break Up of Revenue

Revenue	Eatery	Restaurant	Hotel	Resort	Guest House	G.M.V.N. Tourist Bungalow
Room Sales	N.A.	N.A.	40%	55%	45%	55%
Food Sales	65%	55%	38%	32%	28%	35%
Beverages Sales	35%	45%	22%	13%	27%	10%
Shop Rentals	N.A.	N.A.	N.A.	N.A.	N.A.	N.A.
Service Charge Collection	N.A.	N.A.	N.A.	N.A.	N.A.	N.A.
Other Income	N.A.	N.A.	N.A.	N.A.	N.A.	N.A.

Source : Author's Field Survey undertaken in March 2004. NA : Not Available

Conclusion

Srinagar in Garhwal Himalaya, though known for enough hospitality units, offers great scope for the improvement in this direction. The quality of food, accommodation and the kind of services extended are below standard and thus could not enhance the level of the satisfaction being extended to visitors. Most of the F&B outlets serve food and beverages of common interest, tastes and flavor. Incidentally, the traders envolved in the trade lack technical expertise. Most of the restaurants and hotels are serving Indian and Chinese food without knowing the peculiarities of such cuisines. There is poor arrangement for preparation and they serve typical Garhwali and other local dishes. During the peak season, the spirit of hospitality degrades as the guest services are given least priority. Because of this, most tourists do not set real experience of hospitality internships and technical expertise to the hospitality operators which can be achieved through induction of formal training programs.

References

Express Hotelier & Caterer, July 2004.

FHRAI Magazine, July-August 2003, Vol.4 –Issue 1.

FHRAI Magazine, May-June 2003, Vol.3 –Issue III.

Hotel & Food Service Review Magazine, August 2002, Vol.16 No.8.

Hotel & Food Service Review Magazine, June 2003, Vol.18 No.5.

Kirk, David (1996). *Environmental Management for Hotels*, Butterworth-Heinemann Ltd, Oxford.

Sustainable Tourism Planning and Development, 169-180, 2006
Edited by Bagri, S.C.
Published by Bishen Singh Mahendra Pal Singh, Dehra Dun, India

The Pristine Glory and Scenic Beauty of Orchha

Devesh Nigam & Nidhi Bhatia

Institute of Tourism and Hotel Management
Bundelkhand University, Jhansi

Abstract : Orchha, meaning a "hidden place", certainly lives up to its name. Languishing amid a tangle of scrubby dhak forest, 18 km southeast of Jhansi, the former capital of the Bundela dynasty gets only a small portion of the Khajuraho bound traffic. Architectural gems, however, abound in this town. Clustered around the foot of the exotic ruins, a sleepy village of neatly painted houses, market stalls, and a couple of Heritage properties with attractive government hotels provide most of the basic amenities. Being bestowed with all the ingredients of becoming a popular destination, this place lacks the attention and its deserved presence on the tourist map of India. This paper specifically makes an attempt to discover and awaken the potential of this sleepy village on the banks of river Betwa.

Key Words: Orchha, architecture, temple, tourist.

Introduction

Orchha is beautifully preserved piece of ancient glory and majestic treasure an island on river Betwa. Tourists come here from far & wide distances to seek a real solace in their mind, heart and soul to get the real joy of life. The entire Orchha township complex which includes ancient temples, majestic palaces, forts and fortress and the serene places of beauty around Betwa is spread over an area of one square kilometer. It has a population of about 2000 inhabitants only, and can be reached in a period of half an hour by bus or taxi from Jhansi.

There is no dearth of accommodation for the Indian and foreign tourists coming to Orchha. The *Sheesh Mahal Palace* has been transformed into a hotel to offer a royal welcome and courtesy to the visitors. The palace rooms offered to the tourists are spacious and airy. The suites on the upper floor are much larger in their sizes and present a grand view of scenic beauty all around, with ancient temples, derelict palaces afforested hills, extolling Betwa and fortresses. Small groups and families could stay in cottages by the side of river Betwa. Each of the cottages is a large but single bedroom unit with attached bathroom and a beautiful garden, from where the music of the streams of river Betwa can be heard with the great delight.

The Physical Setting

Occupying almost 2080 sq. mts. of the central plains in India, the Orchha stretches over northern Madhya Pradesh (MP). Bounded to the north by the Yamuna River and to the south by the hills of the Vindhyanand Malwa Plateau, the region presents a unique set of geologic and geographic characteristics which have had profound effects on human development in the region. It is situated at latitude of 25º to 21º North and Longitude at 78º-40º East, within the Newari Tehsil of district Tikamgarh, under divisional head quarter of Sagar. It is 8 km from Jhansi on way to Khajuraho National Highway.

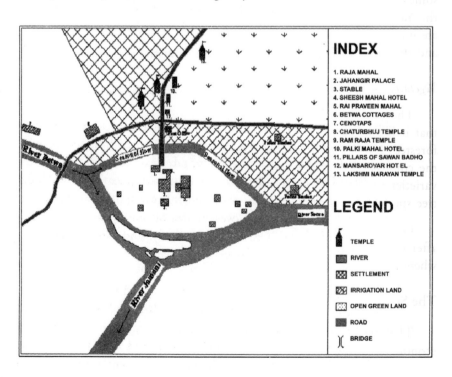

INDEX

1. RAJA MAHAL
2. JAHANGIR PALACE
3. STABLE
4. SHEESH MAHAL HOTEL
5. RAI PRAVEEN MAHAL
6. BETWA COTTAGES
7. CENOTAPS
8. CHATURBHUJ TEMPLE
9. RAM RAJA TEMPLE
10. PALKI MAHAL HOTEL
11. PILLARS OF SAWAN BADHO
12. MANSAROVAR HOT EL
13. LAKSHMI NARAYAN TEMPLE

LEGEND

TEMPLE
RIVER
SETTLEMENT
IRRIGATION LAND
OPEN GREEN LAND
ROAD
BRIDGE

Climate

Orchha generally experiences a semi-arid climate and is notorious for experiencing droughts in summer and disastrous floods during the monsoon. As with the rest of the Indian sub-continent, the Orchha sees two main seasons: monsoon and dry. The monsoon brings over 90% of the annual rainfall between the months of June to September, with the highest precipitation occurring in July and August. On an average, it receives anywhere from 75 cm to 125 cm of rain each year. Daily temperatures also fluctuate depending on the time of the year. Peak summer (May - June) brings excessively high temperatures, often topping 40°C, as the hot, dry *Loo* winds sweep in from the desert. During the winter months (December - February) daytime temperatures are quite pleasant reaching highs between 16.5°C and 21°C. Nighttime brings much cooler temperatures and frost has been known to occur on the coldest evenings.

Drainage

Drainage in the region occurs principally from north to south, with some local variation depending on topography. The main tributaries of the Yamuna are the Betwa, Jamani and Dhasan Rivers, most of which are important sources of irrigation water. Monsoon brings heavy flooding and the highest flows in all the rivers and tributaries.

Vegetation and Soils

The natural vegetation in the Orchha reflects the semi-arid climate that it is subject to during most of the year. The region was previously forested, but intensive harvesting over the past several centuries has left the countryside denuded of its forest land. *Khardai,* teak and different varieties of acacia (*dhak, semal, salai* and *babul)* are the most common tree species, although only the latter two have any economic benefit.

Grasses are predominant in the rocky plains and hills, particularly after the monsoon, although scrub and brush species are also common where more water is available for their growth.

The Social Set-Up

The people of the Orchha have remained both politically and economically separated. As such the area has one of the lowest levels of economic and human development in the country. Indeed, the remoteness of the region has prevented the development of basic infrastructure such as roads, electricity, water and sanitation services, and telephone lines. The lack of these services has only perpetuated the poverty cycle in the region.

Population

There is a gradual population growth in Orchha since 1951. The population increased from 831 in 1951 to 1010 in the year 1961 with 1226 in 1971, according to the 1981 census the population was 1855 which increased upto 5786 (1991 Indian Census) with about 1045 households. However on the basis of random sampling the population as on date is 10,000.

Orchha: Population

Year	Population
1951	831
1961	1010
1971	1226
1981	1861
1991	5786
2005	10,000

About a third of its working population subsists on agriculture while 30% are engaged in small business and tourist related activities and about 20% are engaged as contractual labour. The houses are built along the few main roads of the town. Typically the built form of the town is not obtrusive in scale with the monuments, but stricter heritage controls in terms of street frontages and heights need to be put in place to promote homogeneity and lack of incongruence in new developments. However it is noticed that 54% of the total population of Orchha migrated from the near by places in search of employment and are residing in rented houses.

There is a tremendous increase in the literacy rate after 1981due to the advent of migrants and increase in education facilities, though the female literacy rate is very low in the region. The literacy rate for male and females over the years is clearly specified in the table below:

Orchha: Literacy Rate

Literacy	1961	1971	1981	1991
Male	56%	47%	48%	82%
Female	13%	15%	23%	45%

There is an outstanding increase in employment opportunities due to Tourism and its related activities, more and more people are taking over employment directly or indirectly related to this industry the reason behind is lack of good agricultural land and good income and opportunities in the said industry. This clearly depicts the changing face of Orchha from rural level to urbanisation.

Back of the Beyond

Orchha was founded in 1531 by Rudra Pratap, a valiant Bundela Rajput king. The origin of the Bundela dynasty in the 11th century is traced to a Rajput prince who offered himself as a sacrifice to the mountain goddess *Vrindavasini*; it is said that she stopped him and named him *'Bundela'* (one who offered blood). The dynasty ruled over the area between the Yamuna and Narmada rivers. Garhkurar, once the capital of the Bundela Rajas, fell to the Tughlaq just as that dynasty was weakening. Into the vacuum that they left, the Bundelas again expanded, moving their base to Orchha (meaning hidden).

The golden age of Orchha had been in 16th and 17th century and in that period, a number of monuments were created by Raja Bir Singh. It was the period when *Jehangir Mahal* was constructed with the honour of the friendship of then Mughal king with Raja Bir Singh. The earlier Raj Mahal was constructed by Madhukar Shah,The predecessor of Raja Bir Singh. It stand by the side of Jehangir Mahal and depicts its own ancient glory. Its exquisite frescoes in the interior with profound simplicity outwards, are appreciated by visitors coming to Orchha.

Jehangir Mahal is marvelous in its look as a memorable and historical site of that age, depicting its glory. It is blessed by pleasant sites of the river and the countryside around. It becomes more and more exciting as we move from its lower to upper levels. Raja Birendra Singh was favourite to Jehangir and ruled Orchha from 1603-1627. He was the king who gave refuge to prince Salim when he revolted against Emperor Akbar. This resulted into the wrath of Emperor Akbar who ruined the Rajput Kingdom of Orchha by attacking through his forces. However, Raja Birendra Singh could manage to escape and in 1605 when Prince Salim ascended to the Mughal throne and become emperor Jehangir, Raja Birendra Singh once again become one of the most powerful figures of his time. It was in 1606 that Jehangir visited Orchha and the famous Jehangir Mahal was built in his honour.

The wrath of the Mughal emperor *Shahjahan* and *Aurangzeb* had fallen from time to time on Orchha as soon Jehangir died. Orchha was invaded by Shahjahan and Aurangzeb from time to time, but the glory of this famous Rajput kingdom couldn't be curved by attacks of Mughal forces and Orchha remained very strong till 1783, when for administrative reasons the capital was shifted to Tikamgarh.

By 1803, the Mughal emperor had almost dwindled and the British East India Company took control of most of the part of India. The remaining state including the Rajput kingdom of Orchha had come under the British patronage who took over their defense at their cost. By that time, Jhansi has emerged as a bigger city than Orchha. Although the Jhansi fort was build much earlier by Raja Birendra Singh, but the · importance of Jhansi fort grew more and more along with importance of the city of Jhansi. When the British East India Company become the defense-custodian of the kings, they become weak to defend themselves and at that time the British passed a law to take over all those states of the kings who had no male heir. The successor of this Rajput kingdom was Lakshmibai and when she was deprived of her right to rule the state, she revolted and fought a heroic battle against the British and defended the Rajput kingdom, till she become a martyr. Since than the Rajput kingdom including those of Jhansi and Orchha was annexed by the British East India Company and become the part of British emperor in India.

ATTRACTIONS

Jehangir Mahal

The exquisite *Jehangir Mahal* is of a very impressive size and is a part of the fort area. It is a fine example of elaborate domes and trellis work.

The fort remains one of the golden periods of Orchha, when it was constructed in the honour of emperor Jehangir by the then Rajput king. Orchha's single most admired palace, the Jehangir Mahal, was built by Bir Singh Deo as a monumental welcome present for the Mughal emperor Jehangir when he paid a state visit in the 17th century. Entered through an ornate ceremonial gateway, the east-facing facade is encrusted with turquoise tiles. Two stone elephants flank the stairway, holding bells in their trunks to announce the arrival of the Raja. Three storeys of elegant hanging balconies, terraces, apartments and onion domes are piled around a central courtyard. This palace, however, is sort of more airy and lighted since it has countless windows and pierced stone screens looking out over the skyline to the west, and a sea of treetops and ruined temples in the other direction.

Jehangir Mahal

Raj Mahal

The *Raj Mahal* is much older and stands by the side of Jehangir Mahal. These royal residences are much of the same style, with large square shaped courtyard, and verandahs with spacious rooms on all sides. The construction of the first building across the medieval granite bridge, the Raj Mahal was started by Rudra Pratap, and completed by one of his successors, Madhukar Shah. This leads on to the Sheesh Mahal. The two rectangular courtyards inside, the second, was formerly used by the

Bundela queens. One can find the fragments of mirror-inlay and vibrant painting plastered over their walls and ceilings. Some of the friezes are still in remarkable condition.

Another palace of elegance is *Rai Parveen Mahal*, a small palace adjoining the two places within the fort area. This palace is named after the famous poetess, musician, dancer and a beautiful coutesan Rai Parveen of Orchha kingdom. It is a small, double-storeyed brick apartment built by Raja Indramani for his concubine in the mid-1670. This building lies to the North of the Sheesh Mahal. The building, set amid the lawns of the Anand Mahal gardens, it has a main assembly hall on the ground floor (used to host music and dance performances), a boudoir upstairs, and cool underground apartments.

The Temples

There are a number of temples around the township of Orchha but the principal amongst them is Ram Raja temple which is architecturally unique, massive and with soaring spires. The temple is dedicated to Lord Rama, the god incarnate who is always taken as the king of this place. The temple has a large square shape with open space in front of it, where the material needed for worship of deity such as flowers, sweets are sold. The shops cater to the needs of the tourists and pilgrims, who went to worship lord Rama. As soon as the temple bell rings, the chanting of arti starts the entire population of township flocks.

The other famous temples are *Chaturbhuj temple* and *Lakshminarayan temple* which are both side by side and interlinked. The *Lakshminarayan* temple has exquisite frescoes on the walls and roofs, and are very finely composed painting of the scenes visualized from the Holy Scriptures. The courtyard of the temple is of a unique triangular design.

Cenotaphs

Apart from the famous temples and forts, Orchha is also having a cluster of cenotaphs. Out of them, fourteen cenotaphs are unique in their design and structures. There are two major clusters and one of them is located by the side of the river and known a Kanchona ghat. These cenotaphs are built in the memory of great persons of profound respect in their present or past.

Chaturbhuj temple

Cenotaphs on the Bank of River Betwa

Tourism in Orchha

Today Orchha is most famous for its architectural heritage and its pilgrimage stature. Orchha has many temples, many of it disused now. But it is most famous for the *Ram Raja* temple is a sacred Hindu pilgrimage and receives devotees regularly. The town receives as many as 25,000 foreign tourists and over 2-3 lakh domestic visitors annually.

While daily visitors to the town range from 1000 to 3000 during the peak season from September to March. The ingress of devotees on certain religious festivals range from 10,000 to 20,000 per day. However, the daily number of visitors to Ram temple range from 1500 to 3000 and on certain important Hindu festivals like the *Makar Sankranti, Basant Panchami, Shivratri, Ram navami, Kartik Purnima* and *Vivaha Panchami* the number of devotees who throng to Orchha range in thousands. The temple and its medieval heritage is very much a part of the fabric of the town. On the basis of random sampling it is received that aviate a large number of visitors visited different attractions of Orchha.

	Month	Approximate Tourist Arrivals in 2004
Festivals		
Shiv Ratri	March	20,000
Ram Navmi	April	100,000
Vivah Panchami	November-December	30,000
Fairs		
Makar Sankranti	January	50,000
Basant Panchami	February	20,000–25,000
Kartik Poornima	October-December	20,000

The tourist destination appeal of Orchha is not limited only to *Heritage* but its also playing a significant role in *Adventure and Religious* tourism activities, it has good scope for water sports being on the banks of river Betwa and the only place in India where Lord Rama is worshipped as a king. In Orchha an annual festival of music, dance and drama is held every year, where in Ramlila is enacted by the cultural organizations 'The Sri Ram Bhartiya Kala Kendra', besides having the provision of various folk and classical dances.

Orchha is also famous for a Sanctuary: This Orchha wildlife sanctuary spreads in an area of 46 sq. kms and came into being in 1994 by the *State Department of Forest* to preserve the natural beauty of this beautiful town and conserving its flora and fauna. Principal floras that flourish in the sanctuary are Teak, Palash, Khair etc. The principal fauna that inhabit the sanctuary are Spotted Deer, Blue Bull, Peacock, Wild Pig, Monkey, Jackal etc.

For the last few years MPSTDC is holding tourism festivals at Orchha and Panchmari. An amount of Rs. 100.00 lakhs has been proposed during the Tenth Plan for this activity. The Central Tourism Development has also agreed in principle to sanction 16 new schemes of dwelling units for tourists, water sports facility and refurbishment of monuments. Plans are also in the pipeline to improve the water-sport facilities at Shivpuri, Dhubhela, Orchha and the Chambal area. Refurbishment of the Monuments.

Conclusion

Orchha is known for monuments, and religious temples and a major stopover for tourist visiting Khajurao. The place is well off the beaten track and a wonderful stopover for a day or two. The ruins of the temples and palaces are spectacular, in particular the Jahangir Mahal and the Lakshmi Narayan Mandir, not only for their architectural merit but for the views of the surrounding countryside. The new Wildlife Park, whilst not exactly teeming with wildlife, has great scenery and wonderful views over the river and temples pointing up through the surrounding forest. Thus, even though Orchha is a small village it offers moderate kind of services to the tourist visiting there. There is a lot of scope for further development and improvement as far as quality of basic infrastructural facilities is concerned. Though the experiences gathered, show that the tourist are satisfied from their visit but there are certain areas like telecom service, shopping facilities and guiding facilities has to be improved. Orchha as a destination has immense potential to attract visitors. It is due to this reason the tourist visiting Orchha believes they should visit it again with a longer duration of stay. However proposed accommodation at Orchha should also include five star and four star type of hotels in order to cater luxury class tourists. The condition of roads to reach Orchha and within Orchha must be improved. Proper Parking facilities should be provided at all places of interest. The historical monuments are loosing their charm. Proper measures are to be taken for their maintenance and protection. Cultural events, like fairs and festivals should be organized round the year and special provision is to be made of Son-et-Lumiere (sound and light) shows at Jahangir Mahal, Rai Parveen Mahal. As almost all the tourists believe in recommending Orchha to their friends and relatives as a place to visit. This fact itself show that in the near future with all the efforts and measures taken in order to improve facilities at Orchha it will definitely able to satisfied the expectations of the tourist in a more better way.

References

Centre for Science and the Environment (1999). *The Citizen's Fifth Report: Part II Statistical Database*. CSE: New Delhi, 256p.

Deshpande, Aruna (2003). *150 Fascinating Destinations of India,Crest* Publishing House New Delhi http://www.mptourism.com/dest/orchha.html, http://9.1911encyclopedia.org/O/OR/ORCHHA.htm

Development Alternatives (1999). *Reversing the Downward Spiral: Understanding the influence of livelihood systems on the resource base in Bundelkhand*. Development Alternatives: New Delhi, 118p.

Government of India (2000). *India 2000 : A Reference Annual*. Publications Division, Ministry of Information and Broadcasting, Government of India, p. 321.

National Geographic Society of India (1989). "Bundelkhand Region". *India: A regional geography*. R.L. Singh, Ed. UBS Publishers' Distributors Ltd.: New Delhi, pp. 597-622.

http://9.1911 encyclopedia.org/O/OR/ORCHHA.htm

http://www.mptourrism.com/dest/orchha.html

Rawlins, Barbara, *et al.* April (1999). *Checkdam Assessment Study: Final Report* Development Alternatives Bundelkhand Region. 53p + annexes.

Sustainable Tourism Planning and Development, 181-195, 2006
Edited by Bagri, S.C.
Published by Bishen Singh Mahendra Pal Singh, Dehra Dun, India

Yoga for Wellness: An Emerging Trend in Alternative Tourism

Prachi Rastogi

Research Scholar & Assistant Editor
Centre for Tourism Research & Development
A-965/6 Indira Nagar, Lucknow - 226016, India

Abstract : Psychology has made its appearance on the stage of western science only in the last century. After developing elaborate sciences of the external world and conquering nature, man has at last started to turn his curiosity back toward himself. Individuals with long working hours, fragmentation of communities and traditions have exacerbated feelings of isolation, depression and stress. This leads to an exploration of ones inner being, his behaviour, his motivation, and his mind. Thus from the viewpoint of maintenance and improvement of physical, psychological and spiritual health an alternative form of Tourism known as Wellness Tourism came into picture. Yoga appeared to be one of the oldest disciplines contributing to the study of voluntary physical and mental control and the induction of altered state of consciousness. The purpose of this paper is to establish yoga as a discipline of wellness and its contribution to a new form of tourism called 'health tourism'.

Introduction

Gone are the days when leisure, happiness and peace were not to be purchased from outside, they came in naturally as man could find these existing around him. The small joys of day-to-day life were enough to keep him going. He was satisfied and contended with the little that he had. But today in this post modern era of global consumerism, with the advancement in science and technology, development of modern industries, a restless activity has taken hold of once so sedentary human society.

As a devotee to *Mammon* man is constantly pursuing wealth. In his insatiable desire of amassing money he has lost his inner harmony. He is no longer happy, his life has become increasingly automated and functionalized; he feels the monotony of daily routine, the cold rationality of the factories, offices, apartments and transport, shrinking human contact, the repression of feelings and the loss of nature and naturalness. He feels that life has been reduced to a mere existence, leading to stress, physical and mental exhaustion, emptiness and boredom. Thus in quest of this lost happiness he is ready to pay any price. His only aim being to switch off and fill up. He seeks for solace and serenity; a remedy that will help him get rid of all his mental agonies. He attempts for all kinds of modern, ultra modern techniques but to no avail. Helplessly, he then turns to a holistic way of life in order to de-stress and rejuvenate his senses. This he tries to achieve through meditation, yoga, ayurveda and other therapies that are burgeoning in the market. There are about 150 new age therapies that provide healing and upliftment of the body, mind and soul. The pill of wellness is all about a mind-body-soul balance. We are gradually adopting an organic lifestyle, wellness homes, wellness offices and wellness travel.

The Vedas talked about health lifestyle eons ago. However, the first person to package the term 'wellness' in the modern context, in the 1950s was American physician, Dr Halbert Dunn, with his book 'High Level Wellness' (Banerjee 2004). Studies into 'wellness tourism' (Gilbert and Abdullah, 2002; Mueller and Kaufmann, 2001) show that the well being of a tourist is an under researched area. The research within the hotel sector on wellness programme revealed an expanding supply and an insufficient demand for wellness programmes. Wellness can be understood as a state where mind and soul unite to safeguard the body against the attack of depression, stress, strain and disease. It is a natural, non-invasive treatment system designed to affect the whole person, not just the symptom or disease and to assist the body's natural ability to balance, regulate, heal and maintain itself. These wellness holidays come in a variety of flavours, from ayurveda to aqua-balancing, to yoga.

Ayurveda system of medicine aims not just curing disease but also maintaining health, it advocates a life of physical, mental and spiritual discipline. Ayurveda believes in the innate abilities of nature and the body to cure itself. Its medicines are drawn from nature-herbs and plants, animals and mineral products-which detoxify and gel with natural substances of human body.

Yoga as in practice contributes to the concept of wellness. It is a natural and most appropriate method to explore ones inner-being, his behaviour, his motivation and that elusive something called mind.

More than twenty years ago the potential of yogic practices for ensuring well-being was often disdained by the western society, paradoxically, today symposia, conferences, and courses on the usefulness of yoga to recover and maintain both physical and mental health can be found in the curricula of most prominent Institutions of the World serving the Health sciences (Brown, 1977).

Yoga, the science of man, based on ancient Indian wisdom and culture, is an art of living a healthy, balanced, peaceful and contented life. Yoga, being a total integrated system, studies man in his wholeness - body, mind and spirit and is integrated to certain principles, ideas, values, attitudes and a way of life for personal and social benefits.

Yoga represents a pivotal concept in the culture of India. It is the development of a relationship between man and god, between all pervasive divinity and its reflection within individual consciousness.

Yoga is one of the six orthodox systems of Indian philosophy. Its name derived from the Sanskrit root *yuj* meaning to bind, join, direct and concentrate ones attention on how to use and apply. In simple words, yoga means union. It is a systematic approach to becoming one with, or attaining the highest level or state of consciousness of which man is capable of (Swami Rama, 1977).

Yoga has attracted particular attention in part because it appears to be one of the oldest continuous disciplines studying voluntary physical and mental control and the induction of altered state of consciousness.

Effective application of the methods of yoga and the rudimentary understanding of its principles requires not only study of its texts, but also study of oneself. Yoga thus forms the basic, distillation of the essential principles of inner searching. Yoga has traditionally involved the notion that bodily positions and physical postures are intimately linked to personality and emotion.

The psychology of yoga is based on the concept that there are various levels of functioning. We are all aware of a 'body' and 'mind', but these are, from the perspective of Eastern thought, only part of the whole picture. The idea of different levels of being, each able to observe and control the one below, is central. The systematic exploration, development and experimentation with these higher levels are the main functions of meditation and yoga.

There are five principal levels called 'sheaths' in the ancient writings. Each sheath covers and obscures the more subtle awareness that is interior to it. These five levels or 'sheaths' span the whole spectrum of human nature. The continuum that they form makes up a sort of step-wise ladder that is the basis of all growth and evolution (Swami Rama *et al.*, 1979).

Yoga is associated primarily with strange contortions of the body, but the major focus is actually on the alteration of one's self awareness and his relationship to the world. It is a complete system of therapy, which includes work on developing awareness, and control of the physical body, emotions, mind and interpersonal relations. It is not a question of merely closing one's eyes or of sitting in a posture. It involves cultivation of an attitude and approach to life. It must not only be a philosophy to be imbibed but a practical philosophy, which must be lived. It is therefore, not enough to think of yoga but to do it and to live it in our lives. It is also necessary to understand that yoga is not a substitute for action.

There are following six forms of yoga including physical yoga (*Hatha*), devotional (*Bhakti*) or spiritualization of emotion, service or action (*Karma*), *Gyan Yoga* or the yoga of wisdom and intellectual discrimination, and philosophical yoga (*Jnana*). The most comprehensive and scientific yogic system for developing awareness is *Raja* Yoga, the 'royal path'(Swami Rama *et al.* 1979).

There are many different approaches to yoga. Most of them focus on meditation and on holding specific postures (asanas). *Ashtanga* (Power) yoga that focuses on working through the primary series of postures and aims to build stamina, strength and flexibility. *Iyengar*, emphasizes strength. *Hatha* yoga is based on the series of poses, breathing and relaxation. Some postures are held statue like while others involve jumping and movements that build stamina, endurance and co-operation. Yoga puts a lot of emphasis on breathing (pranayama) which helps to focus the mind and promote relaxation (Knight, 2003).

Stages of Yoga

Of these, the lower five, which border on the Psychosomatic Approach, are referred to as external (*Bahiranga*) yoga, popularly known as *Hatha* Yoga, while the upper three, which directly affect the psyche are known as internal (*Antaranga*) yoga, popularly known as *Raja* Yoga (www.somatheraam.com).

Mastery of each of the above step leads to work on a more subtle aspect of our being, beginning with habits and behaviour then proceeding to work on the body, breath and mental functioning.

Yoga therapy integrates a behavioural and introspective approach to growth. In many varieties of behaviour therapy, the therapeutic sessions are begun with a process of 'progressive relaxation'. The yoga postures, in addition to these more direct functions, serve another more subtle purpose in preparing an individual for the practice of yoga.

Yoga also provides cleansing techniques through breathing exercises and facilitates in the elimination of wastes through skin and breath.

In contrast to much of modern psychology, it views roles and personality as superficial and easily changed when one is not caught up at the level of being. It provides a perspective from which one can become detached from the worldly pleasures.

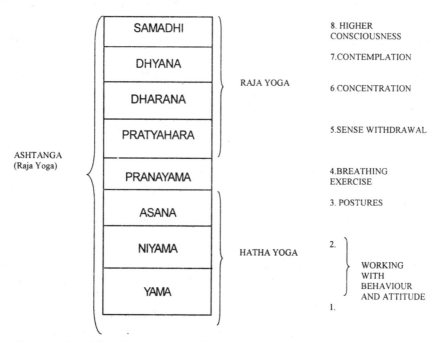

Source: Adapted from Swami Rama *et al.*, 1979

Yoga in Today's World

Many of the countries and cultures that we tend to visit on our spiritual quests are desperate to acquire the standard of living and perceived quality of life enjoyed by western, capitalist societies (Smith, 2003).

In this modern and developing world where stress, tension and anxiety are the root cause of physical and mental exhaustion, yoga provides a sensible, accessible programme incorporating relaxation for the benefit of both mind and body.

Yoga Tourism offers a huge marketing opportunity to India. In India states such as Uttaranchal have developed International Centre of Yoga and organized meditation week, which apart from teaching participants also offers a platform to exchange and share ideas and understand different cultures. The following case study examines how the Indian state of Kerala has attempted to use cultural tourism, focusing on holistic health practices to create a successful image of their destination.

Holistic Holidays: the case of Kerala

Kerala Tourism Development Corporation (KTDC) launched a campaign that intended to promote the Southern Indian state as a tourism destination rich in culture and backwaters. During the late 90s the marketing focus shifted towards cultural heritage of the state; traditional dance forms such as Kathakali, Koodiyattam, temple festivals, boat races and holistic therapies such as Ayurveda, Yoga and meditation were promoted in an attempt to reach an international high yield niche market. In 2000, a high profile promotional campaign - Kerala Travel Mart – 2000 – was launched.

Gradually as Kerala's marketing campaign picked up, international travellers became aware of the states rich culture, traditions, arts and cuisine and international tourist arrivals increased from 69,000 in 1991 to 210,000 in 2000 (Department of Tourism, Government of Kerala). Kerala was the first state in India to have enacted Tourism Conservation, Preservations and Trade Bill to regulate tourism activities in the state and it was initiatives such as these that resulted in Kerala's share of Indians domestic tourism rising from 52,0619 in 1987 to 5,01,3221 in 2000 (Department of Tourism, Government of Kerala). Though the exact state of affairs in the rise of tourist arrival is yet not confirmed it is presumed that Yoga and Ecotourism have been the major contributors.

Table I: Domestic Tourists arrivals to Kerala

Month	Month-wise Arrival Details of Domestic Tourists to Kerala (1987 to 2000)															
	1987	1988	1989	1990	1991	1992	1993	1994	1995	1996	1997	1998	1999	% of Variation over 1998	2000	% of Variation over 1999
Jan.	61837	54627	56948	66255	77962	93010	99472	121338	329248	334179	484975	354406	453729	28.03	454330	0.13
Feb.	52158	48751	59252	55930	69944	81487	83201	104687	283452	307909	408933	312576	402718	28.84	382657	-4.98
March	53228	51825	55777	72108	78039	76611	81297	106195	300534	306910	341863	308514	419911	36.11	369231	-12.07
April	41786	40758	42410	66794	75666	79973	80422	102916	321449	350525	398367	330395	456629	38.21	453194	-0.75
May	37860	44632	48560	77815	77336	92422	93458	104075	355890	484802	524497	347725	441644	27.01	486006	10.04
June	35536	44536	43322	71600	73706	78701	80001	106673	235655	250424	314516	296525	351733	18.62	356260	1.29
July	36922	45643	51715	72862	74121	76787	77469	96783	370480	400327	412655	287957	356893	23.94	361034	1.16
Aug.	37658	43317	49890	69754	74214	79617	85268	86554	362669	402125	387696	367812	367486	-0.09	373599	1.66
Sep.	31568	46514	52931	73794	78500	81809	84524	99724	364752	448715	461166	441951	382841	-13.37	386123	0.86
Oct.	40517	47551	55294	77264	85620	83000	85561	105405	368217	435763	479543	421477	403944	-4.16	435426	7.79
Nov.	40925	53140	55899	79320	90974	85265	88176	85978	324953	359192	377800	429204	411233	-4.19	476877	15.96
Dec.	40624	60756	62250	83029	92909	85458	88387	106394	298357	322131	361390	583172	439526	-24.63	478484	8.86
Total	510619	582050	634248	866525	948991	994140	1027236	1226722	3915656	4403002	4953401	4481714	4888287	9.07	5013221	2.56

Source: Tourist Statistics of Kerala 1996 & Past Volume Department of Tourism, Govt. of Kerala.

There are few resorts in Kerala that offer rejuvenation therapies. For example resorts such as Somatheeram Ayurvedic Beach Resort and Travancore heritage are critical in attracting cultural tourists to the state offering Yoga and Ayurveda treatments and massages to enliven spirit and body.

Rejuvenation packages offered by Resorts

These resorts offer a wide range of therapies including massage, lymphatic drainage, shiatsu, reflexology, reiki and aromatherapy.

Somatheeram resort offers rejuvenation packages and body purification packages. Rates include accommodation, treatments, meals, airport transfers, backwater cruises.

The seaside Travancore Heritage is about a half hour drive from the airport. Programmes: Relaxation (3/5/7 days), Rejuvenation (15/22/29/36 days) and stress-relieving (7 days). Rejuvenation for old age disorders (15/22/29). Rates are inclusive of accommodation, treatments, meals and taxes.

Poovar Island Resort – Packages: Rejuvenation (7/13/20 nights), Body Purification (7/13/20 nights). Rates include accommodation, treatment and meals, Yoga, airport/railway transfers, cruise, taxes, sightseeing.

Coconut Bay about 30 minutes from airport. Treatments: Panchkarma rejuvenation/body purification package (7/14/21/28 days). Package includes accommodation, treatment, meals, airport transfers, taxes and sight seeing (Outlook Traveller, 2003).

Kerala's success in destination promotion inspired other Indian states to take steps towards branding themselves as tourist destinations. For example Rishikesh in Uttaranchal is widely considered as the Yoga Capital of India and they have organized an International Yoga Week. Tourists and travellers searching quietude and inner peace stop to practice Yoga and meditation in this town nestled in the Himalayan foot-hills (www.keralatourism.com).

Yoga can therefore be seen as a powerful brand for states such as Kerala and Uttaranchal to use in their promotional activity and help to reinforce the image of India as a land of inherent spirituality.

Table II: Rejuvenation packages offered by Resorts

S.No	Name of the Resort	Facilities	Duration	Treatment Specialties	Location/Environ	Price
1.	Somatheeram	Accommodation, treatments, meals, airport transfers, backwater cruises.	7/14 days	Body purification therapies	Somatheeram, Chowara P.O., Thiruvananthapuram 0471- 2268101: somatheeram@vsnl.com; www.somatheeram.com	Rs 33,550-1,67,700
2.	Travancore Heritage	Accommodation, treatments, meals and taxes	3-29 days	Relaxation, Stress relieving, Rejuvenation for age old disorders	The Travancore Heritage, Chowara P.O., Thiruvananthapuram 0471-267828-32; travencoreheritage@vsnl.net; www.travencoreheritage.com	Rs 12,700-2,16,850
3.	Poovar Island Resort	Treatment and meals, Yoga, airport/railway transfers, cruise, taxes, sightseeing	7/13/20 days	Rejuvenation and body purification	Poovar Island Resort, K.P.VII/911 Pozhiyoor, Thiruvananthapuram 0471- 212068/9; poovarisland@sify.com; www.floatelsindia.com.	Rs 28,000-69,450
4.	Coconut Bay	Treatment, meals, airport transfers, taxes and sight seeing	7/14/21/ 28 days	Panchkarma Rejuvenation/body purification	Coconut bay, Mulloor P.O., Vizhinjam, Thiruvananthapuram 0471- 2480566,2480668; cocobay@vsnl www.coconutbay.com	Rs 26,220-2,13,900

India: Places offering Yoga

For more pertinent study it may be necessary to give information on some of the packages offered by other Indian states. A few of such resorts have been given below. These places offer extensive yoga courses ranging from one to three weeks (Outlook Traveller, 2003).

- Span Resorts, Manali.

  A luxurious 25-cottage property on the banks of Beas River. Yoga, spa, massages, aroma therapy. Packages: 7 day yoga vacation package includes accommodation, vegetarian meals.

- Yog-Ganga Centre, Dehradun.

  Several intensive 3-week courses each year (asana, pranayama and Yoga philosophy). Payment is by donation.

- Himalayan Iyengar Yoga Centre (HIYC), Dharamshala.

  Located on the beautiful grounds in Dharamkot village, with trees, ponds, and a yoga library. The centre operates until mid-June from September to November.

- Yoga-Centre

  This is a HIYC's centre in Goa. Accommodation and food not provided. The centre offers five-day courses, intensive courses, and teachers' courses. You must register and book in person. Fees and contacts as for HIYC, Dharamshala

- Sri Aurobindo Ashram, Pondicherry.

  The ashram teaches 'internal yoga'

- Sivananda Yoga Vedanta Dhanrvantari Ashram, Kerala.

  Offers 'yoga vacations', on the 1st and 15th of each month, which also include group meditation and chanting. Also available are ayurvedic and massage treatment.

- The Bihar School of Yoga, Munger

  Offers four months comprehensive course.

- Sivananda Ashram, Rishikesh.

  A charitable organization. No charge but the space is limited.

Table III: India places offering Yoga

S.No	Name of the Resort	Facilities	Duration	Treatment Specialties	Location/Environ	Price
1	Span Resorts	Accommodation, vegetarian meals	7 days	Yoga, Spa, Massages, Aroma therapy	Manali 01902-240138, 240538; spanres@del.vsnl.net.in	Rs 16,999 per person on twin sharing 6N/7D; Rs 25,999 for single occupanc
2	Yog-Ganga Centre	-	3-weeks	Asana, Pranayama and Yoga philosophy	The Ashram is near Shahenshah Ashram, 101 Old Rajpur (0135-2733653; telefax 0135-2632793; yoganga@vsnl.com; yoganga@hotmail.com	By donation
3	Himalayan Iyengar Yoga Centre (HIYC)	-	5 days	Yoga and Aromatherapy	HIYC, Village Dharamkot, Dharamshala (01892-21312; info@hiyogacentre.com)	Rs 1500
4	Yoga Centre	-	5 days	Yoga and Aromatherapy	Arambol, Goa	Rs 1500
5	Sri Aurobindo Ashram	-	-	Intensive Yoga	Pondicherry Phone: 0413-22622123	Rs 150 and Rs 1,000
6	Sivananda Yoga Vedanta Dhanvantari Ashram	Ayurveda and massage treatment	Course start on 1st and 15th of every month	Yoga vacations	Sivananda Yoga Vedanta Dhanwantari Ashram, Neyyar Dam P.O., Thiruvananthapuram Dist., Kerala (0471-2273093); yogaIndia@sivananda.org)	Rs 600-400

contd. ...

S.No	Name of the Resort	Facilities	Duration	Treatment Specialties	Location/Environ	Price
7	The Bihar School of Yoga	-	4 month course	Yoga	Secretary, Bihar School of Yoga Ganga Darshan, Fort Munger, Bihar (06344-22430; byb@yogavision.net; www.yogavision.net/main_set.html)	Rs 5000
8	Sivananda Ashram	-	-	Yoga	Divine Life Society, P.O. Shivanandanagar, 249192, District Tehri-Garhwal, Uttaranchal (0135-430040)	Charitable
9	Yoga Niketan	-	Classical asanas	Ashram	Rishikesh Phone: 0135-432227	Rs 225/day
10	Sri Ved Niketan Ashram	-	1 month	Asanas, Pranayama and Meditation	Rishikesh Phone: 0135-433537/430279	Rs 60-150/day

● Yoga Niketan Ashram, Rishikesh

Classes are taught in traditional style: classical asanas with few variations. Attendance at morning and evening yoga and meditation classes is compulsory.

● Sri Ved Niketan Ashram, Rishikesh

Offers gentle yoga instructions with warm-ups, asanas, and pranayama and meditation classes. Classes are held at 8 am, 6:30 and 9 pm. There is also a one-month course seven times a year covering asanas, pranayama and philosophy.

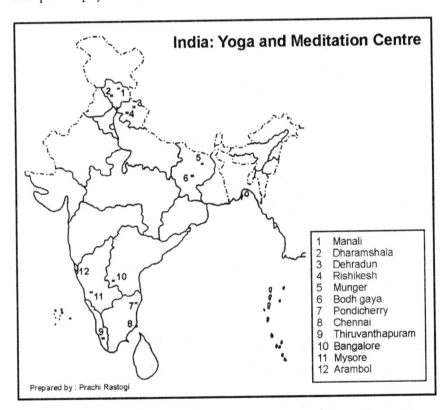

India: Yoga and Meditation Centre

1   Manali
2   Dharamshala
3   Dehradun
4   Rishikesh
5   Munger
6   Bodh gaya
7   Pondicherry
8   Chennai
9   Thiruvanthapuram
10 Bangalore
11 Mysore
12 Arambol

Prepared by : Prachi Rastogi

Conclusions

Life is lived privately, publicly and secretly. The life we lead reflect the choices we make within the bounds of constraints and information. Our genes and income contribute to the opportunities we have. Thus we see that the art of living is the most complicated of all arts as it is

194

based upon the scientific application of the good principles and attitude of a human being.

Today high-octane materialism has created a void in our lives and high-octane wellness has come along to fill it. This new age cult is giving a new meaning to rainbows, crystals, pyramids, feng shui, reiki, aroma oils, candles, aroma bed sheets and organic food. We see that the world of wellness has come full circle. We are going back to our roots with holistic healing methods and a penchant for spiritual satisfaction. Thus we see yoga is basically a way of life, which has been evolved as a system to go beyond the personality - complex and achieve absolute freedom-liberation of the spirit from the matter.

Acknowledgements

I wish to express my gratitude to Professor Tej Vir Singh and Professor Shalini Singh of the Centre for their continuous support and assistance in preparing this paper. I also wish to thank Mr Masood Naqvi for sharing administrative workload and providing me much needed quiet time while working on the manuscript.

References

Brown, B. (1977). Introduction. In J. Funderburk, *Science Studies Yoga*. Himalayan International Institute of Yoga Science and Philosophy, USA.

Banerjee, P. (2004). Wellness is now an industry, the next big boom after IT. *Times of India*, 1st February 2004.

Department of Tourism, Government of Kerala. www.Indiastat.com. Accessed on January 30, 2004.

Gilbert, D. and Abdullah, J. (2002). A Study of the Impact of the Expectation of a Holiday on an Individuals Sense of Well-being. *Journal of Vacation Marketing*. 8(4): 352-361.

Iyengar, BKS (1993). *The Illustrated Light on Yoga* London. Thorsons/ Aquarian.

Knight Ali Jane (2003). Yoga Tourism: Keeping Body and Soul Together (unpublished)

Mueller, H. and Kaufmann, E.L. (2001). Wellness Tourism: Market Analysis of a Special Health Tourism Segment and Implications for the Hotel Industry *Journal of Vacation Marketing*. 7(1): 5–17.

Outlook Traveller, June 2003.

Smith, M. (2003). Holistic Holidays: Tourism and the Reconciliation of Body, Mind, Spirit. *Tourism Recreation Research* 28(1): 103-108

Swami Rama (1977). The Foreword, In Funderburk, J. Science Studies Yoga, Himalayan International Institute of Yoga Science and Philosophy, Honesdale. USA.

Swami, R., Rudolph. B. and Swami, A. (1979). *Yoga and Psychotherapy: The Evolution of Consciousness.* The Himalayan International Institute of Yoga Science and Philosophy, Pennsylvania.

Sustainable Tourism Planning and Development, 197-214, 2006
Edited by Bagri, S.C.
Published by Bishen Singh Mahendra Pal Singh, Dehra Dun, India

Ethiopia: Tourism to be Harnessed for Food Security

Mohit Kukreti

Asst. Professor, Department of Tourism,
University of Gondar, Gondar, Ethiopia

Abstract: Several authors have studied the famine and food insecurity issues, but not much literature is available on using tourism as a tool for harnessing food security in Ethiopia. Hence, this paper is an attempt to correlate tourism with the food security. This paper emphasize that tourism is an effective tool to fight with poverty and food insecurity. For this purpose, the paper discusses the history and causes of famines, and magnitude of food insecurity problems in Ethiopia. This paper further discusses how tourism relates well to the needs of poor; advantage tourism could bring to Ethiopia; policy and institutional engagements in the context of poverty alleviation and food insecurity. Finally, some suggestions to harness tourism for bringing sustainable development and food security in Ethiopia.

Introduction

Before considering the scope of tourism one needs to examine the food insecurity situation in the country and its causes. There are a large number of literatures available on food security and famine and hunger in developing countries. Food security is defined in several ways. (Habethold, 1995). At the simpler level it may be understood as the access by all people at all times to food sufficient for a healthy life (Reutlinger, 1986). Food insecurity obviously is the lack of access to enough food. There are three methodological approaches to the analysis of food insecurity and famine: a) General explanations in terms of drought, war, land degradation, etc. b) scientific explanations which explain about food insecurity and the causes of famine with reference to specific circumstances and people, and c) an eclectic approach which combines these various explanations (Diriba, 1995).

Food insecurity scenario in the world

The current food insecurity scenario in the world reveals that the number of chronically hungry people in developing countries declined by only 19 million between the World Food Summit (WFS) baseline period of 1990-1992 and 1999-2001. This means that WFS goal of reducing the number of undernourished people by half by the year 2015 can now be reached only if annual restrictions can be accelerated to 26 million per year, more than 12 times the pace of 2.1 million per year achieved to date. World wide, FAO estimates that 842 million people were under nourished in 1999-2001. This includes 10 million in the industrialized countries, 34 million in the countries in transition and 798 million in developing countries. At the regional level, the number of undernourished were reduced in Asia and pacific and in Latin America and the Caribbean. In contrast the number continue to rise in Sub-Saharan Africa and in the Near East and North Africa (FAO, 2003).

Food insecurity scenario in Ethiopia

Ethiopia, one of the most famine-prone countries in Africa, has a long history of famine and food shortages that can be traced back to 250 BC. (Webb, P. and J.V. Braun, 1994).

Table I: A historical documentation of the frequency of famine in Ethiopia

Period (AD)	No. of Famine occurred	No. of Famine years
1000 to 1400	4	9
1400 to 1800	4	17
1800 to 1900	8	11
1900 to 2003	18	25

Source : C.A Wood as quoted in the Ethiopian Red Cross Society 1995.

More than half of the Africa's food insecure population lives in Ethiopia and six other countries: Chad, Zaire, Uganda, Zambia and Somalia (Sisay A, 1995). Earlier studies have estimated Ethiopia's food insecure people to be around 40-50 % of the total population (Ibid.37). Most famines and food crises have been geographically concentrated in two broad zones of this country. The first consist of the central and northern highlands, stretching from northern Shewa through Wello and Tigray, and the second is made up of the crescent of low lying agro-pastoral lands ranging from Wello in the north, through Haraghe and

Bale to Sidamo and Gamo Gofa in the south (Webb, P. and J.V. Braun, 1994, p: 21-22).

Table II: Geographical expansion of drought over time

Region	Number of affected Awrajas/Woredas and people during peak drought years				
	1984	1985	1994	2000	2003
Tigray	9	7	54	28	30
	1,331,890	1,429,390	1,085,000	1,717,756	1,831,600
Amhara	21	22	64	55	73
	2,514,850	3,524,460	2,096,000	3,569,820	3,313,299
Oromia	9	16	97	80	113
	233,210	1,020,410	1,935,000	1,942,824	3,110,860
SNNPS	4	8	40	NA	62
	265,810	667,890	840,700		1,114,652

Source : Computed from DPPC, Food Security Profile reports (various issues)

As shown in the table vulnerability to drought tremendously increased in the major regions of the country. Recently major droughts occurred during 1984, 1985, 2000, and 2003. The data shows that in Tigray region nine Woredas were hit by drought in 1984 while the number rose to 54 that is almost six fold in 1994 due to rearrangement or merger of Woredas in Tigray.

The increasing vulnerability to drought and declining coping capacity can be clearly seen by looking at the peak drought years of 1984/85, 1999/2000, and 2002/2003 in table III. From time to time, the country's economy becomes heavily indebted with bad consequences of limiting investment and economic expansion. With slow or stagnating economic growth and a high rate of population growth, the per capita income as a measurement of purchasing power did not improve over the last decades; it rather declined. In the same way, per capita food availability also declined by as much as 57% and 70% in 1999/2000 and 2003 respectively, from its average level in 1980's. The effects of recurrent droughts are partly the carryover effects of previous ones. Although government policies have been pro production since the early 1990's, there are challenges like: weak market integration (low infrastructure and high transportation cost), weak credit management, weather vulnerability, improved farm technology; still continues constraining improved food security in the country.

Table III: Comparison of droughts in 1984/85, 1999/2000 and 2002/ 2003 in Ethiopia

Basic facts	1984/85	1999/2000	2002/2003
Population	45 million (35 million) rural	64 million (47 million rural)	60 million (53 million rural)
External debts (US$)	1.8 billion (35% of GDP)	5.4 billion (84% of GDP)	5.6 billion (90% of GDP)
GDP per capita (US$)	190 (1981 source: World Bank)	118 (2000 source: World Bank)	108 (2001 source: World Bank)
Agricultural production (Projected)	450 kg per capita	193 kg per capita	140 kg per capita
Population affected	8 million (18%); estimated 1 million deaths	10 million (15.6%); estimated 10,000-50,000 deaths	11.3 million (16.8%)
Causes: drought	Sequence of drought in 1977-80 and 1984 (47% of average rainfall in Wollo)	Failure of belg rains 1995-99 followed by belg failure in 2000 in pastoral areas of north eastern & south eastern	Poor belg/meher rains in east 1999-02. In affected areas less than 50% of average rainfall in 2002
Decreased agricultural production	Average 4% decline per year prior to drought; problem of land user right; forced membership in cooperatives, restricted markets, trade and labor movement; low technology	5.9% lower than 1998/99, although policy is pro-production, state ownership of land, population pressure, small holdings, land degradation, poor market integration are part of the causes.	Production decline of approx. 21% from 5 years average; decline in fertilizer use by 17% improved seed by 70% (due to decline in credit use by 30% of 6 years average); continued vulnerability from 1999/2000.

Source : Andy Yates 2003 quoted from the World Food Program (WFP) comparative Analysis 2002

Explanation of food insecurity and famine in Ethiopia has mainly concentrated on food availability and entitlement decline. Most of these explanations are aggregate, as they do not give details of specific areas and situations (Diriba, 1995). Diriba in 1995 concluded that the decline in physical resources, and also the policy framework of the Ethiopian Government, has played a role in exacerbating food insecurity. Webb and JV Braun in 1994 related famine causality in Ethiopia to declining production and availability, military conflict, droughts and crop failures, the agricultural policies of the Marxist regime, prices and restrictions on the market. The main causes of famine in Ethiopia and factors that influence its extent are climatic factors, environment degradation, weak and poorly functioning market systems, development policy failure, and poor agricultural and over all socioeconomic environment.

The Food Security Strategy (FSS) of Ethiopia (FSS, 2002) rests on three pillars such as

a. increasing the availability of food through domestic (own) product,

b. ensuring access to food for food deficit households, and

c. strengthening emergency response capabilities.

The FSS goals could be achieved with the help of the following measures:

- Micro and small-scale enterprise development thorough industrial extension services to create additional employment opportunity in private sector. Here small-scale tourism enterprises could also play a considerable role.

- Improving the efficiency of food marketing and distribution system with the participation of private sector.

- Improved credit services for food insecure rural areas. These credit services could provide advantage of engaging in the present tourism activities in their respective areas.

- Nutritional and health interventions for the public.

- Effect to strengthen the existing capabilities of the government including monitoring, surveillance and warning arrangement, building the capacity of food and relief distribution, strategic reserve of food.

- The need for carefully planned food security assistance from experience of European Union and Sweden.

- Encouraging supplementary employment and income generating schemes. Off farm income generating activities would supplement own production for a considerable number of reasons as a coping mechanism during the periods of food strategy.

From the above discussion, it is evident that although major factors responsible for the food insecurity and poverty are climate, agriculture, etc. But other allied factors also triggers food insecurity problems viz. environment, economic conditions, nutrition and health, infrastructure, energy, industries and technology, employment, foreign exchange etc. These factors could very well be mitigated with the help of contributions from tourism.

Why tourism can relate well to the needs of the poor for fighting food insecurity?

Compared with many other sectors, tourism provides a growth for the countries with a high incidence of poverty, in which they have comparative advantages. It also has potential to generate income directly for poor in places where they live. Therefore, the contribution of tourism to the local economy should not be undervalued. Infact, it has ten kinds of positive economic impacts on livelihoods, any or all of which can form part of a poverty reduction strategy:

- Wages from formal employment of poor in tourism enterprises.

- Earnings from selling goods, services or casual labor and other supplies to tourism enterprises by the poor.

- Dividends and profits arising from locally owned enterprises.

- Collective income which may include profits from community run enterprise, land rental, dividends from a joint venture or levies – these incomes can provide significant development capital and provide finance for corn-grinding mills, a clinic, teachers, housing and school books.

- Many poorest countries are at comparative advantage over developed countries in this sector. They have capital assets of enormous value to the tourism industry such as culture, art, music, landscape, wildlife, and climate. This can include, for example, World heritage Sites, where visits by tourists can generate employment and income for surrounding communities as well as help in their conservation.

- Tourism contributes to the geographical spread of employment to the rural areas, which are away from the main centers of economic activity. Tourism can sometimes provide a source of income in such locations while few other industries can do so.

- Infrastructure gains, for example roads, piped water, electricity and communications, health, safety and security benefiting poor in the locality directly or through support to other sectors.

- Voluntary providing/giving support by tourism enterprises.

- Tax or levy on tourism income or profits with proceeds benefiting poor.

- Tourism employs more women and young people than other industries. Providing economic benefits and independence to women is very important in terms of supporting child development and breaking the cycle of poverty and food insecurity.

Further, there are number of proven strategies in tourism field which can be used to enhance the overall economic benefits to reduce poverty and thereby food insecurity:

- Attracting higher yield market segments
- Increasing tourist length of stay
- Increasing visitor expenditure
- Developing complementary products
- Spreading the benefits of tourism geographically
- Infrastructure and planning gain
- Local management of tourism and partnerships
- Small and medium scale enterprise development
- Reducing seasonality
- Employment and training.

International policy concern about poverty alleviation

The Millennium Development Goals, agreed by all 191 members States of the UN, set the international agenda for the twenty first century. The goals, to be reached by 2015 are to:

- Halve extreme poverty and hunger
- Achieve universal primary education

- Empower women and promote equality between men and women.

- Reduce under-five mortality by two-third.

- Reverse the spread of diseases, especially HIV/AIDS and malaria.

- Create a global partnership for development, with targets for aids, trade and debt relief.

The issue of poverty is central to almost all these goals. Some of them provide an important slant on associated issues that must be borne in mind when developing actions to tackle poverty through tourism, including matter of equality, health, trade and broader agendas for sustainable development.

An increasing number of countries, developed and developing, have begun to recognize the potential of tourism as an agent to deliver on the new global agenda, where poverty alleviation is the top priority, defined in the summits of Doha. The report of the World Summit on Sustainable Developed in Johannesburg, 2002 makes specific reference to tourism to increase benefits for all population in the host communities. The Global Code of Ethics for tourism agreed in 1999 and supported by United Nations, calls for local populations to be associated with tourism activities and to share equitability in the economic, social and cultural benefits they generate. The sustainable Tourism – Elimination of Poverty (ST-EP) initiative launched by WTO with the support of UNCTAD at the Johannesburg Summit provides a basis for practical actions to demonstrate how tourism can be used specifically for the elimination of poverty. The aim is for 5000 small projects to be in place by 2015 (WTO, 2004).

Performance of tourism in Ethiopia

According to World Tourism Organization (WTO) report Africa's tourism development prospects to 2020 are promising. That year it will receive an estimated 77 million tourist, and tourism will be among the economy's most dynamic sectors owing to its ever-more notable contribution to foreign currency earnings to the balance of payments, its creation of direct and indirect employment and its influence on other sectors like agriculture, fishing and handicrafts.

Francesco Frangialli, secretary general of the World Tourism Organization, mentioned Ethiopia to be one of the first countries to be targeted under a United Nations scheme harnessing the country's tourism potential in order to tackle entrenched poverty. Ethiopia would benefit from a WTO-led, development friendly, tourism scheme. The Sustainable Tourism Eliminating Poverty initiative focuses on encouraging sustainable tourism – social, economic and ecological – to ease poverty.

Ethiopia has vast treasures of multiple attractions including seven World Heritage Sites, rich heritage and culture, indigenous flora and fauna, breath taking vistas and this tourism potential could be harnessed in order to tackle entrenched poverty, food insecurity and famine.

According to World Travel and Tourism Council's (WTTC) statistics, the current economic status of Ethiopian tourism industry is promising. (WTTC 2004) It reveals the following:

- **Ethiopia travel and tourism industry** is expected to generate ETB 7,874.1 million (US872.6mn) of economic activity (total demand) in 2004, growing (nominal terms) to ETB 18,345.3 million (US$ 1,633.0mn) by 2014. Travel and Tourism demand is expected to grow by 5.1% per annum, in real terms, between 2004 and 2014.

- **Ethiopia travel and tourism employment** is estimated at 1,450,580 jobs in 2004, 8.1% of total employment, or 1 in every 12.3 jobs. By 2014, this should total 1,753,800 jobs, 7.5% of total employment or 1 in every 13.2 jobs. The 755,971 travel and tourism industry jobs accounts for 4.2% of total employment in 2004 and are forecast at 833,741 jobs or 3.8% of the total by 2014.

- **Ethiopia's travel and tourism industry** is expected to contribute 5.5% to Gross Domestic Product (GDP) in 2004 (ETB, 3,330.7 mn or US$369.1mn), rising in nominal terms to ETB 7,004.4 mn or US$ 623.5 million (5.0 percent of total) by 2014.

- **Ethiopia travels and tourism capital investment** is estimated at ETB 871.2 mn, US$ 96.6 mn or 8.1 % of total investment in year 2004. By 2014, this should reach ETB, 2,330.1 mn, US$198.5 mn or 8.3% of total.

- **Ethiopia's personal travel and tourism** is estimated at ETB 2,221.8 mn, US$ 246.2mn or 4.6% of total personal consumption in year 2004. By 2014, this should reach ETB5, 889.0 mn, US$524.2mn or 5.2% of total consumption. Ethiopia business travel is estimated at ETB 1,386.3mn, US$153.6mn in year 2004. By 2014, this should reach ETB 3,489.4 mn or US$310.6 mn.

- **Visitor's export** plays an important development role for the resident travel and tourism economy. Ethiopia travel and tourism is expected to generate 30.0% of total exports (ETB3, 149.4mn or US$349.0mn) in 2004, growing (nominal terms) to ETB 6,133.8 mn or US$546.0mn (20.4% of total) in 2014.

Review of arrivals and receipts from international inbound tourism in Ethiopia also reveals promising trends that in 1963 total arrivals were 19215, which grew to 64542 arrivals in 1971 with 19669,000 ETB as receipts. In 2002 almost 1,56,327 arrivals were recorded with ETB676100, 000 as receipts. Which means Ethiopia earned almost ETB 4325 per arrival. In the year 2003 the arrival figure rose to 181000 tourists (ETC, 2003).

Ethiopia has six tourist entry ports, by air Addis Ababa and Dire Dawa, by road Moyale, Metema & Galafi and by railways Dawale. In 2002 arrivals to Ethiopia via Bole international airport, Addis Ababa recorded 30.3% from Africa, 26.5% from Europe, 20.3% from Americas, 14.6 % from Middle East, 7.4% from Asia and 0.8% from Oceania (ETC 2003). Regarding the purpose of visit for the years 1990 to 2002 most tourists came for vacation and business. For instance in the year 2002 out of the 156327 arrivals 32% came for vacation, 21% for business, 11% for visiting friends and relatives, 13% for transit, 7% for conference and 16% for reasons not specified.

In year 2000 daily average availability of rooms and beds for tourist class hotels in the country has been 1738 and 3056 respectively while corresponding daily average occupancy has been 836 and 1235. The average length of stay was 2.06 tourist nights. In 2001 the public hotels supplied about 775 thousand room nights and 1.26 million bed nights. The future of tourism is promising in Ethiopia and the Ethiopian tourism Commission (ETC) is seeking a doubling of tourist arrivals in the next five years.

Advantages of tourism to Ethiopia in fighting food insecurity

It must be appreciated that the level of tourism in Ethiopia is low despite considerable potential. A significant impact of poverty and food insecurity through tourism will only be achieved over time through the generation of more tourism. If this is done then tourism could bring number of advantages to Ethiopia in fighting food insecurity:

- As tourism is consumed at the point of production, so there is considerable potential for individuals and micro-enterprises, in urban centers or marginal rural areas to sell additional products like handicrafts and souvenirs or services like guiding, folk dances, music etc. to the consumers.

- Access to international markets is serious problem for developing countries like Ethiopia particularly in traditional sectors like food and agriculture due to tariff and non-tariff barriers. This is not the case for the tourism sector as there are no significant tariff barriers. In fact principal trade barriers to international tourism are visa restrictions and similar taxes imposed by the host countries as a source of revenue. Ethiopia could also earn substantial revenue from the same once tourism is developed.

- Most export industries depend on financial, productive and human capital. Tourism not only depends on these, but also on natural capital (eg. Wildlife, scenery, culture etc.). These are the assets possessed by many food insecure regions in Ethiopia like Amhara, Tigray, and Oromia etc.

- Tourism as an industry is much more diverse than many others and can build upon a wide resource base. This diversity increases the scope for wider participation, and for the informal sectors through livelihood diversification – for example government can encourage farming household to produce handicrafts and embroidered products, which are both qualitative and quantitative in nature.

- Tourism is more labor intensive than other non-agricultural activities, particularly manufacturing. Since, Ethiopia lacks well-developed manufacturing sector so tourism could provide ample employment opportunities.

- Development of domestic tourism could also reduce the gap between food secure and food insecure areas.

- Money earned from tourism could be used for social mobilization for family planning programs, environmental rehabilitation, agriculture and livestock development.

- Ethiopia provides immense investment opportunity in many sectors ranging from cultivation of cash crops such as coffee, oil seeds, food processing activities whose produce can be used for export market, cultivation of flowers, animal husbandry, fishing and irrigation projects, hotels on historic tour routes, national parks accommodations like eco lodges etc.

- If marketed well, marvelous handicrafts of Ethiopia which includes weaving of intricate creations from colored fibers and grasses, the various kinds of hand crosses, church rattles, church paintings and chandeliers of gold, the tankwas (Papyrus canoes) built in Bahirdar to the Berkota a wooden head rest, made by Omotic people of Hamer, Beeme and Geleb among many could provide handsome earnings to poor.

Institutional engagements in Ethiopia to fight food insecurity

To fight poverty and food insecurity problem in Ethiopia different institutional engagements are as follows:

1. **International development agencies:**

   - **World Bank**: The bank has funded a medium term cultural heritage project, which has components on living culture, heritage interpretation and recording the heritage. This project is focus on towns such as Gondar, Auxum, Lallibella and Harar.

   - **UNDP**: UNDP are providing finance to the Ethiopian Government for an agreed program of work spanning 2002-2006. Since, tourism was not a priority of Government, it is not included in this program. How ever, UNDP is supporting the private sector of tourism as part of UN's global Compact, which contains as initiative called growing sustainable business. They are focusing their support on the new Ecotourism Association of Ethiopia, encouraging the association and individual members in their work with local communities and sustainable development.

   - **EU**: European Union provides an important source of funding for Ethiopia. Two specific projects of EU are 1. Funding in association with UNESCO to support conservation of the heritage in Lalibella. 2. A new funding program aimed at Micro and Small Enterprise, which is still being finalized. This will provide grant of 30,000 to 50,000 Euros per project, based on the call for proposals. It could include tourism and handicraft projects.

   - **UNIDO**: UNIDO provides technical assistance to enterprises. Through their integrated program their main focus has been on handicrafts (especially, textiles, leather and food). They provide capacity building, and general assistance to enhance service quality and marketing etc. They are interested in supporting initiatives to strengthen linkages with the tourism sector, and capacity building and support for the development of products that relates to then tourism.

- **JICA:** Japan is the leading source of bilateral assistance to Ethiopia. They can see the tourism potential of Ethiopia and are looking for more government leadership in this sector. In total they spend around $US 40-50 million per annum in Ethiopia. Much of this goes to infrastructure projects.

- **SNV:** The Dutch technical assistance agency SNV is concentrating on three areas of work in Ethiopia – private sector support, natural resource management and local governance. The focus of activity is capacity building and institutional change. They are not currently involved in tourism in Ethiopia but are looking to support this more actively in future as a tool for sustainable livelihoods.

2. **Government:** Ethiopian government through Ethiopian Tourism Commission (ETC) has taken a number of steps to develop infrastructure including the construction of airports at the major tourist sites. It is also engaged in restoration of major cultural and historical sites. However, further measures will be taken to address the low level of development facilities along the tourist sites, wildlife protection and national parks management as well as the low promotion of the country's tourism.

3. **Non-Governmental Organizations:** NGO's throughout Ethiopia tend to concentrate on poverty alleviation, food security, health and education. They play important role in organizing action at local level.

4. **Private sector tourism enterprises:** Although the private sector of Ethiopia is relatively small, it appears to be reasonably organized. The Ethiopian Tour Operators Association has 48 members and is committed to socially and environmentally responsible tourism. Ecotourism Association of Ethiopia also includes some service providers. There are two hotel associations – The Star Hotel Association (32 members) and the Ethiopia Hotels and Restaurant Association (500 members). They are also interested in poverty and sustainability issues.

Along with the efforts of the above-mentioned institutions, emphasis should also be at the joint action at the local level to channel tourism spending towards that poor. This could be done by establishing steering committees for poverty alleviation thorough tourism. These committees would bring together representatives of different international agencies and stake holders- locals authority, tourism service providers, tour-operators, NGO's etc - and be specially charged with developing and implementing action plans. Action would include:

- Generating new ideas and initiatives.

- Winning support and interest from local service providers.

- Coordinating joint action, for example in identifying, supporting and using local suppliers.

- Generating local publicity and providing information to visitors on poverty issue and food insecurity and how they can help.

- Rising support from international our operators and development assistance agencies.

- Lobbying central government and others.

- Disseminating results and achievements.

Conclusion and suggestions

Tourism can make a substantial contribution to the sustainable development of less developed countries facing poverty and food security problems. However, the degree of attention paid to tourism is often limited compared to the agriculture, food manufacturing sector and the export of commodities. Yet, tourism is better placed then many other sectors in relating to the needs of poor. Tourism is an important stimulus even for achieving UN Millennium Declaration to halve poverty in the World's poorer countries by 2015. In the context of Ethiopia too, sustainable tourism development could help achieve the UN Millennium Development Goals in the following manner:

- **Poverty and Hunger:** Tourism is building economies in areas with few other employment opportunities. It is helping in creating a dynamic private sector for investment in allied tourism areas for overall economic development of Ethiopia.

- **Universal Primary Education**: Tourism increases income and thereby increases the demand and potential for education.

- **Gender Equality and Empowerment**: Tourism is providing income generation opportunities for women and female ownership of assets/enterprises. It provides increased exposure to international gender norms.

- **Child Mortality**: Tourism increases income, demand and potential for child health services and nutrition.

- **Maternal Health**: Tourism increases women's income, status and demand for maternal health services.

- **HIV/AIDS. Malaria**: Tourists contributes for increasing income & adds pressure regarding demand for health services

- **Sustainability**: Tourism provides income opportunities and protects against ecological and social degradation.

- **Global Partnership**: Tourism increases country interaction and knowledge/understanding of Ethiopia reality at the global level.

Based on the above; it could be said that tourism can be a catalyst for positive change in development of critical areas like rural communities, education and woman's leadership. It can improve the image of Ethiopia by showing the rich traditions and humanity of Ethiopia, breaking a vicious circle of poverty driven misconception. The Ethiopian government should formulate an overarching enabling framework, which integrates regional and local delivery at the core and incentivises the private sector towards win-win partnership. Also encouraging the international community to drive tourism focused development support and spreading measurable benefits across the economy and around the country.

Some other measures, which are essential for the achievement of a meaningful growth of tourism to make it an effective tool to fight with poverty and food insecurity problem in Ethiopia, are as follows:

- Strengthening of institutional engagement of international development agencies, Government, NGO's and private sector enterprises in Ethiopia to fight food insecurity. Advocate tourism as a creative industry for Africa with African Union AU/NEPAD, WTO-OMT, ADB and development institutions and integrate tourism into African Commission follow-up.

- Establish an effective inter ministerial tourism structure so that Ethiopian Tourism Commission (ETC) could coordinate with Ministry of Finance and Economic Development (MOFED) and Ministry of Trade and Industry (MTI) for the development of economy and thereby fighting food insecurity.

- Join up government programs with a new tourism "satellite account" to maximize the impact on other economic sectors.

- Strengthen the capacity of the Ethiopian Tourism Commission to do more intensive marketing and promotion and to provide effective support to those involved in tourism sector.

- Agreeing on a clear tourism strategy and action plan for the country that embraces poverty alleviation and food insecurity as a key guiding principle. Tourism must be a key component of Ethiopia's Poverty Reduction Strategy Program and Millennium Development Goals PRSP/MDP & Africa Commission follow-up with progressive intensification, boosted by the 2007 Millennium.

- Preparation of site development plan comprising determined carrying capacities of sites. Land implementation modalities to ensure a sustainable tourism development. Involve community stakeholders in sustainable planning.

- Feed in tourism to infrastructure, energy, security and transport programs as well as link rural development, food and hygiene related activities.

- Conduct studies for possible introduction of a set of incentives for those engaged in tourist -trade and encourage both local and foreign visitors.

- Human resource development through short and long-term training by expediting the on going programs. Include education, training, quality service, entrepreneurship and e-skills starting from school levels.

- Encouraging expansion of micro finance institutions to support tourism activities. The Micro and Small Enterprise Development Agency can help especially in handicraft training.

- Put the initial focus on high value, low impact tourism in Ethiopia like MICE tourism, VFR or Diaspora markets as well as high yield culture seeking leisure travelers.

- Overtime the vacation market focusing on eco and adventure tourism will provide the largest pro-development boost in terms of GDP and export income, as well as its spread around the country.

- Identifying and developing the potential tourism resources and activities such as introducing water sports facilities and resort construction around lakes and rivers such as Omo, Wabe-Sheble, Tana, Abaya, Ziway etc. developing trekking, Para gliding, river rafting, jungle safari and eco lodges, village tourism etc.

In essence, all the above measures will enhance the per capita income, GDP, employment opportunities, foreign exchange reserves, infrastructure development, health, education and other socio-economic conditions to reduce poverty and provide food security to Ethiopia.

References

Ashley, C. Boyd, C. and Goodwin, H. (2000), *Pro Poor Tourism: Putting Poverty at the heart of the Tourism Agenda, Natural Resource Perspective* No. 51, ODI, London.

Diriba Getachew (1995). *The Economy at Crossroads: Famine and Food Security in Rural Ethiopia*, Commercial Printing Press, Addis Ababa.

(DPPC) Disaster Prevention and Preparedness Commission (2002). *Vulnerability profile for sixteen highly drought prone areas, SERA project*, Addis Ababa.

Economic Focus, Bulletin of the Ethiopian Economic Association (EEA), August 2003, vol. 5 No.5.

Ethiopia: Sustainable Development and Poverty reduction program, Ministry of Finance and Economic Development, July 2002, Addis Ababa, Ethiopia.

Ethiopian Tourism Commission (ETC), *Tourism Highlights* (2003). ETC Addis Ababa.

Federal Democratic Republic of Ethiopia,' *Sustainable Industrial Development and competitiveness,' Ministry of Trade and Industry, UNDIO 2004*, Vienna.

(FDRE) Federal Democratic Republic of Ethiopia (2002). *Food Security Strategy*, Addis Ababa, Ethiopia.

FAO/WFP (2003). *Undernourishment around the world, counting the hungry latest estimates; Food and Agricultural World Food Program publication.*

Habethold (1995), *Food Security: A brief Review of Concepts and Indicators*, (originally from Maxwell and Smith, 1992) in Demeke M. *et al.* (eds.).

http//www.wttc.org/2004tsa/tsapdf/Ethiopia.pdf

IMF & IDA (1999). *Poverty Reduction Strategy Paper: Operational Issues*, Washington DC.

Kukreti Mohit (2004). Tourism development planning: A case study of Ethiopia, *Focus Chronicle Vol. 4 No. 1,* April 2004, Ethiopia.

Report on the Ethiopian Economy, vol. III 2003/04, Industrialization and industrial policy in Ethiopia, Ethiopian Economic Association, Addis Ababa, Ethiopia July 2004.

Reutlinger, Shlomo (1996). *Poverty and Hunger: Issues and Opinions For Food Insecurity in developing countries,* Washington DC., World Bank.

Roe, D., Goodwin, H. and Ashley, C. (2002). *The Tourism Industry and Poverty Reduction: A Business Primer PPT Briefing* No. 2 March 2002.

Sen A. (1981). *Poverty and famines: An Essay on Entitlement and Deprivation,* Oxford, Oxford University Press.

Sissay Assefa (1995). *Perspective on Agricultural Policy, Rural Poverty and Food Insecurity in Ethiopia',* in Demeke Mulat, Wolday Amha, Simon Ehui and Tesfay Zegeye (eds.) p.37.

Telfer, D.J. and Wall, G. (1996). Linkages between Tourism and Food Production, *Annals of Tourism Research* Vol. 23.

The Ethiopian Red Cross Society (1985). *Hydrological and Metrological Aspects of natural Disaster in Ethiopia, National Water Resource Commission,* paper presented to the disaster prevention symposium, September. 4-7. 1985.

Webb, Patrick and Braun, Joachim Von (1994). *Famine and Food security in Ethiopia: Lessons for Africa,* John Wily & Sons Ltd., England.

World Bank, World Development Report (2004). *Making Services Work for Poor people* A co publication of the World Bank and Oxford University Press.

World Bank (2002). Attacking Poverty: World Development Report 2000/01, OUP Oxford, New York.

(WTO) World Tourism Organization (1999). *Global Code of Ethics for tourism,* WTO, Madrid.

(WTO) World Tourism Organization (2003). *Sustainable Development of Ecotourism: A compilation of Good Practices and SME's,* Madrid, Spain.

(WTO) World Tourism Organization (2004). *Tourism and poverty alleviation in Ethiopia identification of pilot projects (ST-EP programs),* Madrid Spain.

(WTO) World Tourism Organization (2004). *Tourism and poverty alleviation recommendations for actions,* Madrid, Spain.

(WFP) World Food Program (2002). *Comparative Analysis.*

Yates A. (2003). *Food Security in Ethiopia, Fact sheets 2003,* Addis ababa.

ALL INDIA TOURISM TEACHERS ASSOCIATION (AITTA)

List of AITTA (Life) Members

Prof. D.S. Bhardwaj
Dept. of Tourism Management
Kurukshetra University
Kurukshetra - 132119
Haryana.

Prof. Manjula Chaudhary
Dept. of Tourism Management
Kurukshetra University
Kurukshetra - 132119
Haryana.

Prof. K.K. Kamra
Dept. of Tourism Management
Kurukshetra University
Kurukshetra - 132119
Haryana.

Dr. Mohinder Chand
Dept. of Tourism Management
Kurukshetra University
Kurukshetra - 132119
Haryana.

Dr. Ravi Bhushan
Dept. of Tourism Management
Kurukshetra University
Kurukshetra - 132119
Haryana.

Dr. S.S. Boora
Dept. of Tourism Management
Kurukshetra University
Kurukshetra - 132119
Haryana.

Dr. Mukesh Sehgal, Director
M.M. Institute of Computer Technology
& Business Management
Mullana, Ambala
Haryana.

Dr. S.P. Bansal
Chairman, Institute of Vocational Studies
Master of Tourism Administration
H.P. University. Shimla - 171 005.

Ms. Sonia Khan
Lecturer, Institute of Vocational Studies
Master of Tourism Administration
H.P. University, Shimla - 171 005.

Mrs. Sushma Rewal Chugh
Lecturer, Institute of Vocational Studies
Master of Tourism Administration
H.P. University, Shimla - 171 005.

Dr. S.K. Garg
Reader, Dept. of Economics
ICDEOL, Joint Director, IIHS
H.P. University, Shimla - 171 005.

Dr. U.N. Shukla, Lecturer
SPCJ Institute of Management
Dr. B.R. Ambedkar University
Agra.

Mr. H.C. Pandey, Director
ITM, Lucknow
R/o 7-D, Kalyanpur
opp. Kamla Market,
Lucknow - 226 001 (U.P.).

Mr. Dileep M.R.
Lecturer
Dept. of Tourism
Pazhassi Raja College, Pulpally
Wayanad, Kerala - 673579
R/o Surabhi 17/1749 Netaji Road
Pujappura, Trivendrum 695012.

Ms. Prachi Rustogi
Editor
Centre for Tourism Research &
Development
9656, Indira Nagar, Lucknow.

Dr. Usha Aggarwal
Asst. Prof. of History
Govt. P.G. College, Mandsaur
M.P. - 458001.

Prof. Sandeep Kulshrestha
Course Director
IITTM, Govindpuri
Gwalior (M.P.)- 474 011

Dr. R.A. Sharma
Centre for Tourism and Travel
Management Studies
Jiwaji University
Gwalior (M.P.) - 474014.

Dr. K. Rattanan
Asst. Prof. of History
MLB College, Gwalior.

Dr. Mushtaqe Ahmed
Head, Tourism Studies,
Dept. of Commerce
Aligarh Muslim University
Aligarh (U.P.) - 202 002.

Dr. M. Asif Ali Khan
Lecturer
Aligarh Muslim University
Aligarh (U.P.) - 202 002.

Mrs. Sheeba Hamid
Lecturer
Aligarh Muslim University
Aligarh (U.P.) - 202 002.

Prof. Desh Bandhu Gupta
Jammu University
Jammu Tawi, Jammu
(J&K).

Mr. Deepak Raj Gupta
Director,
Centre for Hospitality & Tourism Studies
University of Jammu
Jammu - 180006.

Dr. Rajinder Mishra
Centre for Hospitality & Tourism Studies
University of Jammu
Jammu - 180006.

Ms. Sushma Marva
C/o Sh. Raj Kumar
DDE, University of Jammu
Jammu - 180006.

Ms. Meenakshi Kilam
Lecturer
Dept. of Management Studies
University of Jammu, Jammu -180006.

Dr. Ashok Singh
Incharge -Tourism Studies
Institute of Management Studies
Mohan Lal Sukhadria University
Udaipur, Rajasthan.

Mr. C.M. Parsheera
Lecturer
Institute of Vocational Studies
Master of Tourism Administration
H.P. University,
Shimla (H.P.).

Prof. S.C. Bagri
H.N.B. Garhwal University
Srinagar (Garhwal) - 246174
Uttaranchal.

Prof. D.M. Dutta
Dept. of Business Admn.
University Burdwan
Golapbag Campus,
Burdwan - 713 104, W.B.

Prof. P.K. Yadav
Incharge Hotel Management &
Dean Faculty of Commerce and
Management Studies
Rohilkhand University
Bareilly, U.P.

Dr. Luv Kush Mishra
Incharge Tourism Undergraduate
Studies
Dr. B.R. Ambedkar University,
Agra, U.P.

Prof. O.P. Khandari
Head, Institute of Tourism &
Hotel Management,
Bundelkhand University,
Jhansi.

Prof. S.K. Mishra
IITTM
Visitors Centre, Udyan Marg,
Bhubhneshwar - 751 009.

Dr. M.A. Safique
Lecturer, Tourism Studies
Dept. of Business Admn.
Burdwan University,
Golapbag Campus,
Burdwan
W.B. - 713 104.

Prof. Kalpana Mathur
Incharge Tourism Studies
Faculty of Commerce and Management
J.N. Vyas University
Jodhpur, Rajasthan.

Prof. Kapil Kumar
Director, School of Social Sciences
IGNOU, Maidan Garhi
New Delhi - 110 068.

Prof. Bashir Ahmed
Head, Centre of Tourism Studies
Pondicherry University
R. Venkataraman Nagar
Pondicherry.

Prof. Nishith Rai
Director
Institute of Tourism Studies,
Lucknow University, Badshah Bagh
Lucknow (U.P.) - 226 007.

Prof. Badar Alam Iqwal
Department of Commerce
Aligarh Muslim University
Aligarh (U.P.) - 202 002.

Mr. O.P. Ahuja
Managing Director
Holiday Maker, 6, USO House
Special Institutional Area
Qutab Hotel Road
New Delhi - 110 067.

Dr. Ashref S. Husain
Department of Commerce
Aligarh Muslim University
Aligarh (U.P.) - 202 002.

Mrs. Purnima Chauhan
Secretary – State Electricity
Regulatory Commission,
Khallini, Shimla.

Dr. Vinay Chauhan
Department Tourism Management
Jammu University
Jammu Tawi, Jammu (J&K).

Dr. S.B. Deshmukh
Reader in Geography
Deptt. Of Geography
Shivaji University,
Kolhapur, Maharashtra.

Dr. V.S. Deshmukh,
Lecturer in Geography
Shri Shiv Shahu Mahavidalya
Sarud Tal Sahuwadi,
Distt. Kolhapur, Maharashtra.

Dr. Amar Dev.
Govt. Degree College
Sanjauli, Shimla.

Dr. Pradeep Ahlawat
Faculty Member
Institute of Management Studies &
Research
Maharishi Dayanand University
Rohtak -124001.

Dr. Mukesh Dhunna
Faculty Member
Institute of Management Studies &
Research
Maharishi Dayanand University
Rohtak -124001.

Dr. Amit Khurana
Faculty Member
Institute of Management Studies &
Research
Maharishi Dayanand University,
Rohtak -124001.

Dr. Devesh Nigam
Institute of Tourism & Hotel
Management,
Bundelkhand University, Jhansi.

Dr. Jayant K. Parida
Head and coordinator of MFC
Programme
Utkal University, Banihar,
Bhubneshwar (Orissa) - 751004.

Dr. Prabhjot K. Pradhan
Department of Tourism Studies
Utkal University, Banihar
Bhubneshwar, Orissa -751004.

Dr. Mrs. Reena Singh
Lecturer
Inst. of Management Studies
C-238, Industrial Area
Bulandshahar Road,
Gaziabad (U.P.)

Dr. Ajay Singh
Inst. of Management Studies
C-238, Industrial Area
Bulandshahar Road
Gaziabad (U.P.)

Prof. D. D. Sharma
Technical Teachers' Training Institute
Sector-26, Chandigarh.

Dr. Mukesh Ranga
Lecturer
Institute of Tourism & Management
Bundelkhand University
Jhansi.

Dr. Kulwant Rana
Reader in Commerce
ICDEOL, H.P. University
Shimla - 171 005.

Dr. B.B. Parida
Reader & Head,
Tourism Studies,
Dept. of Business Admn.
The of University Burdwan
Golapbag Campus,
Burdwan -713 104, W.B.

Dr. S. Kabia
Institute of Tourism & Hotel
Management
Bundelkhand University
Jhansi.

Dr. S.K. Gupta
H.N.B. Garhwal University
Srinagar (Garhwal)- 246174
Uttaranchal.

Dr. Punit Gautam
Institute of Tourism & Hotel
Management
Bundelkhand University
Jhansi.

Dr. Sourav Dixit
IITTM, Govindpuri
Gwalior (M.P.) - 474 011.

Dr. Jaiwanty Dimri
Reader, Department of English
HPU, Shimla.

Dr. S. Babu
Department of Tourism Studies
Utkal University, Banihar
Bhubneshwar, Orissa -751004.

Prof. M.R. Bansal
Director
SPCJ Institute of Management Studies
Dr. B.R. Ambadkar University
Agra (U.P.)

Prof. P.K. Jain
Director
Inst. of Mgt. Studies
Mohan Lal Sukhadiya University
Udaipur.

Dr. G.S. Batra
Reader
Deptt. of Mgt.Studies
Panjabi University, Patiala.

Dr. Kulbhushan Chandel
Lecturer
Deptt. of Commerce
HPU, Shimla.

Mr. Pitamber Sharma
International Centre for Integrated
Mountain Development (ICIMOD)
Nepal.

Prof. D.P.S. Verma
QU – 285 B,
Chitrakoot, Uttari Pitampura
Delhi - 110 034.

Prof. R.P. Hooda
Department of Commerce
Kurukshetra University
Kurukshetra.

Dr. Mukta Arora
State Coordinator
Rajasthan State Commission for Women
Government of Rajasthan
35/76, Rajat Path, Mansarovar
Jaipur - 302 020.

Prof. K.C. Singh
Punjab School of Management Studies
Punjabi University
Patiala - 147 002.

Mr. Rajneesh Thapar
Lecturer
Institute of Hotel Management
Kufri, Shimla.

Prof. S.C. Vaidya
Business School of Management
Studies,
Punjab University
Chandigarh.

Dr. B.K. Punia
Department of Business Management Studies,
Guru Jambhashwar University
Hisar, Haryana.

Prof. N.K. Chaddha
Department of Psychology
University of Delhi
Delhi - 110 007.

Mr. Ajit Kumar Shakla
Associate Coordinator Tourism & Travel Management Programme
Department of Commerce
Mahatama Gandhi Kashi Vidyapith
Varanasi - 221 002.

Prof. M.M. Goel
894/13, Housing Board
Kurukshetra - 132 118.

Dr. Sudhir Kumar
Reader in English
Department of English
Punjab University
Chandigarh.

Mr. Rajesh Kumar Sharma
Transport Division
DTDC, Opp. INA Market
Near Delhi Haat
New Delhi - 110 024.

Tarun K. Roy
C/o Mr. Rajesh Kumar Sharma
Transport Division
DTDC, Opp. INA Market
Near Delhi Haat, New Delhi - 110 024.

Dr. K.S. Narayan
Principal
Shri Bhakti College of Hotel Management
Venus Plaza, Adjacent to Airport
Bezumpet, Hyderabad - 500 016.

Sh. Anurag Bhosle
Royal College of Tourism & Hotel Management
In the premesis of Royal Hotel
Mallital, Nainital (Uttaranchal).

Sh. B.K. Bagchi
H.40, Bungalows
Bhopal - 462 004.

Mr. Rajesh N. Ragde
Lecturer, Department of Tourism Admn.
Dr. Babasaheb Ambedkar Marathwada University
Aurangabad - 431 004.

Dr. Ayub Khan
Department of Sociology,
MLB Government College of Excellence,
Gwalior - 474 009.

Dr. Hemant K. Gupta, IFS
Dy. Conservator of Forests (Projects)
Aranya Bhawan, Talland,
Shimla - 171 001.

Prof. Shekhar Pathak
Department of History
DSB Campus
Kumaun University
Nainital (Uttaranchal) - 263 002.

Prof. M. Basheer Ahmed Khan
Centre for Tourism Studies,
Pondicherry University, RU Nagar,
Pondicherry - 605 014.

Dr. Ramesh H. Taxak
Department of Tourism Management
Kurukshetra University,
Kurukshetra.

Dr. Rakesh Dhodi
Lecturer, Centre for Mountain Tourism
& Hospitality Studies
H.N.B. Garhwal University,
Srinagar, Garhwal.

Ms. Rashmi
Lecturer, Centre for Mountain Tourism
& Hospitality Studies
H.N.B. Garhwal University
Srinagar, Garhwal.

Dr. Ashok Kumar
Lecturer, Centre for Mountain Tourism
& Hospitality Studies
H.N.B. Garhwal University
Srinagar, Garhwal.

Mr. Sanjay Dhayani
Placement Officer
Centre for Mountain Tourism &
Hospitality Studies
H.N.B. Garhwal University
Srinagar, Garhwal.

Mr. Sarvesh Uniyal
Tour & Training Organiser
Centre for Mountain Tourism &
Hospitality Studies
H.N.B. Garhwal University
Srinagar, Garhwal.

Prof. Rakesh K. Gupta
H. No. 78, Sec. 15-A,
Chandigarh - 160 015.

Mr. Madan Kak
Sr. Manager Inbound Tour,
TCI, Hotel Metro, N-49
Connaught Circus,
New Delhi - 110 001.

Dr. Mohit Kukreti
Assistant Professor & Head
Department of Tourism Management
P.O. Box 198, University of Gondar,
Gondar, Ethiopia, Africa.

List of Associate Members

Mr. Ashish Atal
Dept. of Tourism
C/o Prof. D.S. Bhardwaj
K.U. Kurukshetra
Haryana.

Surender Marwal
C/o Prof. D.S. Bhardwaj
Research Scholar
Tourism Dept. K.U.
Kurukshetra.

Ranbir Singh
C/o Prof. D.S. Bhardwaj
Research Scholar
Dept. of. Tourism, K.U.
Kurukshetra.

Mr. Prashant Kumar Gautam
C/o Dr. S.P. Bansal
Research Scholar
Institute of Vocational Studies
Master of Tourism Administration
H.P.U. Shimla - 171 005.

Anil Kumar, Student,
C/o Dr. S.P. Bansal
Institute of Vocational Studies,
Master of Tourism Administration
H.P.U. Shimla - 171 005.

Rajesh Kumar, Student,
C/o Dr. S.P. Bansal
Institute of Vocational Studies
Master of Tourism Administration
H.P.U. Shimla - 171 005.

Rajeev Chauhan, **Student,**
C/o Dr. S.P. Bansal
Institute of Vocational Studies
Master of Tourism Administration
H.P.U. Shimla - 171 005.

Akshay Sharma, **Student,**
C/o Dr. S.P. Bansal
Institute of Vocational Studies
Master of Tourism Administration
H.P.U. Shimla - 171 005.

Kamal Kathiat, **Student,**
C/o Dr. S.P. Bansal
Institute of Vocational Studies
Master of Tourism Administration
H.P.U. Shimla - 171 005.

Ms. Nickita Khera, **Student,**
C/o Dr. S.P. Bansal
Institute of Vocational Studies
Master of Tourism Administration
H.P.U. Shimla - 171 005.

Sunil Kumar, **Student,**
C/o Dr. S.P. Bansal
Institute of Vocational Studies
Master of Tourism Administration
H.P.U. Shimla - 171 005.

Ms. Shweta Grover, **Student,**
C/o Dr. S.P. Bansal
Institute of Vocational Studies
Master of Tourism Administration
H.P.U. Shimla - 171 005.

Amrik Singh, **Student,**
C/o Dr. S.P. Bansal
Institute of Vocational Studies
Master of Tourism Administration
H.P.U. Shimla - 171 005.

Mohit Sood, **Student,**
C/o Dr. S.P. Bansal
Institute of Vocational Studies
Master of Tourism Administration
H.P.U. Shimla - 171 005.

Aman Mahajan, **Student,**
C/o Dr. S.P. Bansal
Institute of Vocational Studies
Master of Tourism Administration
H.P.U. Shimla - 171 005.

Amit Sharma, **Student,**
C/o Dr. S.P. Bansal
Institute of Vocational Studies
Master of Tourism Administration
H.P.U. Shimla - 171 005.

Ms. Disha Thakur, **Student**
C/o Dr. S.P. Bansal
Institute of Vocational Studies Master
of Tourism Administration
H.P.U. Shimla - 171 005.

Sandeep Sharma, **Student,**
C/o Dr. S.P. Bansal
Institute of Vocational Studies
Master of Tourism Administration
H.P.U. Shimla - 171 005.

Pratap Chand, **Student,**
C/o Dr. S.P. Bansal
Institute of Vocational Studies
Master of Tourism Administration
H.P.U. Shimla - 171 005.

Ashish Kaundal, **Student,**
C/o Dr. S.P. Bansal
Institute of Vocational Studies
Master of Tourism Administration
H.P.U. Shimla - 171 005.

Ajay Kumar, **Student,**
C/o Dr. S.P. Bansal
Institute of Vocational Studies
Master of Tourism Administration
H.P.U. Shimla - 171 005.

Surender Kumar, **Student,**
C/o Dr. S.P. Bansal
Institute of Vocational Studies
Master of Tourism Administration
H.P.U. Shimla - 171 005.

Virender Singh, **Student**,
C/o Dr. S.P. Bansal
Institute of Vocational Studies
Master of Tourism Administration
H.P.U. Shimla - 171 005.

Abhishek Sharma,
C/o Prof. Desh Bandhu Gupta
Research Scholar
H.N. 1249, Sector No. 6
Nanak Nagar, Jammu - 180006.

Mukesh Sharma,
C/o Prof. Desh Bandhu Gupta
Student VPO Kanhal (Lower)
The. Bishnal, Distt. Jammu - 181132.

Suvidhar Khana, **Student**,
C/o Prof. Desh Bandhu Gupta
12-C, Shastri Nagar, Jammu - 180006.

Abdul Mujeeb Sheikh, **Student**,
C/o Prof. Desh Bandhu Gupta
H.N. 219-F, New Plots 180005,
Jammu.

Sanjeev Kumar Sharma,
C/o Prof. Desh Bandhu Gupta
Student, S/o Sh. Basant Ram Sharma
R/o Ward No. 1 Jawahar Nagar
Distt. Rajauri (J&K).

Neetu Dhar, **Student**,
C/o Prof. Desh Bandhu Gupta
F-334, Gurhev Qarim Nagar
Bakshi Nagar, Jammu.

Poonam Sharma, **Student**,
C/o Prof. Desh Bandhu Gupta
26/1 Chogan Salthian
Panjthairthi, Jammu.

Rishikesh Khajuria, **Student**,
C/o Prof. Desh Bandhu Gupta
Refmbhi Academy
New Plots,
Jammu (Tawi) 180005.

Atul Kumat Sharma,
C/o Prof. Desh Bandhu Gupta
Student, C/o Dr. Jatinder Sharma
H.N. 538, Salwal
Jammu - 180005.

Shair Singh Manhas, **Student**,
C/o Prof. Desh Bandhu Gupta
Q.No. 25, B.No. 4 (Incomplete Block)
Distt. Police Lines,
Gandhi Nagar,
Jammu - 180003.

Pritam Lal Thapa,
C/o Prof. Desh Bandhu Gupta
S/o Sh. Chuni Lal
R/o PTS Vill Sai
P.O. PTS Udhampur - 182103.

Jitendra Mohan Misra
C/o Prof. S.C. Bagri
Centre for Mountain Tourism &
Hospitality Studies
H.N.B. Garhwal University,
Srinagar, Garhwal.

I. Kathirbel
C/o Prof. S.C. Bagri
Centre for Mountain Tourism &
Hospitality Studies
H.N.B. Garhwal University,
Srinagar, Garhwal.

SEMINAR ORGANISING COMMITTEE

Seminar Director	:	S.C. Bagri
Assistant coordinator	:	S.K. Gupta
Publication	:	Rakesh Dhodi Satish Gusain Srinivas Ghildiyal
Hospitality and Accommodation	:	Sanjay Dhayani
Press, Communication and Stage Arrangement	:	Ashok Kumar Rashmi Dhodi
Technical Session	:	Sarvesh Uniyal Jitendra Mohan Mishra Reena Sharma Ragini Dawar
Financial Affairs	:	Saurabh Dixit Kaliram Manoj Raturi
Public Relation and Media Management	:	Subodh Hatwal
Transportation	:	Sanjay Joshi
Registration	:	Jitendra Mohan Mishra